Slave Ship Sailors and Their Captive Cargoes, 1730–1807

Despite the vast literature on the transatlantic slave trade, the role of sailors aboard slave ships has remained unexplored. This book fills that gap by examining every aspect of their working lives, from their reasons for signing on a slaving vessel to their experiences in the Caribbean and the American South after their human cargoes had been sold. It explores how they interacted with men and women of African origin at all of their ports of call, from the Africans they traded with, to the free black seamen who were their crewmates, to the slaves and ex-slaves they mingled with in the port cities of the Americas. Most importantly, it questions their interactions with the captive Africans they were transporting during the dread middle passage, arguing that their work encompassed the commoditization of these people ready for sale.

Emma Christopher gained her PhD from University College London in 2002 and is currently a Postdoctoral Fellow in the School of Historical Studies, Monash University. She has held fellowships from Mystic Seaport Museum, Connecticut; the Huntington Library, California; the National Maritime Museum in London; and the Atlantic World Center at Harvard University. She is the author of several articles on the slave trade and convict transportation. She has travelled extensively in many parts of the world, including wide-ranging travels around areas of West Africa and the Caribbean mentioned in this work.

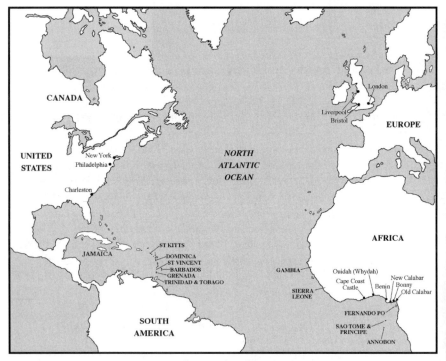

The North Atlantic

Slave Ship Sailors and Their Captive Cargoes, 1730–1807

EMMA CHRISTOPHER

Monash University

CAMBRIDGE
UNIVERSITY PRESS

CAMBRIDGE UNIVERSITY PRESS
Cambridge, New York, Melbourne, Madrid, Cape Town, Singapore, São Paulo

Cambridge University Press
40 West 20th Street, New York, NY 10011-4211, USA

www.cambridge.org
Information on this title: www.cambridge.org/9780521861625

© Emma Christopher 2006

First published 2006

Printed in the United States of America

A catalog record for this publication is available from the British Library.

Library of Congress Cataloging in Publication Data
Christopher, Emma, 1971–
Slave ship sailors and their captive cargoes, 1730–1807 / Emma Christopher.
p. cm.
Includes index.
ISBN-13: 978-0-521-86162-5 (hardback)
ISBN-10: 0-521-86162-4 (hardback)
ISBN-13: 978-0-521-67966-4 (pbk.)
ISBN-10: 0-521-67966-4 (pbk.)
1. Slave trade – Africa – History.   2. Merchant mariners.   3. Slaves.
4. Race relations. I. Title.
HT1321.C48   2006
306.3′62–dc22   2006000225

ISBN-13   978-0-521-86162-5 hardback
ISBN-10   0-521-86162-4 hardback

ISBN-13   978-0-521-67966-4 paperback
ISBN-10   0-521-67966-4 paperback

Contents

Illustrations

Abbreviations

Classifications from the National Archives, UK (PRO)

ADM Admiralty papers
BT   Board of Trade papers
C   Chancery papers
HCA High Court of the Admiralty papers
HO   Home Office papers
PL   Records of the Palatinate of Lancaster
T   Treasury papers
TS   Treasury Solicitor's papers
ZHC Publications of the House of Commons, including some of the
     House of Lords

Acknowledgements

As this work began as my PhD dissertation at University College London, I would first and foremost like to thank Rick Halpern, supervisor, mentor and friend through times both bad and good. During the process of writing the thesis and latterly turning it into a book I have incurred many debts and would like to thank Marcus Rediker, Cassandra Pybus, Paul Lovejoy, Martin Klein, Catherine Hall, David Richardson and Phillip Morgan for contributing in a range of ways.

I have benefited greatly from various grants and fellowships, and would like to thank the Arts and Humanities Research Board for providing doctoral funding; the Royal Historical Society for giving a grant to research in the USA and attend a conference in Nigeria; Mystic Seaport Museum where I was a Paul Cuffe Fellow; the Huntington Library where I held a Mellon Fellowship; the Atlantic World Center at Harvard which awarded me a short-term research fellowship to research in Jamaica; and the National Maritime Museum in London where I was a Caird Fellow. Additionally I am grateful to the history department at the University of Pennsylvania where I was a visiting graduate student and the University of Toronto where I taught during the final year of writing my PhD. Just as this project was being completed for publication I was hired by Monash University in Melbourne, Australia, and I am grateful to Barbara Caine and the other faculty there for making me very welcome.

A host of friends, too numerous to mention, have made the years of writing this book a pleasure. I'm especially grateful to Julia Drake, Enrico Dal Lago, Frank Deserino, Ralph Kingston, Arlene Hui, Susan Guy, Hilde Kempenaers, Pandora Hay, Tammy and Shaun McMahon, Ros Kane, and Bruce and Nicky Johnson. Susan Guy and Hilde Kempenaers also played host to me when I returned to London, as did Laurie Walters in New York, Georgiana Cunningham Reynal in Washington, D.C., and Peter and Margaret Turner when I was researching in Bristol. Hans de Klerk helped with the calculations of the overall number of seamen on slave ships. Amanda Pearse and Craig Kelly have provided love, laughter and boundless friendship and I would be lost without them. I would also like to thank my sister Sarah Hill and my nephew and niece Edward and Aletheia Hill for providing a very welcome distraction at various times, and my brother Richard Christopher for his ongoing encouragement and lately his shared love of history.

My largest debt though is to my parents, Brian and Barbara Christopher, who have provided never-failing support of all kinds through the long years of writing this work. Their input to it went well above and beyond the call of duty, and although it is an extremely inadequate return on my debt to them, it is, nevertheless, for them with much love.

Preface

The most magnificent drama in the last thousand years of human history is the transportation of ten million human beings out of the dark beauty of their mother continent into the new-found Eldorado of the West.

W. E. B. Du Bois[1]

As the three hundred or so captive Africans wallowed below deck, chained two by two, stifling in the heat, the crew of the *Lady Nelson* forgot their imprisoned cargo for a while and began the elaborate maritime ceremony common to the ships of many nations. Sailor Samuel Robinson wrote in his journal that "the old god of the sea is constantly on the lookout for greenhorns" and the ship had to welcome Neptune aboard. Any men who had not crossed the equator before had to perform a forfeit or make a payment of alcohol. This crossing the line ceremony was an essential piece of seaman's lore and ritual, and to them was not just "childish, foolish, stupid" or any of the other adjectives their officers, and landlubbers, used to describe it. It celebrated a world turned upside down, of authority challenged for a day and replaced by power based on sailors' own value system. Instead of the captain being in charge, "Neptune", the oldest and/or most experienced man, held sway for the duration of the ceremony. Seafaring skill rather than social standing, warrant or appointment was the basis of authority. Besides being actors in the "magnificent drama" of slave trading, sailors also performed theatre all of their own as slave ships crossed the ocean.[2]

---

[1] W. E. B. Du Bois, *Black Reconstruction* (London: Frank Cass, 1966) 727.

[2] Samuel Robinson, *A Sailor Boy's Experience Aboard a Slave Ship* (Wigtown: G.C. Book Publishers, 1996) 25–6; Greg Dening, *Mr Bligh's Bad Language: Passion, Power and*

As in other nautical trades, crossing the line differed between slave ships and over time but it always involved satirizing the hegemony of the ship's rulers. Power and authority were ritually lampooned, along with brutality, inhumanity, and even the omnipresent risk of death. Seamen were engaged in the parody of their own working lives. There were several common elements to the ceremony. Firstly those who had not crossed the equator before would be tried by a mock court, during which they were subjected to "insults, humiliations, injustices, erotic oaths, and compromising choices".[3] With the sentences set, each man would then be shaved "by Neptune's barber" as Samuel Robinson recalled. William Butterworth, another slave trade sailor who appears frequently in this book, reported that the "shaving foam" used on the *Hudibras* in 1786 comprised "tar, oil, and the excrement of fowls".[4] Souse and resin were also sometimes added to the mix.

The next element to the ceremony was commonly ducking the "greenhorns" into the deep blue sea. A ducking stool attached to the yardarm was used to lower the men into the water in a parody of hanging. A ship's officers would avoid punishment by paying alcohol or other goods to Neptune, while a sailor might pay off a part of his sentence. For the common seamen though, the number of duckings they withstood was a matter of boasting and pride, an assertion of their right to be accepted into the body of seafarers who were "old salts" and who had ventured widely across the oceans. Meanwhile, the alcohol which was paid to Neptune as forfeits was "merrily drunk by all the rest that had been there before".[5]

Quite what the 300 or so slaves on the *Lady Nelson* or the 360 aboard the *Hudibras* made of these strange rituals is hard to imagine. Probably known to most of those who made the middle passage as captives only as a new and different set of terrifying noises coming from deck, nevertheless the implications of a "world turned upside down" were profoundly changed by the context of transatlantic slavery. Not least, the racial stratification that the slave trade fostered – one unified white race and one

---

Theatre on the Bounty (Cambridge: Cambridge University Press, 1992) 76–80; Marcus Rediker, *Between the Devil and the Deep Blue Sea* (Cambridge: Cambridge University Press, 1987) 186–9.

[3] Dening, *Mr Bligh's Bad Language* 77.

[4] William Butterworth, *Three Years Adventures of a Minor in England, Africa, the West Indies, South-Carolina, and Georgia* (Leeds: Edward Baines, 1822) 14.

[5] Dening, *Mr Bligh's Bad Language* 76–80; Peter Earle, *Sailors: English Merchant Seamen 1650–1775* (London: Methuen, 1998) 96–7; British Library Add Mss 39946; John Newton, *The Journal of a Slave Trader, 1750–1754* Bernard Martin and Mark Spurrell (eds.) (London: The Epworth Press, 1962) 9.

unified black race – was both mirrored and disregarded during the ceremony. Free black seamen or cooks were generally greeted by Neptune just
as any other crewmember would have been, while the vast majority of the
Africans present – those condemned to the doom of the marketplace and
perpetual enslavement – were excluded from the entire event. While the
"world" of the ship "was turned upside down", they were locked below
decks, beneath that world, a symbolic representation of their future place
in the slaveholding societies of the Americas.

Although the historiography on the transatlantic slave trade is vast,
traditionally there has been little place for mention of such maritime rituals. This is understandable, as in trying to untangle the motives, effects,
and data of the trade, all of which have had such a profound effect on the
modern world, the fact that seamen continued their rites while working
aboard slave ships seems irrelevant at best, sickening at worst. Encapsulated in these rituals, however, are some truths about these men who
were so central to the slave trade. Seamen created a world turned upside
down because they were traditionally abused, lowly and powerless. In
some ways they continued to see themselves as such aboard a slave ship –
and indeed these factors were exaggerated by the conditions of the trade
in human beings – although the reality was that they had a great deal of
power over those they transported as captives for sale.

The loyalties, opinions, attitudes and motivations of slave trade seamen are the focus of this book. My starting point is the gap between the
image they have in the history of the slave trade and the way they are
described in the literature on seamen in all trades. In the first they appear
rarely, and then mainly as adjuncts to the will of the captain, as his sub-
ordinates in the violence and cruelty inflicted on the millions of African
captives transported as cargo across the Atlantic Ocean. While in no way
denying the wrongs sailors did to members of their human cargoes, this
view is contradictory to the view of seafarers working in other maritime
trades in the eighteenth and early nineteenth centuries.[6] As will be shown,
there were steadfast divisions operating in the slave trade which decisively
separated sailors from their captains and senior officers. Faced with the
perilous event of a slave revolt, sailors threw these divisions to the winds
to save their own lives as well as, in the process, securing the merchants'

---

[6] Rediker, *Between the Devil*; Marcus Rediker, "Common Seamen and the Histories of
Capitalism and the Working Class" *International Journal of Maritime History* 1 (1989);
Jesse Lemisch, *Jack Tar vs. John Bull: The Role of New York's Seamen in Precipitating
the Revolution* (New York: Garland Press, 1997).

profits. In less extreme situations, however, the common sailor generally had few allegiances to his captain's worldview, much fewer still to those of the trade's financial investors.

Outside of slave trade historiography, the image of eighteenth-century white sailors is one of men who, united by class and professional loyalties, could be more accepting of having black men as colleagues than their non-seafaring peers. Clearly this is hard to reconcile with popular ideas about the seamen who worked aboard slaving vessels. Yet the maritime workforce had always been multiracial in nature as it enticed men from all around the edges of the seas into it in a variety of roles. Combined with a "morbid attachment to their profession" and an ersatz kinship system among sailors, this led to an occupation which often confounded the prevailing racial categorizations in an era when increasingly impermeable divisions of black and white were being formulated.[7] Historians such as Jeffrey Bolster, Julius Scott and David Cecelski have shown how white and black seamen worked alongside each other from Canada down to the Caribbean in ways which sometimes defied the strict racial divisions of eighteenth-century America.[8]

While the focus of Bolster, Scott and Cecelski's work is primarily black seafarers – their interaction with white sailors is largely a secondary concern – the work of Peter Linebaugh and Marcus Rediker takes the image of seaman and slave as colleagues, co-conspirators and allies much further. Building on their earlier work and the tradition of the radical Atlantic, in *The Many-Headed Hydra* they argue that seamen and slaves worked together around the ocean's littoral to oppose the rise of

---

[7] Robinson, *A Sailor Boy's Experience* 32–3; Rediker, *Between the Devil* 243–4.

[8] W. Jeffrey Bolster, *Black Jacks: African American Seamen in the Age of Sail* (Cambridge: Harvard University Press, 1997); W. Jeffrey Bolster, "'To Feel Like a Man': Black Seamen in the Northern States 1800–1860" *Journal of American History* 76 (1990) 1173–1199; W. Jeffrey Bolster, "An Inner Diaspora: Black Sailors Making Selves" Ronald Hoffman, Mechal Sobel and Frederika J. Teute (eds.) *Through a Glass Darkly: Reflections on Personal Identity in Early America* (Chapel Hill: University of North Carolina Press, 1997) 419–448; Julius S. Scott III, "The Common Wind: Currents of Afro-American Communication in the Era of the Haitian Revolution" Unpublished PhD Dissertation, Duke University (1986); Julius S. Scott, "Crisscrossing Empires: Ships, Sailors and Resistance in the Lesser Antilles in the Eighteenth Century" Robert L. Paquette and Stanley L. Engerman (eds.) *The Lesser Antilles in the Age of European Expansion* (Gainsville: University of Florida Press, 1996); Julius S. Scott, "Afro-American Sailors and the International Communication Network: The Case of Newport Bowers" Richard Twomey and Colin Howell (eds.) *Jack Tar in History: Essays in the History of Maritime Life and Labor* (New Brunswick: Acadiensis Press, 1991); David. S. Cecelski, *The Waterman's Song: Slavery and Freedom in North Carolina* (Chapel Hill: University of North Carolina Press, 2001).

capitalism. Along with various other dispossessed groups of people, they view seamen and slaves as having shared loyalties and understandings which they used to unite in opposing the wealthy merchants and planters who oppressed them. Linebaugh and Rediker's argument is multifaceted and their time scale and scope far greater than mine, but nonetheless positioning these arguments within the history of the transatlantic slave trade is challenging.[9]

In trying to understand how these diverse schools of thought apply to the men who worked aboard slaving vessels, this book explores how slave trade sailors expanded their cries for liberty because of their working conditions and terms of employment. As has been acknowledged in other settings, those who experienced slavery in close relief often came to recognize the importance of liberty all the more. Sailors fought any comparison of their condition with that of African captives and took that fight into their larger battle for better pay, fair treatment and liberty from the naval press and merchant crimps around the Atlantic world. At the same time, during the dread middle passage, seamen used their own brutalization and turned it, redoubled, onto those they had under their command. So often under the coercive rule of a slave ship captain, a common seaman could suddenly conceive himself as powerful when standing guard over the hatch of a stinking, fetid, slave hold. Regularly himself ordered to strip off and endure the lash, a sailor rarely showed restraint when ordered to flog a member of the captive cargo.

In participating in the business of the slave trade, seamen were undoubtedly implicated in the formation of racial designations in the late eighteenth century, which created a notion of racial supremacy that ran counter to the way in which seafaring in general operated. The historiographical debate into the formation of "white" as a meaningful racial category consequently has implications for seamen's work aboard slaving vessels. As historians such as David Roediger, Theodore Allen, Matthew Frye Jacobson and Eric Lott have argued, working-class men came to see their white skin as meaningful when they were in close contact with racial slavery in North America.[10] Likewise, white seamen could obviously see

---

[9] Peter Linebaugh and Marcus Rediker, *The Many-Headed Hydra: Sailors, Slaves, Commoners and the Hidden History of the Revolutionary Atlantic* (Boston: Beacon Press, 2000).

[10] David R. Roediger, *The Wages of Whiteness: Race and the Making of the American Working Class* (London: Verso, 1991); Theodore W. Allen, *The Invention of the White Race: The Origin of Racial Oppression in Anglo-America* (London: Verso, 1997); Matthew Frye Jacobson, *Whiteness of a Different Color: European Immigrants and the Alchemy*

the value of their own skin colour, because, whatever their own lack of liberty, it was what ultimately protected them from the slave markets of America and the Caribbean.

Yet white seamen's workmates aboard slaving vessels were of many different ethnic origins and included African, African-American and Afro-Caribbean co-workers. In Africa and the Caribbean sailors formed alliances across the colour-line as that line came to be conceived in the plantation societies to which they sold their human merchandise. The slave trade swept countless Africans and their descendents into the Atlantic labour force as maritime workers, creating allegiances among the seafaring community which could confound the larger racial stratification of plantation societies and were often seen as threatening by the authorities. Just as the paradigm of "transatlantic" has more recently been exchanged for a "circum-Atlantic" viewpoint, so the history of slave trade sailors suggests that their influences and motivations often led simultaneously down multi-directional, and sometimes contradictory, channels.[11]

Exploring his concept of the "black Atlantic", Paul Gilroy describes a ship as "a living, microcultural, micropolitical system in motion" and urges his readers to get aboard. Following in his wake, I can only ask readers to do the same.[12] "The sea" as Derek Walcott declared, "is history".[13]

---

of Race (Cambridge: Harvard University Press, 1998); Eric Lott, *Love and Theft: Black-face Minstrelsy and the American Working Class* (New York: Oxford University Press, 1993).

[11] For example, Joseph Roach, *Cities of the Dead: Circum-Atlantic Performance* (New York: Columbia University Press, 1996); David Armitage, "Three Concepts of Atlantic History" David Armitage and Michael J. Braddick (eds.) *The British Atlantic World, 1500–1800* (Hampshire: Palgrave Macmillan, 2002) 16–18.

[12] Paul Gilroy, *The Black Atlantic: Modernity and Double Consciousness* (Cambridge: Harvard University Press, 1993) 4–5.

[13] Derek Walcott, "The Sea is History" *The Star-Apple Kingdom* (New York: Farrar, Straus and Giroux, 1979).

Introduction

When Irishman James Field Stanfield wrote a poem about the transatlantic slave trade in 1789, he turned to the melodramas of antiquity to explain the scale of the horrors committed. He began by invoking "O heav'nly Muse! with Sybil-bough" to "Lead thro' the horrors of these scenes of woe". He continued:

> Help me to paint the melancholy view,
> The dismal track of ocean to pursue,
> And with the Eagle-eye of Truth pervade
> All the dark mazes of th' *inhuman Trade*.[1]

By 1789 there were many poems written attacking the slave trade, yet quickly Stanfield's poem takes a turn which, while seemingly commonplace, is actually challenging to twenty-first century readers. He writes:

> Shut now from comfort, agoniz'd with grief,
> Hopeless alike of justice, or relief –
> [....]
> Subdu'd by pow'r, by misfortune worn,
> Or by the pangs of hopeless passion torn;
> Weary of griefs no patience can endure.
> They seek the *Lethe* of a mortal cure.

Written alone out of context it seems typical enough, but what is unusual about these words is that Stanfield is not speaking of the Africans who were the victims of the slave trade, but rather, "Neptune's sons", the

[1] James Field Stanfield, *The Guinea Voyage: A Poem in Three Books* (London: James Phillips, 1789).

I

"dauntless crew" who would "steer their vessel through the boist'rous main".[2]

James Field Stanfield had himself been a seaman on a slave ship, and a year prior to publishing this poem had written of his experiences in a book entitled *The Guinea Trade and Letters*.[3] After returning to Britain he became an ardent abolitionist, and indeed the poem's focus is the suffering of those ripped from their homelands for sale in the Americas. He wrote of these people in the lines:

> In painful rows with studious art comprest,
> Smoking they lie, and breathe the humid pest:
> Moisten'd with gore, on the hard platform ground,
> The bare-rubb'd joint soon bursts the painful bound....

Perhaps he spoke of a painful memory when remembering,

> In one long groan the feeble throng unite;
> One strain of anguish wastes the lenthen'd night.[4]

Yet this was not Stanfield's only concern. In his earlier book he had written of the many hardships and inhumanities the seamen had endured on board the slave ship, and the life-threatening circumstances they had faced. In fact, only he and two other crewmen had ultimately survived and returned to Britain. A theme of both his book and his poem was that sailors were denied their liberty in the slave trade, with many being forced aboard slave ships against their will. The lines of his poem express in verse the subject of crimping which he had previously addressed in prose:

> For this tribe a confed'rate take the wing,
> And round resistless youth their poisons fling.
> Polluted dens of infamy they throng,
> With painted vice, to raise the Syren-song;
> With specious arts subdue th' unwary mind,
> Then close their web, and fast their victims bind.
> At length with debts fictitious charge their case,
> And make a *dungeon* stare them in the face.[5]

---

[2] Ibid.
[3] James F. Stanfield, *The Guinea Voyage and Letters* (London, 1807); reprinted in Thomas Howard (ed.) *Black Voyage: Eyewitness Accounts of the Atlantic Slave Trade* (Boston: Little, Brown and Co., 1971).
[4] Stanfield, *A Poem*.
[5] Ibid.

His book had contained a detailed description of how crimping worked, a fate of which he claimed to have personal knowledge. He had written:

There are public houses, under the influence and in the pay of merchants. Every allurement and artifice is held out to entice [sailors] into these infamous dens. Festivity and music lay hold of the deluded senses, prostitution throws in a fascinating spell with too much success, and intoxication generally gives the business its fatal period. In these houses, every temptation to run to debt is most studious offered; this, with an unthinking sailor, is easily brought about.[6]

"When the debt is sufficient for the purpose", he concluded, "a Guinea ship is offered". "Some few, the voluntary woe embrase", he noted in his poem, and even they were enlisting aboard "Sore from false friends, or undeserv'd disgrace". The slave trade, James Field Stanfield clearly believed, was not a business seamen joined from preference.[7]

This linking of seamen's woes to that of slaves sits uneasily with mainstream understanding of the transatlantic slave trade. Much of the popular history, literature and even art of the trade unambiguously posits seamen as abusers. This is perhaps most apparent in popular novels. In Toni Morrison's *Beloved*, Sethe's mother and nurse remember that they were "both taken up many times by the crew". The resulting baby her mother "threw away...on the island".[8] In *Ama*, Manu Herbstein similarly writes of female slaves being raped by the crew of the ship on which his eponymous heroine sailed.[9] Perhaps it is telling that it is Barry Unsworth's *Sacred Hunger*, in which the crew as much as the slaves are the protagonists, which most challenges this image.[10]

Part of the problem is the gap between history and memory, a divide which still creates considerable conflict where the slave trade is concerned.[11] Yet even outside of the tradition in which seamen are the faceless abusers of captive slaves, they rarely appear in the historiography in any detail. Moreover, contrary to Stanfield's implications, the focus of the scholarship has implicitly separated slave from sailor. The study

[handwritten margin note: Gap between history + memory]

---

[6] Stanfield, *A Guinea Voyage and Letters* 56–8.
[7] Ibid. Stanfield, *A Poem*.
[8] (London: Vintage, 1987) 62.
[9] (New York: e-reads, 2001) 283–5, 305–6.
[10] (London: Penguin, 1992).
[11] Bernard Bailyn, "Considering the Slave Trade: History and Memory" *William and Mary Quarterly* 58:1 (2001) 245–52; Ralph A. Austen, "The Slave Trade as History and Memory: Confrontations of Slaving Voyage Documents and Communal Traditions" *William and Mary Quarterly* 58:1 (2001) 224–44.

of profit and loss, numbers and figures, accounts and economics divides the two groups categorically. To historians examining the profits of slave traders, seamen appear in the loss column, slaves – or those that survived at least – in the profit column. For those involved in the attempt to quantify the total number of slaves forcibly taken across the Atlantic, seamen have only recently figured in their calculations.[12]

Thus slave trade sailors generally appear in the wider literature only with cat-o'-nine-tails or branding iron in hand, firing fiercely on rebel slaves, or mercilessly raping a captive African woman. Along with the American or Caribbean slaveowner wielding his whip, a sailor standing over a captive African with a branding iron is part of our collective imagery of almost indescribable inhumanity on a scale, in terms of longevity at least, virtually unsurpassed. Let me be clear that this image of seamen is not incorrect; they were certainly guilty of many of the individual acts of brutality committed aboard slave ships. Sailors were far from uni-dimensional tyrants, however. In fact the suffering of crews was one of the factors Seymour Drescher points to in separating the slave trade from the holocaust and other genocides. Victim and perpetrator were less absolute categories aboard a slave ship than in a prison camp, for example, at least as far as seamen's position was concerned.[13]

Writing in 1789, before the slave trade had become a universally condemned crime and so closely allied with the omnipresent problem of racism, Stanfield's use of the same rhetoric to express the suffering of both sailor and slave was not unusual and reflected this blurring of lines between abused and abuser. The British abolitionist movement composed its arguments in this way, as by focusing on the suffering of seaman as well as African captive, their work aboard slave ships was brought to the fore as an aspect of the trouble with slave trading. Sailors' working conditions, death rates, punishments and a host of other facets of their lives were made public giving them an agency they had not held previously. More crucially, it tied their own suffering to that of the slaves they were paid to transport to market. The ill-treatment of both groups

---

[12] Philip Curtin, *The Atlantic Slave Trade: A Census* (Madison: University of Wisconsin Press, 1969); David Eltis, Stephen D. Behrendt, David Richardson and Herbert S. Klein, *The Transatlantic Slave Trade: A CD-ROM* (Cambridge: Cambridge University Press, 1999) [hereafter cited as Eltis, *CD-ROM* with, where relevant, the ID number of the voyage being discussed].

[13] Seymour Drescher, "The Atlantic Slave Trade and the Holocaust: A Comparative Analysis" Alan S. Rosenbaum (ed.) *Is the Holocaust Unique? Perspectives on Comparative Genocide* (New York: Westview Press, 1969) 65–85.

was antithetical to Christianity, humanity and the progress of the British nation, Thomas Clarkson and his supporters alleged.

Stanfield firmly tied the seamen's lack of liberty to that of slaves. He wrote of a sailor becoming his "own master" upon reaching land, and when he ends his poem with the wish that "British freedom smile on Afric's coast" it gives the impression that it was needed both by the slave trade's lowly employees as well as its victims.[14] This was a new take on an old theme, as sailors had long been considered to be "bondsmen of the sea". The term "galley slave", which originally referred to enslaved oarsmen on Greek or Roman galleys, had come to symbolize any person condemned to drudgery, so closely tied were seafaring and moil in the view of contemporary society. This linguistic linkage of seafaring and slavery was so ubiquitous as to be hackneyed – sailors had long called their time on shore "liberty", their time at sea, by implication, being seen as a period of bondage. The term master referred to both captain and slaveowner. What is notable, though, is that such associations, as Stanfield's writing shows, increased rather than dwindled in the face of actual transatlantic chattel slavery. We can only ponder what sights had caused Captain Edward Thompson of the Royal Navy to compose a poem entitled *To Emma, Extempore; Hyaena, off Gambia, June 4th 1779* in which he wrote of himself as "a mere sea-drudge, a very Guinea slave".[15]

James Field Stanfield and the other men who went to sea aboard slaving vessels saw no irony in comparing their status to that of the trade's African victims. As Stanfield implied in both his book and poem, there were important aspects to seafaring work, especially in the slave trade, which were closely related to the central issue of the era, liberty, which was itself inextricable from slavery and the slave trade. However alien it might seem to the popular image of the transatlantic slave trade, in a variety of ways, seamen, and those engaged aboard slave ships specifically, were the Europeans who lived their lives closest to slavery.

Observers of all creeds have long puzzled over the symbiotic growth of both liberty and slavery in the western world. During the eighteenth century the American mainland colonies declared their freedom and that "all men are created equal" while enshrining slavery and continuing their involvement in the slave trade. Later, the French overthrew the monarchy

---

[14] Stanfield, *A Poem*.

[15] James G. Basker, *Amazing Grace: An Anthology of Poems about Slavery, 1660–1810* (New Haven: Yale University Press, 2002) 283.

in the name of *liberté*, *égalité* and *fraternité*, but that idealism was quickly challenged, not least by events in Saint Domingue. The British continued to have a complacent pride in their own brand of freedom, which they believed had been preserved at the time of the Glorious Revolution. Meanwhile, they were the biggest transporters of slaves across the Atlantic in the eighteenth century.[16]

What exactly was meant by the term liberty in the face of such an increase in slave trading, slavery and a whole host of other forms of unfreedom has been the subject of debate since the words were first uttered. The image of "a swaggering libertine . . . with one hand whipping a negro tied to a liberty-pole, and the other dashing an emaciated Indian to the ground" evokes only some of the shortcomings of the American concept of equality and liberty for all, but the most relevant here.[17] British liberty, with its long standing belief in the freedom to own property, including slaves, and its close association with freedom from central government, was no less problematic for prospects of the abolition of slavery. The Somerset decision of 1772 did not actually make slavery illegal in England as is sometimes claimed. Prior to their decisions in 1807 to illegalize the transatlantic slave trade, both Britain and its former American mainland colonies boasted loudly of their freedoms while profiting from its antithesis. The prolonged fight over who would be eligible for freedom and what this would functionally entail is a theme of this book.

Current estimates of the total number of slaves transported across the Atlantic Ocean by all the trading nations are around 11 million men, women and children. Of these, approximately 9.6 million survived to be sold in the Americas.[18] Almost two-thirds of the total number was shipped between 1698 and 1807.[19] To break this down, in the eighteenth century slave ships which left from British ports purchased, at a bare minimum, 2,302,774 slaves from Africa. These are the ones historians have been able to trace. Approximately twelve per cent of those captives died, either while the ship was still anchored in Africa, or on a voyage – the

---

[16] David Brion Davis, *Slavery and Human Progress* (New York: Oxford University Press, 1984); David Brion Davis, *The Problem of Slavery in the Age of Revolution* (Ithaca: Cornell University Press, 1975) especially 343–468; Orlando Patterson, *Freedom: The Making of Western Culture* (New York: Basic Books, 1991); David Brion Davis, *The Problem of Slavery in Western Culture* (Ithaca: Cornell University Press, 1966); Julian Hoppit, *A Land of Liberty? England 1689–1727* (Oxford: Clarendon Press, 2000).

[17] Davis, *Slavery and Human Progress* 150–1.

[18] David Eltis, "The Volume and Structure of the Transatlantic Slave trade: a Reassessment" *William and Mary Quarterly* 58:1 (2001) 17–46.

[19] David Eltis, *The Rise of African Slavery in the Americas* (Cambridge: Cambridge University Press, 2000) 231.

so-called middle passage – which lasted an average of almost nine weeks.[20] Slave ships which left from what became the United States of America are known to have purchased no less than 130,248 captive Africans during the eighteenth century, of whom at least 111,984 survived to be sold at market.[21] Various British territories also had ships involved in the slave trade. Barbadian ships purchased a minimum of 32,207 captives from Africa during the period 1700–1800, Jamaican slave captains bartered and haggled for another 9,368.[22]

The importation of such vast numbers of African captives changed the Americas profoundly. The black populations of all the British colonies in the Americas rose quickly in the eighteenth century, especially in the West Indies and southern plantation colonies. On the eve of the American Revolution, black people made up only three per cent of the population of New England but more than ninety per cent of the British Caribbean islands. In just the twenty year period from 1750 to 1770 the black population of these islands grew by 139,000, overwhelmingly because of importation rather than natural increase.[23] These enslaved Africans were responsible for the creation of vast wealth, principally from the backbreaking cultivation of sugar and cotton. Slavery was associated in the eighteenth century with "wealth and national greatness".[24] West Indian planters' affluence was legendary; they were the emblematic rich men of the era.

Shipping the sugar, cotton, tobacco and other plantation products to the markets of Europe was also a booming industry. Britain's American colonies were by far its most vigorous trading partners in a period when maritime trades as a whole were expanding rapidly and were among the most progressive and eminent of industries. Although the effect of the slave trade itself on Britain's wealth remains controversial – refuting Eric Williams's arguments, Stanley Engerman, David Eltis and others emphasize the relatively low profits the trade delivered to Britain and North America – many have argued that the accumulation of wealth resulting from all overseas trade was central to the transformation to capitalism.[25]

[20] Eltis, *CD-ROM*
[21] Ibid.
[22] Ibid.
[23] John J. McCusker and Russell R. Menard, *The Economy of British America, 1607–1789* (Chapel Hill: University of North Carolina Press, 1985) 54, 219.
[24] Davis, *Slavery and Human Progress* 73.
[25] Eric Williams, *Capitalism and Slavery* (London: Andre Deutsch, 1st published 1944); David Eltis and Stanley L. Engerman, "The Importance of Slavery and the Slave Trade to Industrializing Britain" *Journal of Economic History* 60:1 (2000) 123–44; McCusker and Menard, *The Economy of British America* 39; Robert Brenner, "The Origins of Capitalist

TABLE 1. *Number of slaves known to have been transported on British slave ships, 1731–1810*

1731–5	1736–40	1741–5	1746–50	1751–5	1756–60	1761–5	1766–70
92,596	111,769	70,322	83,098	122,579	116,812	164,832	180,636

1771–5	1776–80	1781–5	1786–90	1791–5	1796–1800	1800–05	1806–10
205,411	80,594	131,844	154,408	178,161	201,883	213,916	89,472

TABLE 2. *Number of slaves known to have been transported on Rhode Island slave ships, 1731–1810*

1731–5	1736–40	1741–5	1746–50	1751–5	1756–60	1761–5	1766–70
3,968	7,513	3,882	2,776	6,981	5,598	10,636	10,573

1771–5	1776–80	1781–5	1786–90	1791–5	1796–1800	1800–05	1806–10
14,584	70	1,006	3,775	7,436	11,761	10,928	12,910

Note: Tables showing the rise in the number of slaves carried across the Atlantic during the final years of legal slave trading. They also show how much the trade was disrupted by the century's wars, particularly the American Revolutionary War. These figures are taken from David Eltis, Stephen D. Behrendt, David Richardson and Herbert S. Klein, *The Transatlantic Slave Trade: a Database on CD-ROM* (Cambridge: Cambridge University Press, 1999). They naturally understate the total number of slaves carried as they represent only those about whom records have survived.

Seaport towns around the Atlantic Ocean, including the major slaving trading ports, were the "dynamic loci of change" which "predicted the future".[26] Dockworkers, shipbuilders and especially sailors were vital and active professional groups throughout the eighteenth century. Seamen were also one of the most significant segments of the workforce,

Development: a Critique of Neo-Smithian Marxism" *New Left Review* 104 (1977) 25–93; Robert Brenner, "Agrarian Class Structure and Economic Development" *Past and Present* 70 (1976) 30–75; Marcus Rediker, *Between the Devil and the Deep Blue Sea* (Cambridge: Cambridge University Press, 1987) 16–19; T.H. Aston and C.H.E. Philpin, *The Brenner Debate* (Cambridge: Cambridge University Press, 1985); Maurice Dobb, *Studies in the Development of Capitalism* (New York: G. Routledge, 1947); Immanuel Wallerstein, *The Modern World-System II: Mercantilism and the Consolidation of the European World-Economy, 1600–1750* (New York: Academic Press, 1980); Ralph Davis, *The Rise of the Atlantic Economies* (Ithaca: Cornell University Press, 1973).

[26] Gary B. Nash, *The Urban Crucible: the Northern Seaports and the Origin of the American Revolution* (Cambridge: Harvard University Press, 1986) ix; McCusker and Menard, *Economy of British America* 39, 57–8.

particularly in the colonies. There were between 25,000 and 40,000 sailors working out of the North Atlantic seaports at any one time between 1700 and 1750; after that date the figure was at least 60,000.[27] Between approximately 300,000 and 350,000 of them sailed for Africa on slave ships from Britain, British territories, and later the independent United States of America between 1750 and 1807.[28]

Partly because of seamen's central role in the creation of wealth while their liberties remained uncertain, the nature of their work in the eighteenth century is hotly debated by historians. Indeed, the conflation of the suffering of slave and sailor as suggested by James Stanfield is far more familiar to the historiography of maritime workers than it is to that of the slave trade. Marcus Rediker argues that as sailors earned wages for their labour and were divorced from traditional craft skills, they were among the first collective labourers. "The assembly and enclosure of wage labourers on the ship, an early precursor of the factory, initiated a process by which labour was carefully coordinated and synchronized", he writes. Yet as their labour power became a commodity, extra economic force was still crucial to the occupation, both on board ship and in getting them to enrol for such employment. Sailors faced both the pull factor of wages paid, and the rather more direct means of compulsion and naked force. The whip was a prominent tool of repression aboard ship as well as on a plantation.[29]

---

[27] Rediker, *Between the Devil* 78, 290.

[28] This figure is calculated from Eltis, *CD-Rom*. It is calculated from the ships which left from British territory and the USA between these years of which the crew is known. For other ships from British territory the total crew is not known, but the total tonnage is; the average from that where crew and tonnage is known is imputed. For another 192 voyages the crew numbers have been approximated from the total slaves carried or the imputed number of slaves carried. A further average is added for the percentage of British ships, as a percentage of the total, for which no port of departure is listed. The total calculated number is 353,654. This of course is approximate; it is impossible to know how many are missing from this total, and as it uses the dataset's figures purporting to be the crew at the voyage's outset, it misses those who joined during the voyage. The extent to which these missing numbers are offset, or exceeded, by the percentage of men who made more than one slaving voyage is unknown. The number of men who made more than one voyage is the reason for the downward rounding of the figure. The figure does roughly fit with the rough measure of two slaves per ton of ship, and one seaman for every ten slaves. Philip D. Morgan calculated a figure of approximately 330,000 seamen involved in Britain's slave trade from 1680–1780. Philip D. Morgan, "British Encounters with Africans and African-Americans circa 1600–1780" *Strangers within the Realm* Bernard Bailyn and Philip D. Morgan (eds.) (Williamsburg,: Institute of Early American History and Culture, 1991) 160.

[29] Rediker, *Between the Devil* 77–90, 288–98, quote 290.

While Rediker's theories remain contested, it is notable that in refuting the early factory image, other historians use symbolism which is very suggestive in terms of seamen's freedom and their work in the slave trade. Arguing against Rediker, Daniel Vickers writes that the rule of all deep-sea sailing ships bore similarities to "absentee-owner plantations" rather than factories, because of their "captive work forces, their floggings and their terrorism, and their quasi-independent managers".[30] There thus seems to be a reasonably wide agreement that coercion, physical punishment and lack of liberty were central elements to seafaring in the eighteenth century, words which recall those of the seaman and aspirant poet Stanfield.[31]

In fact seamen's liberties were increasingly infringed by the exigencies of the era. A sailor, like a slave, was losing status while creating wealth. The rise of capitalism did not always advance a free labour market, but rather yoked some people's non-freedom to its expansion. Sailors straddled the line. While seafaring was one of the first professions to be paid monthly wages, their liberties were compromised by the manner in which they were recruited. In the absence of enough volunteers, the British state began using the press to compel more and more men to join the Royal Navy. Later, these men were often shunted into the merchant service.[32] At a time when the liberty of all was being asserted, and indeed should, theoretically, have been enhanced by the rise of capitalism, seamen were a group of men whose freedoms were systematically compromised.

Having long been Neptune's bondsmen, in the era of proclaimed liberty and equality seamen challenged both impressment into the Royal Navy and trepanning on board merchant ships by comparing them to slavery. This was a particularly compelling argument in North America, where liberty was supposed to be enjoyed by those of European ancestry. The pressing of men into the British Navy was one of the grievances which led the American mainland colonies to seek their independence from the motherland, and to invoke their own brand of liberty in opposition to

---

[30] Daniel Vickers, "Roundtable – Reviews of Marcus Rediker 'Between the Devil and the Deep Blue Sea: Merchant Seamen, Pirates and the Anglo-American Maritime World 1700–1750'" *International Journal of Maritime History* 1 (1989) 311–36, quote 312; Rediker, "The Common Seamen in the History of Capitalism and the Working Class" *International Journal of Maritime History* (1989) 337–57.

[31] Although N.A.M. Rodger would demur, *The Wooden World: An Anatomy of the Georgian Navy* (London: Fontana Press, 1988). See Chapter 3 on the arguments over whipping and coercion in the Royal Navy.

[32] Rediker, *Between the Devil* 288–90.

what they characterized as the tyranny of the crown. Benjamin Franklin identified sailors as being in positions akin to slavery.[33] Historian Jesse Lemisch claims that "the British government seemed to treat the Sons of Neptune little better than slaves" because of the manner in which they recruited them through the press.[34]

The naval press was hardly less controversial in Britain by the period of the American War of Independence, however. It had only ever been grimly tolerated, but even its status as a necessary evil was challenged when it became seen as a form of state enslavement.[35] In 1780 Captain Thomas Pasley said that sailors were the only British men who were "really slaves" because of the danger of their being pressed against their will onto a naval ship.[36] Increasingly seamen's fight against their obligatory service to the navy became linked to the twin themes of liberty and slavery. In 1794 riots broke out in London specifically against crimping and the naval press, whereupon numerous public houses and individuals who were suspected of being involved in crimping were attacked. The political element to these riots is clear in the handbills produced at the time in which French revolutionary ideas of liberty were intermixed with complaints about the crimps and the military press. A common one mentioned the sufferings of "parents that are made wretched, in having their blooming sons torn from them by these Monsters" and asked, "Is this the land so famed for liberty?"[37]

The linkage between crimping or pressing men aboard ship and actual chattel slavery might seem merely rhetorical but it became part of the pro-slave trade campaign. Those who wished to preserve the slave trade saw in the naval press a defence of their industry. If the loyal, brave British tar could have his freedom summarily removed, then why not a heathen, primitive African they demanded? Slave ship captain Hugh

---

[33] Roediger, *Wages of Whiteness* 29.

[34] Lemisch, *Jack Tar* 24.

[35] N.A.M. Rodger's view of seamen cheerfully accepting the press as a necessary evil is hard to accept uncritically in view of the hatred it provoked, *The Wooden World* 164–82; Nicholas Rogers, "Liberty Road: Opposition to Impressment in Britain during the American War of Independence" Colin Howell and Richard Twomey (eds.) *Jack Tar in History: Essays in the History of Maritime Life and Labor* (New Brunswick: Acadiensis Press, 1991) 60.

[36] Nicholas Rogers, "Vagrancy, Impressment and the Regulation of Labour in Eighteenth Century Britain" *Slavery and Abolition* 15:2 (August 1994) 102–13.

[37] J. Stevenson, "The London 'Crimp' Riots of 1794" *International Review of Social History* 16 (1971) 40–58.

Crow, who had men pressed from his ship in Jamaica, wrote that he had "always considered [impressment] to be, in many points of view, much more arbitrary and cruel than what was named the slave trade".[38] This argument continued after the slave trade was banned in 1807, when there was discontent that the abolitionists' and the nation's ire had not been equally directed at the wrongs done to seamen. Eight years after the slave trade was abolished, a pamphlet was written in the form of a letter to William Wilberforce about the naval press, "calling on him ... to prove those feelings of sensibility expressed in the cause of humanity on negro slavery by acting with the same ardor and zeal in the cause of British seamen".[39]

Apart from sailors' loss of freedom because of their necessity to the nation and its wealth, Greg Dening has put forward a further significant argument. He posits that the characterization of seamen as inferior was founded in their importance to the wealth of Britain. "The more the country became dependent on the exploitation of seamen's brilliant skills", he writes, "the more sure it became that seamen were 'children' – improvident, intemperate, profligate. They were lazy children who could have no politics or independence."[40] In an age when the equality of man was heralded, a sailor's place in such a structure – like that of many other groups, especially those of African origin – was ambiguous.

The tenets of this conjectured inferiority are intriguing in terms of their wider connotations. Seamen were infantilized, an image coined of a jolly Jack Tar who was simple both in mind and habit, needed protection from himself and unthinkingly loyal while also being rebellious. Sailors were also depicted as musical, given to dancing, unable to plan ahead, sexually promiscuous and powerless to control their lascivious impulses. All of these traits, of course, were also part of the repertoire of characteristics which were believed in the Americas to comprise the inferiority of "negroes". The perceived failings of the black man and those who had shipped him and his ancestors across the seas were, rather ironically, characterized in much the same way. What is more, while seamen were separated from the rest of the landlubber population by their dress, language

---

[38] Hugh Crow, *Memoirs of the Late Captain Hugh Crow, of Liverpool*; comprising a narrative of his life, together with descriptive sketches of the western coast of Africa; particularly of Bonny (London: Frank Cass, 1970; 1st published 1830) 72.

[39] Thomas Urquhart, *A Letter to William Wilberforce, Esq, MP, on the Subject of Impressment* (London, 1824).

[40] Greg Dening, *Mr Bligh's Bad Language: Passion, Power and Theatre on the Bounty* (Cambridge: Cambridge University Press, 1992) 56.

and gait, this difference was sometimes described in racial terms.[41] And historians such as Marcus Rediker and Jesse Lemisch suggest that sailors, like slaves, defiantly wore whip marks on their backs as a sign of their autonomy and non-compliance as they subverted the epithet Jack Tar into a term of self-respect.[42]

To Rediker, Lemisch and others, these infringements to sailors' freedom, dignity and standing, and their regimented working practices, profoundly politicized them.[43] They point to seamen's role in the bigger history of the revolutionary Atlantic to support this claim. In fact much of the terminology and symbolism of working-class revolt does come from maritime labour in this era. In 1768 seamen had *struck* the sails of their ships in the River Thames, preventing them from sailing out of London. In the process they had popularized the term "strike" and given the red flag that they had raised "as a permanent bequest to the future proletarian movement".[44] During the Gordon Riots of 1780 – the most "formidable commotion" in Britain for almost a century – sailors were noted to be major actors with their traditional weaponry of cutlasses and marlin spikes being carried by many in the mob.[45] Indeed the "greatest revolutionary portents for England" were naval affairs, when the British fleet was wracked by mutinies at Spithead and the Nore in 1797. E.P. Thompson has argued that these were radical revolts, where the politically aware

[41] Ibid; James Dugan, *The Great Mutiny* (New York: G.P. Putnam's Sons, 1965) 90; Valerie Burton, "The Myth of Bachelor Jack: Masculinity, Patriarchy and Seafaring Labor" *Jack Tar in History: Essays in the History of Maritime Life and Labor* Colin Howell and Richard Twomey (eds.) (New Brunswick: Acadiensis Press, 1991); Daniel Vickers, "An Honest Tar: Ashley Bowen of Marblehead" *New England Quarterly* (December 1996) 531–53.

[42] Rediker, *Between the Devil* 211; Jesse Lemisch, "Jack Tar in the Streets: Merchant Seamen in the Politics of Revolutionary America" *William and Mary Quarterly* 25 (1968) 371–407; Valerie Burton, "Myth of Bachelor Jack" 180.

[43] Marcus Rediker, "Common Seamen and the Histories of Capitalism and the Working Class" *International Journal of Maritime History* 1 (1989) 337–357; Rediker, *Between the Devil* 77–9, 288–98. For those who disagree on this point see Daniel Vickers and Vince Walsh, "Young Men and the Sea: the Sociology of Seafaring in Eighteenth Century Salem Massachusetts" *Social History* 24 (January 1999) 17–38; Daniel Vickers, "Beyond Jack Tar" *William and Mary Quarterly* 3rd Series, 50 (1993) 418–24; Vickers and Cadigan "Roundtable" *International Journal of Maritime History* 1 (1989) 311–36; Michael J. Jarvis, "'In the Eye of All Trade': Maritime Revolution and the Transformation of Bermudian Society, 1612–1800" Unpublished PhD Dissertation, College of William and Mary (1998).

[44] Peter Linebaugh, *The London Hanged: Crime and Civil Society in the Eighteenth Century* (London: Penguin, 1991) 310–11.

[45] Linebaugh, *London Hanged* 335, 342–4; Nicholas Rogers, "The Gordon Riots Revisited" *Canadian Historical Society: Historical Papers* (1988) 16–34.

minority turned "a parochial affair of ship's biscuits" into something far more threatening to the British establishment.[46]

As the Liverpool seamen's strike of 1775 (see Chapter 1) made clear, sailors' work in the transatlantic slave trade contributed to the mass of discontentment which made maritime workers rebel in these ways. The conditions of slave trading led to immense disgruntlement among sailors which fed their non-compliance. What is more, as at other times and in other places, it was these men's closeness to actual chattel slavery which gave added insistence to their fight. When the currency of freedom became more highly prized in the age of revolutions, seamen were in the vanguard of the battle not only because their situation was often compromised by recruitment practices, but also because they knew only too well what a lack of liberty could ultimately entail. Freedom was most highly prized by those closest to enslavement.

This analysis raises questions of racial construction, of whether a coherent identity of whiteness can be said to have paralleled the creation of a unified African identity in the setting of a slave ship. The thesis of David Roediger and others, that it was the ability to imagine themselves as slaves that caused working white men in the age of the American Revolution to clearly self-identify themselves as white, would seem to have a particular application in the case of slave ship seamen. Just as land-based poor working men in the same era, slave ship seamen to some extent could have used the "status and privilege conferred by race ... to make up for alienating and exploitative class relationships".[47] When a sailor stood over an African captive with a whip in his hand his stance displayed only too well the gap between his situation and that of an actual chattel slave, no matter how callous his own treatment at the hands of the ship's officers. However oppressed his situation, during the middle passage he had power over the captive cargo, and that was contingent upon the pallor

---

[46] *The Making of the English Working Class* (New York: Random House, 1964) 167–8; Christopher Lloyd, "New Light on the Mutiny at the Nore" *The Mariner's Mirror* 46:4 (1960) 286–95.

[47] David R. Roediger, *The Wages of Whiteness: Race and the Making of the American Working Class* (London: Verso, 1991) 11–13; Sydney W. Mintz and Richard Price, *The Birth of African-American Culture: An Anthropological Perspective* (Boston: Beacon Press, 1992); Theodore W. Allen, *The Invention of the White Race: The Origin of Racial Oppression in Anglo-America* volume II (London: Verso, 1997) chapter 13; Matthew Frye Jacobson, *Whiteness of a Different Color: European Immigrants and the Alchemy of Race* (Cambridge: Harvard University Press, 1998) 17–21; Eric Arnesen, "Whiteness and the Historians' Imagination" *International Labor and Working Class History* 60 (Fall 2001) 3–32.

of his skin. This was the "public and psychological wage" of whiteness between the wooden walls of a slave ship.[48]

While the creation of whiteness is a useful paradigm through which to explore the racial constructions of slave ship seamen, it does not, however, cover the full complexity of the issues involved. White skin may have protected sailors from transatlantic slavery, but many were enslaved in North Africa after capture by the notorious "Sallee rovers" or Barbary pirates. Into the nineteenth century the crews of British and American slave ships continued to be themselves enslaved in the Maghreb, by which time there were over a million Christian slaves in the region.[49] As Linda Colley has recently reminded us, slavery was "racially promiscuous". Britons (and white North Americans) quite contrary to the words of *Rule Britannia*, "could be slaves – and were".[50]

It was not just that white seamen could be enslaved that complicates the study of whiteness in the Atlantic arena. The fact is that the basis of their enslavement in the Maghreb was their religion and culture rather than their skin colour or ethnicity. This reflected continuing beliefs in England that a person's "race" constituted more than the colour of his skin. Roxann Wheeler has recently argued that "Christianity, civility, and rank were more explicitly important to Briton's assessment of themselves and other people than physical attributes such as skin colour, shape of nose or texture of hair".[51] Kathleen Wilson similarly writes that race was "identified and signified through religion, custom, language, climate, aesthetics and historical time as much as physiognomy and skin colour".[52] Dress was also important; it was "the anchor of identity".[53]

[48] Roediger, *Wages of Whiteness*, 6–13, 20, 30–2; Ira Berlin, *Many Thousands Gone: The First Two Centuries of Slavery in America* (Cambridge: Harvard University Press, 1998).

[49] Ibid. Lancashire Record Office, Journal of James Irving, 1789–1790; Lancashire Record Office, Correspondence of James Irving, 1789–1809; Davis, "Slavery – White, Black, Muslim, Christian"; Robert C. Davis, *Christian Slaves, Muslim Masters: White Slavery in the Mediterranean, Barbary Coast and Italy, 1500–1800* (New York: Macmillan, 2003).

[50] Linda Colley, *Captives: Britain, Empire and the World, 1600–1850* (London: Pimlico, 2003) 43–72, quote 63.

[51] Roxann Wheeler, *The Complexion of Race: Categories of Difference in Eighteenth Century British Culture* (Philadelphia: University of Pennsylvania Press, 2000) 7. See also, Dror Wahrman, *The Making of the Modern Self: Identity and Culture in Eighteenth Century England* (New Haven: Yale University Press, 2004) 86–93, 101–4; Colin Kidd, "Ethnicity in the British Atlantic World, 1688–1830" Kathleen Wilson (ed.) *A New Imperial History: Culture, Identity and Modernity in Britain and the Empire, 1660–1840* (Cambridge: Cambridge University Press, 2004) 260–4.

[52] Kathleen Wilson, *The Island Race: Englishness, Empire and Gender in the Eighteenth Century* (London: Routledge, 2003) 11, 151

[53] Wahrman, *The Making of the Modern Self* 177–8; Wheeler, *Complexion of Race* 14–21.

For seamen who were employed on slave ships, therefore, while they were shown clearly how their skin colour was meaningful and far surpassed other factors in determining a person's status on the western side of the Atlantic, they could also identify with black people who, for example, were Christian, spoke English and/or dressed as seamen, in ways which to some extent cut across the divide of skin colour.

This was important because not all seamen were "white", even if that term is used rather anachronistically to include, say, the many men of Irish origin who worked on British and North American slave ships. Just as in all other long-distance commerce, the slave trade enticed men into it as labourers at its various ports of call, as well as in this case taking men, women and children as goods to be bought and sold. In the same way that the European mercantile forces absorbed countless African merchants into the Atlantic financial network, so on the reverse side they drew in less noble born Africans as seamen, porters, interpreters, cooks, canoemen, sentinels and pilots. What is more, some of those who initially made the Atlantic crossing shackled below decks as human cargo would later return to the seas as seamen, stewards and cooks.

These seamen with darker skin formed an integral part of the entire seafaring community, as well as being central players in the transient societies founded on each sailing ship while it was away from land. The kind of rough, limited acceptance of black seamen by their white counterparts which Jeffrey Bolster has written about in the North American context was also often found on British and American slave ships. They may not have always treated them as equals, but they regarded them as fellow members of the crew, trusted them as co-workers and, on occasion, rebelled with them against a ship's officers.[54]

These bonds may have been strained by the circumstances of the slave trade, but the loyalties and attachments of black seamen, of whom some were African, others African-American or Caribbean, and others still Afro-Britons, were definitely not homogenous either. Often no simple lines of black or white could be drawn aboard a slaving vessel, and an African-American seaman who spoke English, dressed in a sailor's distinctive clothing and was conversant with maritime lore would be seen by his colleagues as entirely separate to the alien, naked, incomprehensible mass of humanity locked in the hold. His own feelings on the matter might have been quite different of course. Nevertheless his cultural ties

---

[54] W. Jeffrey Bolster, *Black Jacks: African American Seamen in the Age of Sail* (Cambridge: Harvard University Press, 1997) 70.

and professional identity in some ways cut across the divisions of skin colour, even in the highly divisive setting of a slave ship.

It becomes clear, therefore, that seamen employed aboard slave ships sailed between worlds in which their situation changed radically. Sailors aboard slaving vessels lived complex lives in which not only were they employed in an industry that was constantly bolstering the cataclysm of American slavery and racism, they also sailed between continents with very different views of racial construction. In Africa they might be disciplined by an African slave merchant or even enslaved to an Islamic master. By the time they crossed the Atlantic to sell their human cargo, those of European heritage gained status as their white skin entitled them to some privileges in the plantation societies of the Americas.

The effects of slave trading on seamen were, ultimately, contradictory. It is not hard to see how a lowly seaman, himself forced against his will onto the vessel and at the mercy of his captain, would turn exploiter to those over whom he held so much power. The most oppressed man in the crew could suddenly conceive himself powerful when, armed with a musket, he faced his shackled charges. Seamen had both a pressing personal interest in quashing slave rebellions – many seamen were killed in such revolts – and also a financial stake, as they would not be paid if the "cargo" was lost. Individual seaman was pitted against individual slave in terms of wages docked for an escapee during a man's watch. Cases where white sailors were implicated in a slave revolt may not have been totally unheard of, but they were highly exceptional and probably reflected a captain's fears as much as the reality of the situation.[55] A slave ship would essentially appear to be a setting in which a man's white skin came to be highly meaningful and imbued with privilege and power.

Yet these were some of the same men who were apparently particularly willing to accept black colleagues even in racially divided North America. Jeffrey Bolster claims that white seamen "empathized with the plight of blacks" in general.[56] Julius S. Scott has argued that in the Caribbean, sailors and slaves often found "common cause". He posits slave trade seamen as major purveyors of information about the French Revolution and British abolitionism to West Indian enslaved field

---

[55] David Eltis, *The Rise of African Slavery in the Americas* (New York: Cambridge University Press, 1999) 157n; Davis, "Slavery – White, Black, Muslim, Christian". See chapter 3 for a discussion of these cases.
[56] Ibid.

hands.[57] David Cecelski has shown how sailors and slaves cooperated, sometimes in ways which allowed the bondsmen to escape to freedom, along the waterways of North Carolina. The maritime world held out the promise of liberty, he argues, because "slavery always frayed at the sea's edge".[58] These attitudes, I suggest, were not antithetical to work in the slave trade, but could co-exist within the same men. The complexities of seafarers' history in the slave trade is that they could, and did, brutally quash slave revolts, whip those who would not dance or eat and commit rape, while in other circumstances their ethics could extend to the kind of acceptance or assistance described by Scott, Bolster and Cecelski.

Part of the contradiction between this image and the more familiar one set out in works which study the victims of the transatlantic slave trade is that for seamen a slave voyage comprised far more than the middle passage. A ship away from land was, in Foucault's terms, a "heterotopia par excellence". It was "a floating piece of space, a place without a place".[59] Away from all usual social boundaries, seamen found themselves suddenly instilled with great power over chained, shackled numbers of people far larger than themselves and in a situation when cruelty could be encouraged or even demanded. The historical consequences of the middle passage are, of course, vast. Yet for seamen it was only part, and a relatively short part, of the much longer journey which was a slave ship's voyage. That encompassed, for them, longer periods of time spent in Africa and the Caribbean in which they worked alongside men of African origin. Both aspects of the entire experience affected them, and in ways which were complex and interwoven, and which could change as the circumstances demanded.

The loyalties and actions of sailors who were employed in the slave trade therefore defy any easy classification. In many ways their actions on shore – fighting for liberty, working alongside black colleagues – seem in direct contradiction to their actions during the voyage westwards across the ocean. Examining the intricate ways in which their work in the slave trade affected their fight for liberty, higher pay and better treatment, and provoked them to be a profession seen as tolerant to black people in the

---

[57] Julius S. Scott III, "The Common Wind: Currents of Afro-American Communication in the Era of the Haitian Revolution" Unpublished PhD Dissertation, Duke University (1986) 64–5, 135, 169.

[58] David. S. Cecelski, *The Waterman's Song: Slavery and Freedom in North Carolina* (Chapel Hill: University of North Carolina Press, 2001).

[59] Michel Foucault, "Of Other Spaces" in Nicholas Mirzoeff (ed.) *The Visual Culture Reader* (London: Routledge, 1998) 236.

Americas is a central theme of this study. As David Eltis writes, "the relationship between those charged with carrying the slaves to the Americas and the African slaves themselves was among the most complicated of all forms of human interaction".[60] Unravelling some of these complexities is the aim of the chapters which follow.

In attempting this task, a wide range of sources have been consulted, very few of which are unproblematic. Journals left by common seamen who sailed on slave ships are relatively rare. Most sailors were illiterate, or certainly not able to write more than their name and a few odd words. As a consequence, those who left eloquent, detailed accounts of their time at sea were by their very nature atypical. Yet these journals provide fascinating insight into the lives of seamen. Aside from James Field Stanfield's book, already mentioned, often used in this work are the accounts left by Samuel Robinson and William Butterworth. Robinson sailed on the slave ship *Lady Nelson* in 1801, Butterworth on the *Hudibras* – a ship named after a poem which had depicted Africans as "demonic other[s], in league with the Devil" – sailed in 1786. A number of other journals, both published and unpublished, have also been consulted.[61]

It is impossible to examine the lives of slave trade sailors without turning to the notes, arguments and evidence that Thomas Clarkson collected when fighting for the abolition of the trade. These are fascinating as they offer minute details into the suffering of seamen and their opinions towards the slave trade. Naturally, however, both these and the later evidence of many such men at the parliamentary enquiry into the slave trade have to be read in light of the aim they hoped to achieve. They were marshalling their evidence to show the trade in its worst possible light. Nevertheless, they are a remarkable source in that often lowly, illiterate seamen got to express their grievances in their own words.

Other sources, and possibly the ones which have provoked the most controversy, are the records of the High Court of the Admiralty, and the various Vice-Admiralty Court records. Along with newspaper reports, a

---

[60] *The Rise of African Slavery in the Americas* (Cambridge: Cambridge University Press, 2000) 156.

[61] Samuel Robinson, *A Sailor Boy's Experience Aboard a Slave Ship* (Wigtown: G.C. Book Publishers, 1996; 1st published 1867); William Butterworth, *Three Years Adventures of a Minor in England, Africa, the West Indies, South-Carolina, and Georgia* (Leeds: Edward Baines, 1822); Basker, *Amazing Grace* 8; William Richardson, *A Mariner of England: An Account of the Career of William Richardson from Cabin Boy in the Merchant Service to Warrant Officer in the Royal Navy 1780–1817* Colonel Spencer Childers (ed.) (London: John Murray, 1908); John Hoxse, *The Yankee Tar: An Authentic Narrative of the Voyages and Hardships of John Hoxse* (Northampton: John Metcalf, 1740).

problem with these is that they record the aberrant. Rarely did a commonplace slaving voyage without any particular horrors make it into the newspapers in the form of seamen's letters; never were they reported on to the admiralty courts. The evidence offered in these sources is, furthermore, often fragmentary and hard to evaluate, as the contemporary judgement is missing. Yet they still "offer an unparalleled glimpse into the rough and rowdy world of the deep-sea sailor".[62] To take up the challenge to observe seamen at work and ashore, these sources must be searched, whatever their limitations.

[62] Rediker, *Between the Devil* 315–6.

PART ONE

SAILORS AND SLAVE SHIPS

The crew are not human beings but things,
"manufactured men"
... their permanent condition is sordidness.[1]

[1] C.L.R. James, *Mariners, Renegades and Castaways: The Story of Herman Melville and the World We Live In* (London: Allison and Busby, 1985) 22.

I

Slaving Merchants and Merchant Seamen

In 1775, Liverpool, Britain's major slave trading port, was wracked with protests against slaving merchants. It was the largest riot the country had suffered for some years. Around 1,000 sailors, each wearing a red ribbon in his hat, took to the streets and marched in protest behind a red or "Bloody Flag".[1] The mob made no secret of whom they reviled, threatening "hostile visits" to all merchants involved in the slave trade. First they visited Thomas Ratcliffe, financier of the slave ships *Townside* and *Little Ben*, and then moved onto Thomas Yate, who partially funded the *Derby*'s slaving voyages. Later the homes of William James, who invested in more than 130 slaving voyages from the 1750s to the 1770s, and John Simmons, who had become a merchant after captaining several slave ships, were attacked. Slaver captains were also at risk. Captain Henry Billinge, who commanded seven slaving voyages, later testified that he was hit by an armed seaman named Thomas Pearson after the latter heard a woman in the crowd identify Billinge as "a Guinea Captain".[2]

The seamen's outrage had apparently been sparked by a single act. The trouble began on board the slave ship *Derby*, bound for Angola and Jamaica when the investors in the voyage, including Thomas Yate, had attempted to cut the wages of seamen who had already been hired. The crisis brewing in North America had detrimentally affected trade in

[1] R. Barrie Rose, "A Liverpool Sailors' Strike in the Eighteenth Century" *Transactions of the Lancashire and Cheshire Antiquarian Society* 68 (1958) 85–92; PL 27/5, Information of Thomas Green, 5 September 1775.
[2] PL 27/5, Information of Henry Billinge, 27 September 1775.

23

Liverpool leaving many seamen unemployed. The merchants of the *Derby*, faced with a glut of possible employees, decided to cut the wages of seamen despite the fact that they had already enlisted on the ship. Payment would be reduced from thirty to twenty shillings per month, well below normal rates in the "Guinea trade". The twenty-five or so sailors aboard refused to accept the wage cut and struck the ship's sails, preventing it from departing for Africa. Unfortunately, in the mayhem that followed some damage was caused to the sails and nine of the company were put in jail.[3]

This act of attempting to reduce the sailors' wages and then imprisoning the strikers proved to be the catalyst for an unleashing of a display of detestation among the town for the slave trade and those whom it had made wealthy. By the end of the first day 3,000 seamen had assembled in Liverpool city centre to demand their colleagues' release and had "forced themselves into a Ring with intent...to form a Combination for raising their Wages".[4] After slaver merchants' homes were attacked they turned their fury onto the Exchange, the administrative building where the eighty-one slave ships that returned home to Liverpool in 1775 reported the details of their voyages. The violence used was unwavering as sailors assailed this symbol of authority and commerce with weaponry including cannons taken from the whaleship *Betty*, which was in the harbour alongside the *Derby*. A reputed leader of the seamen, George Hill, allegedly declared that he would not be satisfied until the building was razed to the ground.[5]

Many of the working class of Liverpool had close ties to the slave trade and the riotous mob comprised a wide section of the population of the city. In the aftermath of the rebellion collections were taken throughout the town for the seamen, showing widespread sympathy and solidarity with their cause. One of the protestors, who would later be tried for her part in the trouble, was an illiterate woman named Elizabeth Schofield who had apparently been heard, "with a Shout and Flourish of her Hatt, to call to the massed gang of seamen, 'Now My Boys, Fire away of the Door (meaning the Gaol Door) and let the Prisoners Free'".[6] Clearly the protestors had the sympathy and support of many outside the immediate ranks of seamen.

---

[3] Rose, "Liverpool Sailors' Strike"; Eltis, *CD-ROM*, 29523.
[4] Ibid. PL 27/5, Information of James Waring, 4 September 1775.
[5] PL 27/5, Information of Cuthbert Bisbowery, 2 September 1775.
[6] PL 27/5, Information of Constable James Smoult, 5 September 1775.

The event terrified the authorities so greatly that they rented guards from a neighbouring town to go and suppress the uprising. There was no compromise. The soldiers fired at the mob, killing and wounding a number of the protestors.[7] What particularly alarmed the government was that the rebellion was more than just an enraged riot. The seamen of Liverpool were politicized as well as violent, illustrated by their red ribbons and the red flag of activism behind which they marched.

Worryingly for the establishment, the riot invoked memories of the Boston Tea Party less than two years earlier. "I could not think but we had Boston here", wrote a journalist upon observing the conflict.[8] Sailors had been involved in the burgeoning unrest in the American colonies for a decade since the Stamp Act had caused colonial maritime activity to stagnate. Many sailors had taken to the streets, their political motivations and economic needs intertwined. With the American colonies still in open rebellion, the British government could not countenance domestic unrest, especially not in so profitable a port as Liverpool. Maritime industry was central to the prosperity of the island nation.

In the American colonies it had been the pressing of American seamen into the British navy, symbolized as their lack of personal freedom, which was the particular *bête noire*. This then widened to encompass protests against sailors' poor pay and appalling conditions and treatment. Jesse Lemisch summed up what the seamen protestors in America wanted with one word: "justice".[9] This formulation also has a particular application for understanding what specifically caused the Liverpool seamen to loathe the slave trade to such an extent. The catalyst for the revolt was clearly the attempt to reduce the wages of the crew of the *Derby*, but it is apparent from subsequent events that the hostility of common seamen and even other residents of Liverpool towards the slave trade and its merchants cut much deeper than that one specific incident. Poor pay was the fuel that had fanned the flames of discontent, but lack of liberty and poor working

---

[7] Richard Brooke, *Liverpool as It Was During the Last Quarter of the Eighteenth Century, 1775–1800* (Liverpool: J. Mawdsley and Son, 1853) 323–45; Rose, "Sailors' Strike"; Eltis, CD-ROM suggests that these reports are confused as to the captain of the ship on which the strike started, as they claim that the *Derby*'s captain was named Yates. The CD-ROM however suggests that the *Derby*'s captain in 1775 was Luke Mann, and although a man named Peter Yates was working as a slaver captain out of Liverpool in this period, it is likely that the confusion lies with the fact that two of the *Derby*'s owners are listed as John and Thomas Yate. See voyage 92523.

[8] Rose, "Sailors' Strike".

[9] Jesse Lemisch, *Jack Tar vs. John Bull: The Role of New York's Seamen in Precipitating the Revolution* (New York: Garland Press, 1997) 155.

conditions were also certainly identifiable grievances of Liverpool's slaver seamen, and for reasons which resulted specifically from the organization of the trade.

In fact the circumstances of slave trading in Liverpool in the 1770s suggest that the demand for freedom as well as fair pay was closely related to the level of antipathy seamen held for slave merchants. Because slave ships were unpleasant working environments filled with risk, many seamen did not voluntarily opt to make a slaving voyage if other work was available. Rare among maritime trades in the late eighteenth century, slave ship captains often had to resort to crimps to make up their crew, a situation directly linked to sailors' poor treatment and conditions on slave ships. Crimps were a renegade, civilian force performing the same job that the press did for naval ships. Unlike the naval press, however, their work was not government-sanctioned and they often resorted to trickery involving alcohol, prostitutes, debt and various other techniques to trepan men on board slavers. Clearly no more reconcilable to the concept of liberty than the press, and with far less to justify it in terms of national necessity and civic duty, seamen added the use of crimps – resulting from atrocious treatment – to their grievances against slaving merchants.

There was another aspect to seamen's protests, though. The complaints of seamen against the slave trade, and indeed against other trades, did not just have immediate, direct origins. In a much wider sense the slave trade had caused sailors to resent their working situations. It is one of the ironies of history that the trade which supplied millions of Africans in chains to the Americas to be sold as slaves was among the first to pay its own workers regular wages.[10] That seamen in Liverpool were prepared to take to the streets to fight for higher wages in a profession where their victims would earn none appears to further heighten the paradox. The concurrent obsession with liberty among seamen pushes the coincidences too far. Just as men and ships were swept around the ocean by the wind and the tides, so too were tales of suffering in this most abhorrent of trades. Such information created a heightened estimation of what it meant to be free, and a deepening hostility regarding the economic power that seamen lacked. Those who worked as seamen on board slave ships were at the forefront of battles for liberty, better pay and "justice" and were fully cognizant of the changing nature of free wage labour, while its antithesis was created by their toil. Slavery and the slave trade had amplified the

---

[10] Arthur L. Stinchcombe, *Sugar Island Slavery in the Age of Enlightenment: The Political Economy of the Caribbean World* (Princeton, NJ: Princeton University Press, 1995).

importance of fair pay, good treatment and personal freedom around the Atlantic world by the mid-1770s. Seamen wanted what they felt was their rightful share of all three assets.

Isaac Parker experienced the extremes that seafaring had to offer in the eighteenth century. As a sailor on the Liverpool slave ship *Latham* that transported 308 slaves from Old Calabar and Bonny to Barbados and Grenada in the 1760s he complained of being so short of food that he deserted. He left the ship in Africa, where he lived with an African trader's son, and went with him up river in canoes "fitted out with ammunition, cutlasses, pistols, powder and ball, and two guns, which were three-pounders, fixed upon a block of wood". Hiding until night, they ransacked villages, kidnapping the inhabitants for sale to European captains. Unusually for the late eighteenth century, Isaac Parker took part directly in the initial enslavement process itself. Yet this is not the end of Parker's story, for three years after these events he signed on a ship called *Endeavour*. As a boatswain's mate under Captain James Cook, Parker toured the uncharted lands of New Zealand and Australia's eastern coast, and returned home feted as a hero, doubtless glowing in the reflected glory of one of England's greatest explorers.[11]

Parker's fellow seaman, Richard Drake, had rather different life experiences. He not only worked as a slave trade sailor, but also personally endured considerable misery below decks. Of his misfortune, which began at a young age, he gave the following heartrending account:

I never saw my father. He was a seafaring man . . . lost in a gale four months after his marriage to my mother, a daughter of a spinner in one of the cotton mills at Stockford, England. I can just remember her and also a room full of strange people, a red box and a man standing beside it, talking in a loud voice; then a dismal walk through the rain, to a field where some men had just finished digging a hole in the ground.

After that Drake's home was the workhouse, until he went overseas at the age of twelve. He travelled to America as one of 450 Irish immigrants crowded into steerage on the ship *Polly*, whose sailors "knocked [him] about". Drake remembered the voyage as "pestilential" as "whole families literally wallowed in poisonous filth . . . their tattered garments . . . incrusted and impregnated with the most offensive matter". Only 186 of the original number survived the typhus and dysentery that

[11] ZHC 1/84 123–5, 131; Eltis, *CD-ROM*, 91292; National Library of Australia and the Australian National Maritime Museum, *Endeavour, Captain Cook's Journal 1768–71: A CD-ROM* (National Library of Australia, 1999).

broke out in the horrendous conditions. Then at the age of fourteen he went on board the slave ship *Coralline* and remained engaged in the trade even after it passed out of legality.[12]

Within these stories lies the central contradiction at the heart of seamen's histories, for they were at once perpetrators and victims, heroes and villains. Exploiters of men and women who were forced onto their ships or who lived in the ports they visited, the seamen themselves were also brutally exploited by the merchants and captains who employed them. Committing many of the baser acts that made the middle passage such an unforgettable outrage against humanity, they themselves were contemporaneously viewed as peripheral, abject members of society. Two of the most well known slaver captains of the era both considered sailors in these terms. John Newton wrote to the Reverend D. Jennings from his slaving voyage in 1750 that sailors were "the refuse and dregs of the nation," that many were from jail, and that he spent much time while in Africa pondering on their "unhappy degeneracy".[13] Hugh Crow, who sailed half a century later, stated that seamen were "the very dregs of the community".[14]

These sentiments were obviously shared by merchants, as one investor in slaving voyages expressed his belief that "half the fellows who ship themselves for Seamen are little better than pick Pocketts".[15] If we were to look for a more marginalized occupational group than seamen it would be hard to find one outside of criminal groups, or, of course, slaves. Most seafaring men were recruited from "the lowest ranks of society", that is, men whose families formed part of the hugely swelling ranks of the urban poor, and who had little choice but to eke out a living earning meagre wages however they could.[16] It was a profession cleaved by divisions of class as well as gender. Men who went to sea "were overwhelmingly of humble birth".[17]

Even for penniless seamen, though, slave trading was regarded as an uncommonly abhorrent occupation. A satirical seaman's prayer published

---

[12] Richard Drake, *Revelations of a Slave Smuggler* (New York: 1860); reprinted in George Francis Dow, *Slave Ships and Slaving* (Salem: Marine Research Society, 1927) 189; he probably meant Stockport rather than Stockford.

[13] Liverpool RO 920 MD 409: Letters from John Newton to Rev. D. Jennings, 1750–1760.

[14] Hugh Crow, *Memoirs of the Late Captain Hugh Crow of Liverpool* (London: Frank Cass, 1970) 169n.

[15] Davis Davenport Papers, MIC 392, Liverpool University Library.

[16] Ralph Davis, *The Rise of the English Shipping Industry in the 17th and 18th Centuries* (London, MacMillan and Co., 1962) 114.

[17] Rediker, *Between the Devil* 155–6.

in 1801 asked not only for plentiful brandy and tobacco, "handsome Doxies", and forgiveness for blasphemy and cursing, but also that the penitent be saved from the "Guinea-man and the Tender".[18] Although clearly intended to be light-hearted, the humour of this petition lay of course in the sardonic observation of reality. Slave ships were notorious for reeking so badly that other ships at sea could smell them before they could see them, and the filth and disease were so infamous that they in many ways were the most hated of berths for seamen. With very high mortality rates – resulting variously from the disease environments in Africa and the Caribbean, mistreatment and slave revolt as well as all the usual dangers of the seas – only needy or imprudent men would enlist on a slave ship in a junior position. It was not unknown for a ship to lose all her original crew, as happened to the *Depsey* of London in the late 1750s, its the *Virginia* of Boston in the 1760s, and numerous other vessels.[19] Seamen would have heard rumours of such horrors, and not only feared death but also loathed on principle the idea of becoming a calculated number in a ship's log alongside dead slaves. The *Comte du Norde*'s log, for example, noted "departed this life Daniel Broad, Seamen no. 12" and then "Buried a woman girl slave, no. 33".[20] Those tars who surreptitiously threw their dead colleagues overboard so as not to alert the slaves to their weakness spread legend-making tales of their appalling circumstances all around the docks – if they were themselves lucky enough to survive.[21]

Boys who had gone to sea for romantic reasons did end up in the slave trade, but generally only because of trickery or other misfortune. Samuel Robinson had taken a fancy to sea life because of the "long yarns" an acquaintance had told "after being on a voyage to the West Indies". Before long, however, his "ocean paradise [was] shorn of its beams" by his experiences on board the *Lady Nelson*.[22] Similarly Rhode Island seaman John Hoxse took a berth on the slaver *Lady Eliza* to escape his shore-bound position as a ship's carpenter. Yet he, like Robinson, soon became extremely disenchanted with the job, and by the time he published

---

[18] L. Woodward, *The Sailor's Prayer* (London: R. Ackerman, 1801).
[19] *Pennsylvania Gazette* 12 July 1759; *Pennsylvania Gazette* 25 July 1765; Eltis CD-ROM, 25232; Richard H. Steckel and Richard A. Jensen, "New Evidence on the Causes of Slave and Crew Mortality in the Atlantic Slave Trade" *Journal of Economic History* 46 (1986) 55–77.
[20] Liverpool RO 387 MD 62/1.
[21] British Library Add Mss 39946.
[22] Samuel Robinson, *A Sailor Boy's Experience Aboard a Slave Ship* (Wiltshire: Cromwell Press, 1996) 87, 12.

his memoirs he had become a confirmed abolitionist.[23] William Butterworth had decided upon a career at sea after being impressed at the sight of his cousin wearing a naval uniform. It was not his intention to make a "guinea voyage" though. He and a fellow runaway were shown kindness by a man recruiting for a slave ship and were tricked on board despite an old seaman's attempts to warn them of the horrors of slave trading.[24]

Most common sailors joined slave ships out of immediate financial need, or were from seafaring families and had been apprenticed in their early teens and knew no other life. John McCarten was the son of a Liverpool seaman and had been apprenticed to a sailmaker before he joined the *Fisher*.[25] Others went to sea to escape ruin. Robert Barker had been apprenticed to Thomas Holland of Liverpool at the age of fourteen, and later worked as a barge builder before signing on the slave ship *Tryal*. One of his shipmates on a later slaving voyage was John Richardson who, according to his mother, had gone to sea after he had given "himself up to lewd women" and drink.[26] Silas Told signed on board the slaver *Royal George* after his father had died on a previous slaving voyage, leaving his mother and siblings in much reduced circumstances.[27] When John Wilson testified before the High Court of the Admiralty he related that he had first gone to sea at the age of twelve on the schooner *Ann* and then transferred to the *Tarleton* at the River Congo. Wilson's father had been a ship's carpenter, and the family lived in Liverpool, so it is not unlikely that his father had made slaving voyages before him. By the time Wilson first went to sea both his parents were dead, so his alternatives were probably minimal.[28]

Although the slave trade was generally an industry seamen loathed, during periods when the number of tars far exceeded the available work – in rare episodes of peace, for example – a position on a slave ship would obviously be readily accepted in preference to none at all. Many seamen doubtless just happened to be offered employment on a slave ship when

[23] John Hoxse, *The Yankee Tar: An Authentic Narrative of the Voyages and Hardships of John Hoxse* (Northampton: John Metcalf, 1840) 9; 13–14.
[24] William Butterworth, *Three Years Adventures of a Minor* (Leeds: Edward Baines, 1822) 1–2, 6–7.
[25] *Cornwall Chronicle* [Jamaica] 23 June 1792.
[26] Robert Barker, *The Unfortunate Shipwright, or Cruel Captain: Being a Faithful Narrative of the Unparallel'd Sufferings of Robert Barker, Late Carpenter on Board the* Thetis Snow, *of Bristol, in a Voyage to the Coast of Guinea and Antigua* (London: Printed for, and sold by the Sufferer, 1760) 5, 3.
[27] Silas Told, *Life of Mr. Silas Told* (London, 1976) 4.
[28] HCA 1/25.

their wages from their previous venture had been spent and they were again in dire need. These rather incautious, rough and ready men were hardly the kind to prepare in advance a post in a more desirable business. In Liverpool, furthermore, as perhaps also with Bristol in earlier decades, the slave trade was simply part of life, a trade seamen from the town were inured to from childhood. It seems, among these hard-bitten and long-suffering men, to have been considered something of a necessary evil.

Sailors who later gave evidence to Thomas Clarkson about conditions on board slave ships gave many reasons why they had embarked on a voyage in this trade. Although most spoke of crimps and trickery, others did offer different reasons for their decision. James Bowen, who would later become captain of the *Russell,* related that on his first two slaving voyages he had been too young to really take notice of the trade, but others joined, he thought, because they had no idea how badly they would be treated. Much more rarely, a sailor on board the *Sally* had apparently "been sent on board to cure his extravagance, and to mend his manners". Henry Ellison, who made no less than ten slaving voyages, mostly during the 1760s, was more objective than most in explaining to Thomas Clarkson why seamen joined slave ships. Prepared to admit that some seamen voluntarily went into the slave trade, he gave the following reasons. Some, he said, "have been every other voyage but that to Guinea, and they are desirous of trying it: others, because they have an affection for an old ship-mate, who had perhaps shipped himself for Guinea, and they are willing to be with him". Most though, said Ellison, went from financial necessity or having been crimped.[29]

Although Peter Earle denies that many seamen were recruited by crimps in the second half of the eighteenth century, there are frequent examples of this occurring in the slave trade, with many seamen complaining to Thomas Clarkson that they had suffered from the activities of such men.[30] Rather than just kidnapping men off the streets or directly from inbound ships as the naval press did, crimps more often worked in collusion with local publicans and landlords. Seamen generally signed securities for their board and lodging with innkeepers who then endeavoured to make the men spend as much money as possible through "intoxication, prostitution and debauchery". Then when they had incurred a huge bill

[29] Clarkson, *Substance of the Evidence* 42, 47, 58, 38.
[30] Earle, *Sailors* 29–30; Clarkson, *Substance of the Evidence*; Rodger, *The Wooden World* 184–5.

they were sold to slave ships for their debts, their only alternative being jail.[31]

Sailor James Morley related that he knew of a publican named Sullivan in Bristol who deliberately got sailors into debt and then offered them a choice between "Guinea service or gaol".[32] Another seaman, James Towne, concluded that the major method of procuring sailors for slave ships was by using their tendency towards "drunkenness and indebtedness" to ensnare them.[33] In his book *Liverpool and Slavery* "A Genuine Dicky Sam" described sailors getting drunk in a pub called The Sailor's Block, then waking up to find themselves on board a slave ship "bound to Africa, slaving, fevers, tortures and death".[34] A seaman named Thompson was told that he had engaged for a voyage solely to the West Indies and then found himself bound for Africa.[35] William Butterworth, who was entrapped into serving on a slaving vessel when he was a young boy, related that he and a friend had been "easy prey to these dealers in human flesh".[36] His terminology was not too much of an exaggeration, for crimps apparently received around £3 or £4 for an able-seaman.[37]

So slave trade sailors were not only trapped on the ship in the usual way that all seamen were, with the only escape – not infrequently resorted to – being either desertion when they reached shore or a headlong suicidal leap overboard. More than this, sailors in the slave trade were sometimes sent on board these vessels against their will. This loss of liberty was the cause of tremendous acrimony among seamen, and the men involved in this racket in workers were especially hated. During the Gordon Riots of 1780 at least twenty crimping houses were assaulted and the sailors held therein freed.[38] Crimping was simply irreconcilable with the revolutionary ideal of freedom.[39] The paradox of being forced, against one's free will, to sail to Africa on a slaving voyage, would not have been lost on some

[31] Clarkson, *Grievances* 15–18.
[32] ZHC 1/84 f.160, Evidence of James Morley.
[33] ZHC 1/87 f.26, Evidence of James Towne.
[34] *Liverpool and Slavery: An Historical Account of the Liverpool-African Slave Trade* Compiled from various sources and authentic documents. . .With an interesting plate of the famous slave ship the "Brookes" of Liverpool (Liverpool: A. Bowker & Son, 1884) 20–1.
[35] Clarkson, *Substance of the Evidence* 24.
[36] Butterworth, *Three Years* 6.
[37] Crow, *Memoirs* 90.
[38] Linebaugh, *London Hanged* 335, 342–4.
[39] Nicholas Rogers, "Liberty Road: Opposition to Impressment in Britain during the American War of Independence" Colin Howell and Richard Twomey (eds.) *Jack Tar in History: Essays in the History of Maritime Life and Labor* (New Brunswick: Acadiensis Press, 1991) 60.

of the sailors who woke up with sore heads to find themselves enlisted on a slave ship's muster roll.

The recruitment of seamen was in contrast to the way that captains and surgeons were engaged for a slaving voyage. Only they could apply for positions and negotiate terms with the merchant directly, thus finding work in ways far more genteel than the recruitment of common seamen. The appointed captain of the ship was then in charge of engaging sailors for the voyage ahead, the status of the sailors being too low to occupy the time of the merchant. It was the captain who straddled the world between merchant capitalism and maritime concerns.

A captain was hired for a slaving voyage in ways far more akin to twenty-first-century recruitment. Throughout the late eighteenth century prospective captains wrote polite letters to slaving merchants offering their services. In August 1764, for example, Joseph Wanton of Newport wrote to the Brown brothers of Providence enquiring if they would like to employ him as master of their brig *Sally*. Wanton stated that he was "well aquainted and well experienced in the Ginea Trade all Down the Coasts" and was ready to "Come up to providence and fitt her with what Dispatch will Sute you".[40] In 1790 John Marshall, possibly already the veteran of eight slaving voyages, wrote to James Rogers offering his services as the master of a slave ship. He apparently had been waiting to see if war was imminent because he was hoping for the higher wages the government would have paid in that eventuality.[41]

The only other people who sailed on slavers who had this kind of leeway of negotiation were surgeons. An act of 1788 required that every British slave ship carry a doctor, but even before this most had done so. Merchant James Rogers struggled to get a surgeon for his ship the *Trelawney* and in the end had to acquiesce to the wage and privilege demands of James Burton. He also had to pay three guineas for Burton's medical certificate as he had never been a slave ship surgeon before.[42] John Loughlin who wrote to Rogers in 1790 was also obviously a man who had never been in the Guinea trade before as he demanded his "expenses of Passing Surgeons Hall" as well as "£4.10 per month two Negroes free of all costs ... and Coach hire from London to Bristol".[43] Rogers could

[40] Darold D. Wax, "The Browns of Providence and the Slaving Voyage of the Brig *Sally*, 1764–1765" *American Neptune* 32 (1972) 171–9.
[41] C107/9: Papers of James Rogers; Eltis, CD-ROM: 17654, 17702, 17760, 17815, 17850, 17931, 17979 and 81208 all have a John Marshall listed as the captain of the vessel.
[42] C107/7.
[43] C107/9.

have saved the certificate fee if he had engaged John Walker instead, as his offer of service included the information that he had already sailed on three slaving voyages, one to the windward coast and two to Bonny, as an employee of a Mr. James.[44] Although doctors were not required by law on American ships, some did carry them. One of the first fiscal costs the *Resource* bore, for example, was the cash paid "to take Doctor Knowles from Gaol".[45]

Unlike sailors, there was considerable incentive for men to become involved in slaving voyages as a captain or a senior officer as the profits they accrued could be substantial. Of course officers were paid very much more than the men they commanded in all maritime trades, but the gap between the relative wealth of sailors and the ship's officers was wider in the slave trade than in others. This was not so much due to their actual wage rates, but because of the practice of allowing the ship's senior officers to take a number of "privilege" slaves, free of the costs of "freight", to be sold on their own account. These were usually the higher-priced males who were under the sole ownership of the officer allowed them, and who would be sold for his own advantage rather than contributing to the profits of the ship. The right to carry such men was almost always restricted to the captain, surgeon and chief mate, and thus beyond the prospects of most ordinary seamen. The carpenter of the *Blackmore* in 1730 had the right to take a privilege slave across the Atlantic with him but this was unusual.[46] The number of slaves an officer could take as his privilege varied but could amount to a very substantial extra earning for the seller.[47] And the possible gain from privilege slaves grew immensely during the late eighteenth and early nineteenth centuries. The average gross sale price more than doubled just in the period from the 1760s to 1807, and so the value of privilege arrangements also doubled.[48]

---

[44] C107/9.

[45] Coughtry, *Papers* A/2/19/968.

[46] Davis, *Rise of* 149.

[47] Inevitably there was controversy about this between officers and merchants, with claims that it was common practice for men to take privilege slaves over and above those sanctioned by their employers. Other merchants were apparently worried that their officers would take slaves from the general number as their own if their original privilege slaves died during the voyage. Captain William Snelgrave was ordered by his employer to put "his own mark" on his privilege slaves, while Captain John Fowler of the *Molly* was ordered to brand his own slaves or "bear an equal proportion of the Mortality". Bank of England, Humphrey Morice Papers, 7/10; Bristol Record Office, Bright Family Records, the snow *Molly* 1750.

[48] Roger Anstey, *The Atlantic Slave Trade and British Abolition* (London: MacMillan, 1775) 47; Robin Blackburn, *The Making of New World Slavery: From the Baroque to the Modern, 1492–1800* (London: Verso, 1997) 510.

Equally, sometimes merchants paid out considerable amounts to captains as commission rather than allowing them privilege slaves. The investors in the *Perseverance* that departed from Liverpool in 1798 recorded that after the voyage was completed they paid Captain John Lawson £1,500, while the chief mate and surgeon together gained another £150 in privilege. To put this into perspective, the second-hand purchase of the ship had cost £1,700, and the total wages for the captain and his crew of fifty-six men crew (on a voyage that had already lasted 249 days by the time it reached Tobago) amounted to £2,650.[49]

While profits from privileges and commission grew during the late eighteenth century, wages for seamen remained remarkably stable. They rarely amounted to more than twenty-five shillings per month in peacetime, at least in the capital city. In times of war, with the demand for manpower much higher and the risks far greater, as much as sixty or even seventy shillings might be earned on a ship bound out of London.[50] On the whole, sailors generally earned approximately one-fifth per month of their captain's pay, with other officers somewhere between the two amounts, before privileges and commission were taken into account. On the *Sally*, which left Liverpool for the Windward and Gold Coasts in 1768, for example, Commander David Tuohy earned £5 per month, his chief mate Matthew Flannagan £4 per month, and the common seamen earned £1 15s in the same time.[51] When commission or privilege was added, however, the gap was vastly greater. Furthermore, those who were allowed the perquisite of carrying privilege slaves, or earning commission on all slaves sold, were much more thoroughly a part of the Atlantic world economy on a level other than that of consumer. It tied the captain and his mate into the success of the ship's voyage, and the world of slave trading in general, far more tangibly than the wages paid to common seamen. Their wages, rather, were suffused with the commonplace simplicity of money due for work performed, a fiscal rationale that both transcended and mitigated the horror of the work for which they were being paid.

For the vast majority of common seamen their chances of ever becoming wealthy from slave trading were extremely slim. Although many had minor ventures of their own trading small amounts of produce or alcohol during the course of a voyage, few ever broke away from poverty and want. The effects of sailors who died at sea generally comprised a few

---

[49] Birmingham RO Galton 564; Eltis, *CD-ROM*, 83068, seven men are known to have died during the voyage, and another deserted.
[50] Davis, *Rise of* 137; Rodgers, *The Wooden World* 126–7.
[51] Liverpool RO 380 TUO 4/3: Papers of the ship *Sally*.

worn items of clothing and a knife, which were auctioned off among his crewmates for the benefit of any dependants he left behind. Slave ship captains, by comparison, left far more considerable bequests. Captain Lewis of the *Racehorse*, for example, who died at the African coast in the 1750s left not only his clothes but also a ring valued at five guineas and £150 to each of his sisters.[52] For those who captained slaving vessels half a century later as the trade reached its denouement, gains from the trade could be far more substantial still.

The real way of accruing vast wealth from slave trading, though, was for a man to accumulate enough from his days at sea to retire onshore and indulge in the far safer profession of slave merchant. Far and away greater than the amounts left by captains, let alone common seamen, some slaving merchants secured amongst the largest self-made fortunes of their day. Liverpool merchants Thomas Leyland and John Earle both left around £100,000 upon their deaths in the early eighteenth century.[53] Some were wealthy enough to build country estates or establish the banking facilities in their towns.[54] These were the sizeable gains that slave ship captains aspired to: the wealth to set themselves up in business and then ascend the ranks of society, revelling in the power which often went with it. Relatively few would make it, but many considered the risks involved worth taking. It was the returns from privilege and commission that allowed a captain to dream of retiring from the sea, becoming a merchant, and thus gaining the possibility of entering the ranks of the wealthy.

If there had been general social mobility within the slave trade, with promotion theoretically accessible to all, then naturally such gains would also have been within the reach of all, at least in terms of their ambitions. Seamen might have been tied to the ideology of slave trading to a greater degree because they sought their fortunes in the trade. The chance of promotion, however, was not equally open to all, so this was simply not the case. Despite the high mortality rates for the majority of seamen there were limited opportunities to rise up the ranks of command beyond the junior mate positions. Of men who progressed from second mate to captain during the course of a voyage because of the death of their

---

[52] John Newton, *The Journal of a Slave Trader, 1750–1754* Bernard Martin and Mark Spurrell (eds.) (London: The Epworth Press, 1962) 91–2.

[53] Francis E. Hyde, *Liverpool and the* Mersey: *Development of a Port 1700–1970* (Devon, 1971) 17.

[54] Madge Dresser, "Squares of Distinction, Webs of Interest: Gentility, Urban Development and the Slave Trade in Bristol c. 1673–1820" *Slavery and Abolition* 21:3 (2000) 21–47.

superiors, fewer than half appear to have gone on to captain a slave ship subsequently.[55] The overwhelming majority of both common seamen and their captains were young men so there was clearly a limited chance for major promotion.

A typical example of the career path of a slave trade seaman of impoverished background comes from the parliamentary enquiry into the slave trade. James Morley sailed on the *Eagle* to Angola in 1760 when he was only nine or ten years old, and on the *Amelia* three years later to Old Calabar working as a servant on both voyages. Then, by 1767, he was "before the mast" on the *Marcus* which also sailed to Old Calabar and then to St. Kitts. By his fourth slaving voyage, on the *Tom* to Gabon under Captain Matthews he had become a gunner. On his final two voyages in the 1770s he worked as a gunner and a junior mate.[56] As this was a large number of slaving voyages for any one man to take, progression past the ranks of junior officer, and thus the opportunity to earn substantially higher wages, was simply beyond his grasp. For many, disease, an accident or some other (often occupation-specific) misfortune prematurely ended their careers anyway. For all too many there would be no return from the tropics at all. The bones of seamen, like those of so many captive Africans, were frequently cast to eternity at the bottom of the Atlantic Ocean.

The key to success in becoming a slave ship captain was not hard work or longevity or even sobriety, although these things helped. Rather connections were what mattered, especially those of consanguinity. The best way to become a slave ship captain, with all the possibility for wealth that that offered, was to be the son or nephew of a slaving merchant. George Greaves, who captained six voyages to Africa between 1786 and 1797 was the son of a merchant named William Greaves. His contemporary Robert Forbes, who also led six slaving voyages from 1786 to 1791, was the son of Edward Forbes who had been listed as an Africa merchant in Liverpool as far back as the 1750s. Gerard Backhouse, who captained eight slaving vessels from the *Robert* in 1773 to the *Squirrel* in 1789, was almost certainly related to the brothers Daniel and John Backhouse, who were among Liverpool's most prominent and wealthy slave traders.[57] In the American colonies too this pattern was common. Robert Champlin

---

[55] Calculated for Liverpool vessels. Eltis, *CD-ROM*.

[56] ZHC 1/84 150.

[57] Davis, *Rise of* 117–18; Stephen D. Behrendt, "The Captains of the British Slave Trade, 1785–1807" *Transactions of the Historical Society of Lancashire and Cheshire* 40 (1991) 79–140.

who captained the *Adventure* in 1773–4 belonged to one of the big Narragansett planter and merchant families.[58]

Also common were men who followed in their father's footsteps as slaver captains. Some men had their sons working with them on board slave ships, obviously priming them for a life in command. William Woodville, who captained the *Sam*, had his son William Junior with him when he left Liverpool in 1782, as did Joseph Williams on the *Ruby*, which departed from Bristol five years later. Two years after that William Fairfield's son was writing home from sea to his mother to tell of the sorry loss of his "Honour'd Parent", the captain of the Rhode Island ship *Felicity* who was killed in a slave revolt.[59] Even more common than this was for a captain to apprentice his sons to his contemporaries. Similarly, men who worked in other maritime-related industries often followed this course of action. This gave their sons the chance that they would progress very quickly once their apprenticeship was served to the more lucrative positions among a ship's officers.

Thus the career of being a slave ship captain seems to have been something of a closed shop. Ambrose Lace, who captained seven slave ships in the 1750s and '60s delivering approximately two thousand Africans to the Americas, later became wealthy enough to establish himself as a merchant in Liverpool. His son William became a slave ship captain, commanding nine voyages to Africa and the Americas with cargoes of human beings.[60] A captain who later became a slave merchant, David Tuohy, wrote to his brother telling him of the loss of his son Ned from one of his ships in 1778. "If he had lived he would have been captain in less than 3 years" he wrote to the grieved father.[61] Stories like that of William "Billy" Boats, a foundling who made his fortune in the slave and privateering businesses and died as a wealthy merchant, were highly unusual.[62] Some seamen

---

[58] Verner Crane, *A Rhode Island Slaver: The Trade Book of the Sloop Adventure, 1773–4* (Providence, 1922) intro.

[59] Behrendt, "Captains"; BT 6/11: the brig *Ruby*; Lorenzo J. Greene, "Mutiny on the Slave Ships" *Phylon* 5 (1944) 346–54.

[60] Behrendt, "Captains" 85; Eltis, *CD-ROM*.

[61] Liverpool RO 380 TUO 2/1: Papers of David Tuohy.

[62] Boats had been found abandoned as a small baby on board a vessel at Liverpool, hence his name, and was later apprenticed to a captain after growing up in an orphanage. He made seven slaving voyages as captain, first of the *Byrne* in the 1740s, and then of the *Knight* during the 1750s. After retiring from sea and becoming a merchant, one of his ships captured a Spanish vessel loaded with gold, upon which Boats apparently ran through the streets of Liverpool shouting, "Billy Boates [sic]! Born a beggar, die a Lord!" Daniel P. Mannix and Malcolm Cowley, *Black Cargoes: A History of the Atlantic Slave Trade 1518–1865* (New York: Penguin, 1962) 131–2; Eltis, *CD-ROM*; Gomer Williams, *The*

were set upon a "rapid track" of promotion from their early days at sea, whereas for others the highest they could realistically hope to progress to was one of the lower mate positions. The real social and economic status leap, to captain, was beyond the scope of the ordinary man. Slave ship captains generally came from far less lowly backgrounds than the men they commanded.

There was another relatively common way to be appointed the captain of a slaving vessel in the last decades of the British trade. This was to be firstly a slave ship surgeon, and then to move on to captaincy. This interesting development appears to have come about largely because of regulations about the experience that captains of slave ships were required to have. Surgeons, rarely impressed into the Royal Navy, literate and experienced, were able to fill the requirements for captain as few others were. Stephen Behrendt has found thirty-six men who served as both surgeons and captains on slave ships during the 1785–1807 period.[63] John Knox, for example, who testified before Parliament during the enquiry into the slave trade, stated that he had been a surgeon for seven or eight years, and then a captain for about the same period again.[64] The master of the *Zong* on its infamously murderous voyage was alleged to have been a surgeon, and never before to have captained a ship.[65] Even though medical knowledge was extremely rudimentary compared to today, these men had to undergo education and training, which meant that they came from a different background from the generality of common seamen. Latin-speaking William Chancellor, who was the doctor on board the *Wolf*, expressed this when he claimed that he had suffered more than most from the conditions on board "because [of] the manner in wch I was bred".[66]

Chancellor's comment also hints at another gap between seaman and officer. The cultural separation between the "haves" and the "have-nots" in Britain in this period extended to profound dissimilarities over the way money should be spent. Many of the richer elements of society felt that the inability to spend money wisely was the sole source of the financial woes of the large swath of society that were practically destitute.[67] This was

---

Liverpool Privateers, with an Account of the Liverpool Slave Trade (London: Heineman, 1897) 484–6. Some letters from Boats while on the African coast are in T 70/1476.

[63] Behrendt, "Captains" 98.

[64] ZHC 1/82 73.

[65] National Maritime Museum, File 19, *Zong* records.

[66] Darold D. Wax, "A Philadelphia Surgeon on a Slaving Voyage to Africa, 1749–1751" *Pennsylvania Magazine of History and Biography* 92 (1968) 465–93.

[67] Paul Langford, "Uses of Eighteenth Century Politeness" *Transactions of the Royal Historical Society* 12 (2002) 311–31; Paul Langford, *A Polite and Commercial People: England*

exaggerated even more where seamen were concerned, as they also stereo-typically had their own peculiar maritime ethos that promoted enjoying life on shore while their money lasted with little thought for the future, and then returning to sea to begin the cycle again.

Many contemporary observers wrote of sailors living their lives in such a reckless way, and especially of their irresponsibility with regard to money. Thomas Clarkson, with vastly more compassion over their plight, and not a little condescension, claimed that a seaman's fondness for spending wildly was because while on board ship he had everything provided for him, so did not have to "look about him here and there, nor any calculation to enter into to see that ends meet". "Thus a child, when a cabin boy", thought Clarkson, "he continues a child when a man at the mast, as far as any thought of his own maintenance [was] concerned."[68] Nicolas Owen, who made several slaving voyages, agreed with the end result if not the reasoning, writing, "saylors are commonly mery, hartey people and wares out the difficultey of a voyage with patience, but upon their return lay out the fruits of their labour in debaucherys, without consideration of future wants."[69]

This is clearly part of the stereotype of Jack Tars that was pervasive at the time. James Field Stanfield, however, was more specific in attributing the tendency of seamen to squander their wages and live rashly to the horrors of slave trading. He wrote:

Imagine to yourself . . . a poor worn-out wretch, after the miseries and sickness of a *slaving voyage* – after a long want of every cheering beverage – now first set ashore – his own master – among people of his own color and language – with money in his pocket, and temptations to excess on every side: picture this – and for a moment recollect the unsuspecting, thoughtless, dissipated propensity that marks the character of an English sailor, and you must conclude the consequences as unavoidable – that the feeble remains left by the cruelty and disease of an *African voyage*, are speedily sacrificed by intemperance[70] [emphasis in original].

1727–1783 (Oxford: Clarendon Press, 1989); John Brewer, *The Pleasures of the Imagination: English Culture in the Eighteenth Century* (London: HarperCollins, 1997); Peter Earle, *The Making of the English Middle Class: Business, Society and Family Life in London, 1660–1730* (London: Methuen, 1989).

[68] Thomas Clarkson, *Grievances of Our Mercantile Seamen: A National and Crying Evil* (Ipswich, 1845) 9.

[69] Nicholas Owen, *Journal of a Slave Dealer* Eveline Martin (ed.) (London: George Routledge and Sons, 1930) 63.

[70] James Field Stanfield, *Observations on a Guinea Voyage: A Series of Letters Addressed to the Reverend Thomas Clarkson* (London: James Phillips, 1788) 2–3.

FIGURE 1. Sailors drinking aboard ship. Notice the black seaman at the back. Reprinted with permission of Mary Evans Picture Library, London.

While there is very little evidence to suggest what items men from slave ships spent their money on when they went ashore, the few examples of crew accounts on board slaving vessels which are extant suggest that this view should be treated with caution. Certainly they show that alcohol and tobacco were common purchases, but this is not the entire story. Many seamen also paid for additional articles of clothing, knives and other tools, things which were needed for their personal comfort, survival and work.

The crew accounts of the *Lyon* frigate, which left Liverpool for Africa in May 1761, show that purchases of rum, tobacco and clothing were the most common. Some quantities of alcohol purchased were exceedingly large for one person's use: the carpenter, for example, bought fourteen gallons of brandy within a seven and a half month period, suggesting that he was engaged in private trading. These accounts also reveal some far more unfortunate circumstances, however. John Kelsey was charged for a "New St. George's Ensign" as he had "worn out [the original] with sleeping in it" presumably lacking anything else to keep him warm. John

Williams paid 15 shillings for "sick lodgings on shoar". All paid "hospital money".[71]

The expenditure accounts on board the Rhode Island ship *Resource*, which transported slaves to Montevideo in 1806, suggest less alcohol and more clothing were purchased on this ship, possibly due to its much later sailing date and its American origin. Seaman John Country bought two shirts for $3.33, a month later bought a "Nankin Jacket" for $4 and another two months later purchased another three shirts for $5. Another sailor, Lewis Seriff, purchased two shirts, a jacket, some trousers and a "Jack Nife." Their fellow sailor George Maccomber apparently needed three knives during the voyage, "2 Jacknives" on 20 June and a further "Knief" on 17 September. Such needs seem to have been shared by sailors of other racial origins: a man recorded only as "Henry the Sandwich Islander" purchased shoes for $2, stockings, a "Baze shirt," a pea jacket for $9 and "1 Jack Knief Small Size". Meanwhile the cabin steward, recorded only as "Arsree–Chinese" also purchased stockings and trousers near the start of the voyage. Even the slave, Cipeo or Sippeo, who was a member of the crew, had an account of this type, showing that he purchased a baize shirt, some trousers, a checked shirt, and two jack knives.[72]

These ships' petty accounts reveal another aspect of the triangular trade's unpopularity among sailors. In the slave trade, there were not only the usual ways for seamen to lose money, but also some specific to "guinea" ships. Captains invented creative means by which sailors were reminded of their place as the dominant group in relation to the slaves they shipped, while at the same time reinforcing their lowly position in terms of capitalism. Many of the *Lyon*'s men had part of their wages deducted for African captives who had escaped while they were on watch duty. Seamen John Bruce, for example, paid £1 10s – approximately one month's wages – for "part of a slave lost at sea". William Gamsby, the fourth mate, was charged the value of an "18th part of a Man slave lost" and for "part of a new Yawll and 2 Slaves lost". The cook, William Sharp, was charged for a "7th part" of two male slaves who had run away during his watch, and later again for another two slaves who managed to escape.[73]

[71] HCA 15/55.

[72] Jay Coughtry (ed.) *Papers of the American Slave Trade* (Bethesda, MD: University Publications of America, 1996) Series A/ Part 2/Reel 19 Frame 968–Reel 20 Frame 107.

[73] HCA 15/55.

The *Lyon*'s captain was not alone in charging his men for lost slaves. The captain of the *Spy* tried to deduct £3 from each of his seamen for two female slaves who had thrown themselves overboard and were eaten by sharks at Bonny, adding insult to injury to men who had just been impressed onto *HMS Nemesis*.[74] Captain Hollingsworth of the *Henry* also planned to deduct the value of a slave woman who threw herself overboard during the middle passage from his men's wages after they reached Grenada, but was persuaded to offset this loss from the gain of having stolen a man at Fernando Po.[75] It seems likely that this was quite a common practice, a cost-cutting measure inflicted by captains and hated by seamen. It also, of course, brought seamen and slaves into direct conflict during the course of a slaving voyage.

Although it was a long established practice in maritime industry as a whole to only pay seamen once the freight had been earned for the owners, the risk of not being paid at all in the slave trade increased because of the added dangers. These included the hazards of slave revolt, attack by free Africans or another European nation, or being lost on one of the sandbars that made landing treacherous at several West African harbours. Of course these risks were also feared by the merchants and captains whose financial losses would far outweigh those of sailors in absolute terms. Slave trading was always a high-risk venture. Nevertheless, many merchants deemed the odds worth the risk for their own potential gains could be vast. For seamen, unless the ship took a prize during battle, they had no such hope of considerable accumulation of money to counterbalance the huge hazards they faced. Even the cost of the seaman's chest with his clothing, hammock and a few meagre possessions would on average take a further twelve months of toil on successful voyages to replace.[76]

Another reason that seamen felt cheated out of their dues while on a slaving voyage was the payment of part of their wages in the West Indies in local currency. This was commonly given at the same rate as they would have been paid in sterling, even though colonial currency was worth substantially less. Most seamen were content to take any payment they could and often used the money to procure alcohol and women in the Caribbean, or even to abscond from the ship altogether (see Chapter 6). David Wilkes, second mate of the *Union*, even sued in the

---

[74] William Richardson, *A Mariner of England: An Account of the Career of William Richardson from Cabin Boy in the Merchant Service to Warrant Officer in the Royal Navy, 1780–1817* Colonel Spencer Childers (ed.) (London: John Murray, 1908) 66.

[75] Clarkson, *Substance of the Evidence* 128.

[76] Peter Earle, *Sailors: English Merchant Seamen 1650–1775* (London: Methuen, 1998) 57.

Vice-Admiralty Court of Virginia to be paid what was owed to him at that time.[77]

Many men, however, fervently resented what they saw as an underhanded way of paying them less and were prepared to fight for payment in sterling. Isaac Parker, who would later sign on board Cook's *Endeavour*, was imprisoned in the West Indies for refusing to accept colonial currency.[78] The surgeon of the *Recovery* complained to the ship's owner Walter Jacks that he had been paid "currency for sterling".[79] There was clearly an advantage for merchants to pay their hired men in less valuable colonial currency. Captain William Earle of the *Chesterfield* in 1751, for example, was instructed to "pay what seamen's wages they'll take in the West Indies".[80] This, then, casts new light on arguments, which have raged since the parliamentary enquiry into slaving, as to whether the slave trade paid higher wages than other long-distance trades because of the additional dangers and unpleasantness. Even if seamen were indeed paid around ten shillings more in the slave trade than in other trades as some have claimed, it is not at all clear that this was in fact passed on to them in real terms.[81] The *perceived* higher wages, could, nevertheless, have attracted seamen to slave ships at the outset of a voyage.

The truth was that even if they did not spend all of their wages on alcohol, nicotine and prostitutes, or have to pay for runaway slaves and their own health care, sailors were extremely hard pressed to support a family on the wages paid to them. Studies of seamen in early America found that although a captain's pay would support a family, a mate's would only just do so. Common seamen, therefore, could not hope to support a family on their wages alone.[82] Billy G. Smith found examples of sailors' families in Philadelphia during the second half of the eighteenth century who survived from almshouse charity and were too poor to bury their own children.[83] Ruth Herndon has discovered that sailors in Rhode Island were also frequently too poor to support their own families, and often

---

[77] George Reese (ed.) *Proceedings in the Court of the Vice-Admiralty of Virginia 1698–1775* (Richmond, VA: Virginia State Library, 1983) 91–3.

[78] ZHC 1/84 136.

[79] HCA 1/61 ff.166–70.

[80] Merseyside Maritime Museum, D/Earle/1/1.

[81] ZHC 1/82 105; ZHC 1/85 55.

[82] Daniel Vickers and Vince Walsh, "Young Men and the Sea: the Sociology of Seafaring in 18th Century Salem, Massachusetts" *Social History* 24 (1999) 17–38.

[83] Billy G. Smith, "The Vicissitudes of Fortune: The Careers of Laboring Men in Philadelphia, 1750–1800" Stephen Innes (ed.) *Work and Labor in Early America* (Chapel Hill, NC: Institute of Early American History and Culture, 1988) 236–7.

had to rely on town charity for survival.[84] In Britain the wives and children of seamen were frequently found in workhouses, waiting hopefully for their husbands and fathers to return from a voyage. The alternatives were bleak. So many of these women were forced into prostitution while their husbands were away that society recognized little difference between the two groups. Poor seamen's wives formed such a ubiquitous part of society that ballads were sung about their plight.[85]

The only way that a sailor could support his family during his long absence at sea was through advance wages, and this became another highly contentious issue in the last decades of the eighteenth century. In May 1783 *Gentleman's Magazine* reported that "a body of sailors, to the number of 5 or 600, paraded the streets" of Bristol "with music and colours". They were demanding an advance on their wages. The following year the magazine again reported trouble, when "A body of sailors, ship carpenters, &c, assembled before the Queen's House".[86] Commonly, men hired by slaving vessels would have one or two months' wages advanced to them before the ship set sail. For many who were single this meant that they had the finances to go on one last carousal before departure, but for those with families it meant that wives and children had to survive for the duration of the voyage – normally around a year – on only one or two months' pay. In the meantime they were left to hope that he would not spend all his income on alcohol and women while on shore leave, and also would not run up a large amount on his on-ship account.

The reasons merchants were resistant to paying large sums to seamen in advance are obvious, quite apart from the large outlay involved. Sailor George Bishop took his advance wages and then deserted before the ship even set sail. His would-be colleague Samuel Hooley had a cash advance on his wages, and then during the voyage bought two and a quarter gallons of brandy, three pairs of trousers and two shirts. When he also had his hospital money and charges for "a 12th part of a slave lost" deducted from his wages due, he actually owed £2 17s 9d at the end of the

---

[84] Ruth Wallis Herndon, "The Domestic Cost of Seafaring: Town Leaders and Seamen's Families in Eighteenth Century Rhode Island" Margaret S. Creighton and Lisa Norling (eds.) *Iron Men, Wooden Women: Gender and Seafaring in the Atlantic World 1700–1920* (Baltimore: Johns Hopkins University Press, 1996) 57.

[85] Suzanne J. Stark, *Female Tars: Women aboard Ship in the Age of Sail* (London: Pimlico, 1998) 23–4, 27; David Cordingly, *Women Sailors and Sailors' Women: An Untold Maritime History* (New York: Random, 2001) 19–21.

[86] *Gentleman's Magazine* May 1783; *Gentleman's Magazine* November 1784.

voyage.[87] Giving money to a seaman's family during the voyage rather than giving out a large advance before his departure did not surmount these problems. On the muster roll of the *Colonel*'s 1793 voyage it is noted that sailor James White absconded in the Bahamas, so being "indebted to the owners" because of the "monthly money left his wife".[88]

Part of the unwillingness to support wives and children while the sailor was away did not relate to fiscal matters per se, however, but rather can be attributed to the capitalist ethic that employers were no longer responsible for the whole family of an employee. This was part of the larger picture that had seen smaller ports edged out of the British slave trade by the major powers of Liverpool and London, so that lowly sailors were rarely commanded by men they had had any relationship with on land.[89] Even Liverpool, by far the smaller of the two cities, had little left of the village environment that would have seen men go to sea with those they had known all their lives in the kind of vertical rather than horizontal societal structure known in smaller ports and other time periods.

Records from Bristol, where slave trading activity peaked in the 1720s and '30s, suggest that slave trading in that city was characterized by a more paternalistic approach towards its employees. The Merchant Venturers' Society hospital records reveal that they often paid to support men who had been injured on slaving voyages, and occasionally even provided pensions for the widows and/or children of seamen killed while making the triangular voyage. Frequently former sailors appealed that they had been blinded, wounded in revolts or had suffered from leg ulcers while working on board slave ships and consequently were unable to support themselves and their families anymore. A black seaman named John Quaco claimed a pension from the society having paid into "this charity" for all of his twenty-one years at sea. Widows told pitiful stories of their husbands being killed by slaves during fights with enemy vessels or even by their own crewmates. It is clear that the extent of the relief provided by

[87] HCA 15/55.

[88] BT 98/55 f.276.

[89] By the latter part of the eighteenth century the small ports of Britain had almost entirely been excluded from the trade in slaves, and even Bristol had fallen back from its peak in the late 1720s. The vast majority of Britain's slave ships, more than seventy-two per cent, left from the urban areas of Liverpool or London, Eltis, *CD-ROM*; M. M. Schofield, "The Slave Trade from Lancashire and the Ports Outside Liverpool c.1750–c.1790" *Transactions of the Historical Society of Lancashire and Cheshire* 126 (1976) 30–72; Nigel Tattersfield, *The Forgotten Trade: Comprising the Log of the* Daniel *and* Henry *of 1700 and Accounts of the Slave Trade from the Minor Ports of England, 1698–1725* (London: Pimlico, 1998).

this scheme went beyond that of the seamen's sixpences which paid sick expenses for men in other ports. While there was an "increased social distance between the 'rulers' and the 'ruled'" in Bristol by the mid-eighteenth century, its maritime industries still operated on more paternalistic ethics than those of the much larger cities of London and Liverpool.[90]

The slave trade of North America too almost certainly ran on more personal and patriarchal notions than that of Britain's main ports, as the major slave trading centres of Rhode Island were vastly smaller towns. Ships that left from there were more likely to have employed men who were known to each other in a social setting. Nonetheless, paternalistic bonds were breaking down all around the Atlantic world in this era. By the late eighteenth century there was little chance that the captain of a slave ship would write home asking his wife to check on the wives of his men, as happened in other trades and in other centuries. The social gulf between the trade's authorities and its common seamen was vast.

There was, in fact, a conscious effort on the part of the maritime merchants at the end of the eighteenth century to distance themselves from seamen. Eager to slough off their reputation for being "as rough mannered as their sailors" they spent their newly created wealth in ways which, they hoped, displayed their gentility.[91] In Liverpool small numbers of men and their families grew wealthy from slave trading, while a large mass of downtrodden, subjugated men lived hand-to-mouth existences down by the seafront. Merchants who made profits from slave trading built elaborate homes, sought positions of power and lived lives they felt would bestow that quintessentially Georgian value of respectability upon them. It was as if they hoped it would purify their fortunes from the dual stains of slavery and trade.

There are two examples of the families of seamen who died on slaving voyages asking the employing merchant for details of their deaths and getting little response. In 1792 George MacLaurin's brother wrote asking when exactly his sibling had died on the African coast so that their father could put it in the family bible.[92] He received no answer. In similar circumstances, a merchant named Thomas Leyland, wrote to John Berry of

[90] Merchant Seamen's Hospital Minute Book, 1747–1789, Merchant Venturers' Hall, Bristol; Merchant Seamen's Hospital, Certificates for Financial Help, Merchant Venturers' Hall, Bristol. The petition of John Quaco is number 123. Gerald Francis Lorentz, "Bristol Fashion: The Maritime Culture of Bristol, 1650–1700" Unpublished PhD Thesis, University of Toronto (1997).
[91] Dresser, "Squares of Distinction".
[92] C107/10.

Soho, London, in 1788 offering little sympathy for the death of a seaman who presumably was Berry's kin. He hastily dismissed the enquirer by reporting that the logbook of the ship the man had sailed on, the *Enterprize*, had been lost in Jamaica.[93] Leyland was an investor in more than seventy slave ships between 1782 and 1807 employing countless seamen and doubtless had little individual concern for the men.[94]

There was still a residue of paternalist sentiment that had characterized worker–employer relations in an earlier era, but it was becoming increasingly rare. A Liverpool merchant named Robert Bostock ordered Captain James Fryer, whom he had employed to command the slaver *Bess,* that "you must behave . . . Like a Father and not like a Brute", but this seems to have been related to Fryer's fear that one crewmember in particular would prove unsuited to the job in hand.[95] It was the absence of this kind of paternalism that Thomas Clarkson, who used the ill-treatment of seamen as a central tenet of his argument against the slave trade, saw as so wrong. He agitated for the rather unrealistic aim that captains would see themselves as fathers to the seamen, and the latter as children or servants to their captains.[96] On the whole, however, the class divisions in Britain were such that contact between the two groups was generally minimal. Common seamen were largely divorced from the world of merchant and captain.

When seamen took to the streets of Liverpool in 1775 they were protesting their lot in the slave trading industry as much as the single issue of the reduction of wages on board the *Derby*. In their view, slaving merchants were growing wealthy while they and their families starved, and were living lives filled with luxury while they were forced onto ships against their will and bore the marks of slaver captains' punishments on their backs. Slave trading was a dangerous, corrupt and filthy industry and seamen felt that they unfairly suffered its hardships, while at the same time barely sharing in its spoils. As slave ship seaman John Hoxse noted, merchants got sailors to do the "dirty work" of slaving for them, while their own hands remained unsullied.[97]

The larger picture, however, of which seamen were perhaps only dimly aware, suggests that slave trading had also caused their grievances on a much larger scale. As the slave trade provided the wealth for its investors

[93] Liverpool RO 387 MD 59: Letter Book of Thomas Leyland, May 1786–September 1788.
[94] Eltis, *CD-ROM.*
[95] Liverpool RO 387 MD 55.
[96] Clarkson, *Grievances* 18.
[97] Hoxse, *Yankee Tar,* 14.

to aspire to respectability and to distance themselves through their riches from the trade by which they had grown prosperous, it also linked poverty to lack of freedom. The fact that the white men whose own freedom was most in doubt understood the nature of true slavery through first-hand contact profoundly affected the nature of freedom in the Atlantic world. Often lacking the liberty, humane treatment and wages which should have separated them from actual slavery, they unsurprisingly fought for them at every opportunity.[98]

These most well travelled and worldly wise of men not only encountered the realities of African enslavement, they also saw its antipodal creation up close. As liberty took on a new tenure, seamen on board slave ships were uniquely placed to process this information and adapt it to their own long-running fight against authority, as they were quite literally in the eye of the storm of this transition. What they never seem to have forgotten, and indeed could not forget given the circumstances of those they transported below decks, was that self-determination and payment that allowed a decent standard of living were central to ideas of liberty. What is more, they knew that any political and social rights they won would be essentially meaningless without the economic resources to support them.

In fact poverty itself had been transformed by three centuries of slave trading. In the Americas at least, being impoverished increasingly had racialized implications. Ruth Herndon's study of seamen in Rhode Island has led her to state that "when white men could not adequately govern or provide for their households, they joined a dependent class already inhabited by black men."[99] Her findings have wider implications, for this racialization of dependence had relevance across the ocean in Europe. Dependence everywhere had become tainted with the lack of freedom associated with slavery, and so repellent. Wealth meant personal independence and self-determination. Just as men in North America had personal knowledge of black slaves' lives with which to compare their own, so for those who had been employed in the "triangular trade" these matters took on a significance above and beyond the hunger pangs of poverty. They knew that this inability to support their own families was a form of dependence and they vehemently resented it. The ethos of white manhood,

---

[98] Paul Craven and Douglas Hay, "The Criminalization of 'Free' Labour: Master and Servant in Comparative Perspective" Paul E. Lovejoy and Nicholas Rogers (eds.) *Unfree Labour in the Development of the Atlantic World* (Essex: Frank Cass, 1994).

[99] Herndon, "The Domestic Cost of Seafaring" 57.

deemed eighteenth-century Anglo-American society, was to be the master not only of yourself but also your wife, your family and your servants.

For the protesters on the streets of Liverpool and Boston, fair pay and liberty were indivisible parts of the larger idea of justice. The transition to capitalism theoretically ensured the primacy of labour that was both free and waged, but seamen felt that they were badly treated on both counts. Moreover, they were uniquely positioned to understand what lack of these assets meant, and to appreciate that the implications doubled and then again redoubled as the last decades of the eighteenth century progressed. As the age of revolution advanced, ever more African captives were transported across the Atlantic for sale in the Americas. Liberty became a rallying cry for many factions and groups, but its growing importance was intrinsically linked to its opposite, enslavement. The issues that compelled men to march the streets of the major port cities around the Atlantic rim demanding better pay and freedom from all kinds of oppression were central implications of the slave trade. As seamen demanded justice, liberty and fair pay, the spectre of racism loomed ever larger on the horizons of the Atlantic.

2

The Multiracial Crews of Slave Ships

The rebellion on the slave ship *Amity* occurred when the ship was heading eastward across the Atlantic having set sail from Norfolk, Virginia in the summer of 1785. Two slaves known as Dick and Will were involved; the latter, we are told, was "an exceeding good looking boy". From what part of the African coast they had originally been forcibly shipped is not known, what we do know is that when this rebellion occurred the two men were on their way back towards Africa. Having left the African continent one-year previously, they were labouring as seamen on board the *Amity* at the time they rebelled, or "turned pyrate" as their contemporaries may have phrased it, for their captor was also their captain. James Duncason was their master in both uses of the word, being both their slave owner and the commander of the ship on which they were working. Their rebellion was simultaneously both sailor mutiny and slave insurrection.

Dick and Will's fellow mutineers are equally fascinating for they really were a motley crew representing many strains of Atlantic rebellion. There was a mulatto Bostonian named Stuart who sported a cut on his nose and a scar on his forehead. John Mathew and Alexander Evans were Irishmen, reported in stereotypes common to both their nationality and their profession to "have a good deal of the brogue" and to be "very subject to liquor". Richard Squire, possibly their leader, was an Englishman of about thirty years of age who claimed to have been a lieutenant aboard the *USS General Washington*. The last known rebel, and also the oldest man by a decade was John Boadman, described as having a "black complexion" and being "about five feet seven inches high". Equally interesting is the ethnicity of those who were cast off in the ship's longboat as the rebellion progressed, for the three men set adrift along with the captain, mate and boatswain were all said to be "black boys".[1]

When the owners of the *Amity* named the vessel after the virtue or blessing of friendship, a rebellion fomented among its multiethnic crew was obviously not what they had in mind. Yet the crews of many slave ships were racially mixed. Despite the fact that slave trading ministered to the rise of one of the most odious and destructive racist creeds the world has known, the slave trade, just like other deep-sea trades of the era, employed a multiracial workforce. As the *Amity*'s crew suggests, this was far more complex than any simple division of black and white. Undoubtedly Africans such as Dick and Will would have had different attitudes about identity and race than the "mulatto" American Stuart, while the position of the two Irishmen in any such simplistic formulation is ambiguous. While slave ships fed the racism of the Americas with every cargo of captives they delivered, the implications of race aboard the vessels themselves, at least among their crews, were far more complex.

Quite simply, the popular image of a slave ship as being divided strictly along lines of black and white does not stand up to scrutiny. While those traded as chattels across the Atlantic Ocean were all of African origin, the very real threat of Barbary slavery to ships' crews meant that bondage was not considered the unique preserve of people with darker skin.[2] Likewise, being a slave trader was far from the domain solely of pale skinned people. As well as African slave merchants who sold captives to the ships, many who actually made the middle passage among the ranks of workers rather than captives were also not white. There were men, and occasionally women, of African origin among the crews of slavers, joining ships at each corner of the "triangular voyage". Occasionally there were Asian or indigenous American men. Also working aboard British and North American slave ships were many sailors of Irish, Italian or other origins which were not always considered white in the late eighteenth century.[3]

Some of the only seamen who saw the issue in terms of black and white were Americans, both black and white themselves who came from societies in which these were increasingly coming to be meaningful categorizations. Even then, however, such perceptions were challenged by

---

[1] *Pennsylvania Gazette* 31 August 1785, 7 September 1785.

[2] Linda Colley, *Captives: Britain, Empire and the World, 1600–1850* (London: Pimlico, 2003) 63.

[3] Jacobson, *Whiteness of a Different Color*; Noel Ignatiev, *How the Irish became White* (New York: Routledge, 1995); Thomas A. Guglielmo, *White on Arrival: Italians, Race, Color, and Power in Chicago, 1890–1945* (New York: Oxford University Press, 2004).

the realities of the slave trade. A black American of several generations standing would have a totally different understanding of ethnicity than an African, and possibly even a black Briton, regardless of whether they shared a skin tone. Whiteness was no more cohesive. Race was not perceived in the same way among Britain's working classes as it was, for example, among their countrymen who formed the plantation aristocracy of the West Indies. Language, religion, culture and other factors such as status comprised ideas of race as much as skin colour. In London the black working classes were colleagues, friends, spouses and bedfellows to their white counterparts with surprisingly little comment, while they were wholly unknown in some other parts of the country.[4] For the many men who worked on British and American slave ships who were of Irish origin, the issue is more complex still. Their position with regard to whiteness was tenuous and not necessarily constant as they moved around the Atlantic Ocean.

Part of the reason for the perceived separateness of British sailors from the rest of the population, which was sometimes described in racial terms, was that the profession incorporated men from many parts of the world. Their strongest affinity was often with their fellow tars who were from many racial backgrounds. Thus the kind of self-identification of working men as white, as described by David Roediger and other historians, has an ambiguous relationship to the history of the slave trade's workers.[5] While it might be presumed that a slave ship was one of the environments in which there was the most to be gained by creating a sense of whiteness, in fact seamen who worked in the industry were of many different ethnicities. Many did not have the ability to include themselves into a formulation of whiteness even if they had so wished. Even for those who could have done so, their perception of themselves as part of a professional group comprising men of many backgrounds sometimes limited the influence of a shared identity based on skin tone.

Race, we know, is historically and socially constructed. Racial categorization was changing throughout the period that this book covers, particularly in what became the United States, where influxes of immigrants

---

[4] Stephen J. Braidwood, *Black Poor and White Philanthropists: London's Blacks and the Foundation of the Sierra Leone Settlement, 1786–1791* (Liverpool: Liverpool University Press, 1994) 73–4; Norma Myers, "In Search of the Invisible: British Black Family and Community, 1780–1830" *Slavery and Abolition* 13:3 (December 1992) 156–80.

[5] David R. Roediger, *The Wages of Whiteness: Race and the Making of the American Working Class* (London: Verso, 1991) especially 11–13; Matthew Frye Jacobson, *Whiteness of a Different Color: European Immigrants and the Alchemy of Race* (Cambridge: Harvard University Press, 1998) 17–21.

changed perceptions discernibly.[6] But identities were also flexible in other ways in the eighteenth century Atlantic. A man might see himself as belonging to his own village and kin group, then to his region, then as a Igbo, ally himself with his shipmates, form friendships across tribal lines with those sharing his suffering, and then still be delighted to hear his native tongue spoken in the slave markets of the Caribbean, all within the course of a single journey. Another man might start off a subjugated Celt, find himself a proud crewman on a ship called *Betty*, stand with whip in hand engaged in the oppression of Africans, become a free white man in the Americas with all the benefits that conveyed, and return home to being, once again, a subjugated Irishman.

This chapter explores what led men of African origin, from all parts of the Atlantic world, to be engaged on board slave ships, and their relations with their white crewmates. In so doing, it aims to unravel the many convolutions of race and racial formation among the seamen of late eighteenth century slave ships. Barbara Field's observation that racial attitudes were "promiscuous critters" which could coexist with their apparent opposite within any one person or social group is a necessary insight to understand the lives of slave trade seamen.[7] Engaged in the process of enslavement, and guilty of many acts of gross inhumanity towards those they carried as their captive cargoes, nonetheless it is also a fact that seamen were considered by many of their contemporaries to be peculiarly accepting of co-workers of other ethnicities.

Jeffrey Bolster's *Black Jacks* has transformed understanding of black seamen and their lives. Revealing not only what led black men to jobs at sea and what their lives were like, Bolster also contends that white sailors in the Atlantic world were among the most accepting of blacks as colleagues, often working alongside them as equals. His skilful, nuanced argument shows that while it would be wrong to view white seamen as necessarily charitable towards black men, they nevertheless shared an egalitarian union with fellow members of their profession that could include men of African origin. This, indeed, was a factor in making maritime work tolerable for black workers.[8] It is a viewpoint shared by Julius

---

[6] Jacobson, *Whiteness of a Different Color* 1–38; Theodore W. Allen, *The Invention of the White Race: The Origin of Racial Oppression in Anglo-America* volume II (London: Verso, 1997) chapter 13

[7] Quoted in Roediger, *Wages of Whiteness* 24.

[8] W. Jeffrey Bolster, *Black Jacks: African American Seamen in the Age of Sail* (Cambridge: Harvard University Press, 1997) 70.

S. Scott, who quotes a contemporary observer who noted that "sailors and Negroes are ever on the most amicable terms", sharing "mutual confidence and familiarity".[9]

Although the work of Bolster and other historians such as Ira Dye, Martha Putney and James Farr has acknowledged anew the huge contribution to maritime industry made by black men, their place on board slaving vessels remains veiled.[10] Outside academe the slave trade has become symbolic of all who have suffered or do suffer as the result of racism, making this a highly contentious issue. It may be very hard from a present-day perspective to understand why black men would sign on board slaving vessels, but this is to misunderstand the contemporary situation and to discount the predicament of their lives. A unified black identity was being formed in the Americas, but did not extend to Africa. On a more practical level, the lack of other possibilities meant that some black men simply had to return to the seas in order to feed themselves, and that sometimes meant signing on board a slaver. The transatlantic slave trade created a vacuum that drew men and women out of Africa, but it also simultaneously contrived a particularly invidious form of racism which provided its victims with very narrow choices and few opportunities in the societies into which they were sold.

One of the only options for men who either escaped their bondage or were manumitted was to go to sea. Seafaring was a rare occupation

---

[9] Julius S. Scott III, "The Common Wind: Currents of Afro-American Communication in the Era of the Haitian Revolution" unpublished PhD Dissertation, Duke University (1986) 64–5.

[10] Bolster, *Black Jacks*; W. Jeffrey Bolster, "'To Feel Like a Man': Black Seamen in the Northern States 1800–1860" *Journal of American History* 76 (1990) 1173–99; W. Jeffrey Bolster, "An Inner Diaspora: Black Sailors Making Selves" Ronald Hoffman, Mechal Sobel and Frederika J. Teute (eds.) *Through a Glass Darkly: Reflections on Personal Identity in Early America* (Chapel Hill: University of North Carolina Press, 1997) 419–48; Dye, "Early American Merchant Seafarers"; Martha S. Putney, "Black Merchant Seamen of Newport, 1803–65: A Case Study in Foreign Commerce" *Journal of Negro History* 57:2 (April 1972) 156–68; Martha S. Putney, *Black Sailors: Afro-American merchant Seamen and Whalemen prior to the Civil War* (New York: Greenwood Press, 1987); James Farr, "A Slow Boat to Nowhere: The Multi-Racial Crews of the American Whaling Industry" *Journal of Negro History* 68 (1983) 159–70; James Farr, *Black Odyssey: The Seafaring Traditions of Afro-Americans* (New York: P. Lang, 1989). For England's black seamen see Norma Myers, "Servant, Sailor, Soldier, Taylor, Beggarman: Black Survival in White Society 1780–1830" *Immigrants and Minorities* 12:1 (March 1993) 47–74; Ian Duffield, "'I asked how the Vessel Could go': The Contradictory Experiences of African and African Diaspora Mariners and Port Workers in Britain c.1750–1850" in Anne Kershen (ed.) *Language, Labour and Migration* (Burlington, Vermont: Ashgate Publishing, 2000) 121–54.

in being open to free blacks in eighteenth-century America; many whaling ships' crews were around half African-American.[11] Fredrick Douglass escaped from his enslavement dressed as a seaman and Olaudah Equiano worked for some time in that profession. For generations of African-Americans who had been born free, mostly in the northern states, maritime employment remained one of their best, or only, choices. The lure of the sea was partly its escape potential – a characteristic it has been imbued with in men's minds since time immemorial – but also that seafaring by its nature challenged many of the assumptions of colour enshrined by society on land. Free black sailors were issued with seamen's protection certificates by the United States government after 1796, attesting that they were "citizens" despite the fact that this was more than they could ever claim on land in this period.[12] Those who went to the sea as freemen symbolized not only endurance, but also reclaimed the ocean as a setting for regaining liberty as well as the scene of the African diaspora's wretched ordeal.

Beyond these reasons, a primary factor that made nautical employment accessible to men of African origin was that the internationalism of seafaring made it tolerant to men of other ethnic backgrounds. Swept along by the ebb and flow of the tide, the ships involved in deep-sea trades have always involved the exchange of workers as well as goods, disease, culture and genes. Just as lascars worked on East Indiamen, having being caught up in the transnational trading systems moving cotton and spices across the globe, so Africans joined slaving vessels as free workers as well as captive trading goods. It is implausible that they would not have done so, as the internationalism such men brought to the occupation was a defining trait of deep-sea employment. In a period generally characterized by intense regionalism and parochialism, it was partly a seaman's worldly character and cosmopolitan make-up that set him apart from his non-seagoing peers.[13] Maritime culture, as well as employment, was transoceanic.

African men, and their understanding of the world, were therefore incorporated into the seafaring domain more easily than others partly

---

[11] Farr, "Slow Boat to Nowhere" 159–70.
[12] Bolster, *Black Jacks* 1–2; Rhode Island Historical Society, Seamen's Protection Certificates.
[13] Philip D. Morgan "British Encounters with Africans and African-Americans circa 1600–1780" Bernard Bailyn and Philip D. Morgan (eds.) *Strangers within the Realm: Cultural Margins of the First British Empire* (Williamsburg: Institute of Early American History and Culture, 1991) 59, 46.

because of the transatlantic trade in slaves. To put it another way, black seamen were tolerated and accepted by their co-workers of European origin partly because the slave trade carried so many people of African origin into the maritime labour force. Men do not go and interact with other peoples in the name of trade over such a vast period of time without assimilating far more than the goods they have purchased. That the "goods" they acquired in this particular case were men, women and children does not alter this basic fact. West African ports became well-known places to hordes of sailors, their inhabitants familiar. By the eighteenth century African culture mingled on the margins of nautical societal norms, most appreciably in the form of sea shanties. As early as 1743 a European seaman was reported to have sung a "negro song" at court martial.[14]

Moreover, the European mercantile forces behind the trade absorbed countless African merchants into the Atlantic's financial networks, and also drew in less noble born Africans as seamen, porters, interpreters, cooks, canoemen, sentinels and pilots. Africans too became members of the seafaring rabble which was employed on ships that plied their trade around the Atlantic's shores. Seamen's "fictive kinship" system and "mutual responsibilities and protections" towards each other, incorporated men of many different racial origins.[15] Those who joined slave ships in Africa became integral parts of a multiracial crew.

Like latter-day "Atlantic Creoles", Africans enlisted on slave ships in a variety of roles, showing the "linguistic dexterity, cultural plasticity and social agility" which made them the most feared kind of Africans among American planters.[16] By illustrating that Africans were employable in maritime occupations just like men of any other ethnicity, they gave lie to the vaunted justification of slaveowners who distanced themselves from the actual enslavement process by seeing their human acquisitions as imported goods. The numbers of men of African origin who laboured on board slave ships (as opposed to being captives on them) might be tiny, but they were a visible section of the mass of men. To white sailors,

---

[14] L. G. Carr Laughton, "Shantying and Shanties" *Mariner's Mirror* 9 (1923) 48–74; Roger D. Abrahams, *Deep the Water, Shallow the Shore: Three Essays on Shantying in the West Indies* (Austin: University of Texas Press, 1974).

[15] Nicolas Owen, *Journal of a Slave Dealer* Eveline Martin (ed.) (London: George Routledge and Sons, 1930) 63; Marcus Rediker, *Between the Devil and the Deep Blue Sea* (Cambridge: Cambridge University Press, 1987) 243–4.

[16] Ira Berlin, "From Creole to African: Atlantic Creoles and the Origins of African-American Society in Mainland North America" *William and Mary Quarterly* 53:2 (April 1996) 251–88, quote 263.

what is more, they were men who they relied on in storms, shipwreck, attack by the enemy, slave revolt or a host of other life and death situations. They shared privations, watches, dances, punishments and joy at landfall. Black seamen were not saleable goods to their crewmates, they were brother tars.

As historians such as Paul Lovejoy, Catherine Coquery-Vidrovich and Peter Gutkind have found, African workers were essential to slaving vessels while they were at the African coast. Enjoying some control over trade and their working lives, they withheld their labour for more money, were aware of their position and formed a relatively unified group.[17] Some of these men joined the ships on a more permanent basis, lured by the same mixture of potential financial gain and lack of other opportunities that had entrapped many European sailors into a career at sea. Some of those hired by European slaving vessels as linguists or interpreters did not just stay with the ship while it was anchored in West Africa, but also crossed the Atlantic Ocean with the rest of the crew.[18] And not all the men worked in these uniquely African roles. There were free African sailors too. One factor in Africa wrote home to Britain claiming that "Fante sailors from the Gold Coast, who whenever their services are required, readily enter on Board any English ship whose crew has been weakened by mortality, and return in it on the ensuing voyage."[19] There was no sense of shared African identity that would have morally precluded them from doing so.

This willingness was certainly not restricted to the Fante. Captain William Barns of the *Lightning* added two Africans to his crew at Annabon whom he named Black Tom and Bigg Tom. They were both discharged from the ship back home in Liverpool, after the ship had delivered 328 Cabinda-bought slaves to St. Vincent. Another 95 slaves originally purchased did not make the Caribbean.[20] The *Polly*, commanded by John Ainsworth, also gained two men at Annabon whom he endowed with their place of origin as a surname, recording them as Jem Anabona and Mat Anabona. How they were treated in relation to, and interacted with, the four French prisoners listed on its muster roll can only be imagined.[21]

---

[17] Catherine Coquery-Vidrovitch and Paul E. Lovejoy (eds.) *The Workers of the African Trade* (Beverly Hills: Sage, 1985); and Peter C. W. Gutkind's chapter therein, "Trade and Labor in Early Precolonial African History: The Canoemen of Southern Ghana" 25–50.

[18] Elizabeth Donnan, *Documents Illustrative of the History of the Slave Trade to America* (Washington D.C.: Carnegie Institute, 1935) IV 370–2.

[19] BT 6/7.

[20] BT 98/58 f.88; Eltis, *CD-ROM*.

[21] BT 98/61 f.159.

The *Woolton* and its captain William Sherwood also gained a man there named Manuel who is recorded with simply the word "black" in the rank list.[22] This seems to have been a relatively common place to enlist more seamen, perhaps because as a small island its men were accustomed to sea-going ventures.

The men who joined slave ships as sailors, servants and cooks were almost certainly from along the Atlantic littoral, in contrast to the slaves they transported who, by the eighteenth century, mostly came from far inland. Some African tribal groups from along the coast had excellent seafaring skills, which often far surpassed those of the European visitors. Small wonder that captains, who had generally selected their original crew from a diseased and malnourished pool of men, thought it a great opportunity if they could replace any who had already died with these capable men. They did not generally record their origins, however, so the ethnicity of many who laboured on board slaving vessels can only be assumed. The Liverpool vessel *Two Sisters,* for example, took four men named Ambree, Baggy, Bassanta and Banna aboard while in Africa in 1800. As this ship loaded its captive cargo on the Windward Coast it is likely that the men were also from this region of Africa, but this cannot be proven. What is known is that they travelled with the ship to Demarara and were discharged when the ship got back to Liverpool.[23]

For all those Africans who signed on board slaving vessels as free seamen, at least as many joined in the extremely humble position of cook. This was one of the lowliest positions aboard a sailing ship, and consequently one which few sailors wanted. There were specifics about the position of cook among the crew that marked it out as suitable for Africans in captains' minds. First of all, it was lowly, thankless and acutely unpleasant in the heat of the tropics. Secondly, it was a position that lay outside the main body of the crew, and could be alienating and solitary. One historian wrote that cooks on all ships were men who had been crippled by an accident, or were disabled in some way, and as those crowded beneath the decks of a slave ship could testify, having black skin was judged to be a peculiar kind of disability among transatlantic white society.[24] In addition there was considered to be something slightly effeminate about being a cook, so it was a job ensured not to challenge the white man's sense of

[22] BT 98/66 f.14.
[23] BT 98/61 f.187; Eltis, *CD-ROM.*
[24] Ralph Davis, *The Rise of the English Shipping Industry in the 17th and 18th Centuries* (London: MacMillan and Co., 1962) 121.

supreme masculinity when faced with largely naked men they viewed as strangely libidinous.[25]

Undoubtedly to see the position in the most positive light, there is cause to think that some traders wanted African food to be cooked for their captive passengers, with many at the time believing that the Africans' hatred for ships' food such as salt beef and hard tack caused problems such as "bloody flux" and even "melancholy" among the slaves. Some of the largest slave ships may even have employed an African to cook for the slaves, while a man of European origin produced food for the crew. There is no doubt that Europeans feared that Africans had special knowledge about toxic substances, and would poison them if given the chance.[26] Yet given the number of African men employed as cooks on slave ships this consideration seems to have been put aside in favour of the supposition that a black crewmember would be loyal to the crew not the captives.

Whether Africans joined as cook or seaman, they certainly took risks by enlisting on slavers. Their willingness to go on board was no doubt over-optimistically judged by the English factor quoted above. A letter from another British factor expresses their fears and rather more candidly identifies the risks they took. Joseph Debat wrote to the African Committee in England from James Fort, Accra, on 17 February 1764, "One of the Black Freemen who Shipped himself on board the Ross Capt. Tear is safe returned as he is Next Heir to the Crown of a Neighbouring Kingdom." "It is", he continued, a "fortunate Event, tending to Encrease that Confidence Necessary on all Occasions to be Preserved by the Natives."[27] The implication, of course, is that many potential African seamen did not trust slave ships' captains to honour their freedom when the ship reached its American destination.

They had good reason, for there are cases where free African sailors were sold as slaves, such as the two free black seamen sold at Newport, Rhode Island in the late 1780s by Captain Moses Smith.[28] Similarly, the African who had "liv'd among the English on the Coast of Guiney, and [could] speak some English" had probably been deceived by Captain

[25] Winthrop Jordan, *White Over Black: American Attitudes toward the Negro 1500–1812* (New York: W.W. Norton, 1968) 4–6.

[26] John McLeod, for example, feared being poisoned by his cook named Cudjoe and so ate only eggs while he was being fed by him, *A Voyage to Africa: With Some Account of the Manners and Customs of the Dahomian People* (London: John Murray, 1820) 87. The unnamed sailor who left an account of his voyage on board the *Florida* in 1753–4 also wrote that he had been warned by the other seamen on board the ship not to drink African palm wine as it could be poisoned. British Library Add Mss 39946.

[27] T 70/31.

[28] Donnan, *Documents* III 341.

Wilkinson of the *Jane,* to whom he went to dispute his status after being sold at Maryland in 1760.[29] Even if not betrayed by their employing captain, circumstances might prevail against them, such as happened to two free Senegalese seamen who were sold from the slaver *Amelia* in 1777 at Hispaniola after French privateers captured the ship.[30] Any black seaman employed aboard a ship, and especially a slave ship, was in danger of being sent to the Caribbean for sale if an enemy privateer took his vessel. The designation of prisoner of war could belong exclusively to those with white skin.[31]

A free African seaman named Amissa who was sold at Jamaica was eventually more fortunate. While he was engaged rowing slaves ashore at that island he discovered that he too had been sold, just like those he had helped to transport. The captain had double-crossed him, and sold him into slavery after having extracted his labour to help work the ship. To cover his duplicity the captain, named only as "E.", told Amissa's countrymen in Africa on his next voyage that he had died. Later, however, Amissa was reported to be alive and his friends and family – who were clearly people of authority and standing – demanded that he be returned home. It was reported that the son of a "gold taker" named Quaw went out with Captain E. to identify Amissa and arrange for his redemption. After around three years enslavement in Jamaica, Amissa was taken to London, where his case was laid before the African Committee who arranged for the captain's prosecution. At trial the judge awarded "exemplary damages" of several hundred pounds. When the *Gentleman's Magazine* reported the case, it explained simply to its readers that Amissa had been "hired as a sailor, to help navigate the ship", suggesting that it was a far from unique practice. The rarity of the case was that he regained his freedom and presumably was returned to Africa, not the nature of the contract he had first made with a slaver captain, or the fact that this contract had been broken in the most perfidious, calculating way.[32]

While the potential to be enslaved suggests that the experiences of African seamen in the slave trade were distinct from their European colleagues, there is evidence that white seamen sometimes fought against such treachery on the part of their officers. This shows the nuances of

---

[29] *Maryland Gazette* 23 October 1760; quoted in Lathan A. Windley, *Runaway Slave Advertisements: A Documentary History from the 1730s to 1790* (Westport: Greenwood Press, 1983) volume 2, 39.

[30] Bolster, *Black Jacks* 52.

[31] Macaulay, 'Journal', file 25, 19 January – 22 May 1798.

[32] Bolster, *Black Jacks* 52–3; *Gentleman's Magazine* March 1779; *London Chronicle* 6–9 March 1779. Reports of the damages awarded varied from £300 to £500.

white seamen's attitudes, for seemingly they were prepared to play their part in the trade in slaves, but extended their kinship and protection over those Africans who were their colleagues not their cargo. Interacting with Africans of all spheres while their ship was purchasing its unwilling passengers, they evidently had an understanding of slavery and its relationship to dark skin far more complex than people in the societies where they would sell their victims.

When Captain Jenkin Evans of the *Hudibras* treacherously sold one of his African men known as Bristol at Grenada, at least one of his seamen felt that a great wrong had been done. Sailor William Butterworth did not forget his old shipmate, who had expected to continue with the ship to England. When Butterworth subsequently visited the island on another journey, he tried in vain to find out why Bristol had been sold at Grenada. Although he failed to help Bristol right the wrong done to him, he met up with him on the nearby tiny island of Carriacou. Evidently Butterworth's loyalty to Bristol lasted far beyond the transatlantic crossing. Even writing years later after the trade had become illegal, Butterworth made no great claims about the immorality of the slavery. Bristol, however, in his mind, was very badly treated. He was not a slave in Butterworth's estimation, but a treasured crewmate.[33]

Perhaps Butterworth's loyalty was based, at least in part, on the fact that Bristol had shown his own allegiances in the most immediate of ways. Twice during the voyage he had informed on conspiracies among the slaves. Once he reported that two of the male slaves had knives, whereupon they were taken on deck and flogged, their wounds being rubbed with a mix of "cayenne pepper, salt, and beef brine". During the actual revolt that broke out, Bristol was firmly on the side of the seamen. For their part, if Butterworth is at all representative of the other sailors on the ship, then they repaid this loyalty by taking Bristol into their seafaring alliance, even though that ultimately failed to save him from the fate of plantation slavery.[34]

This revolt actually shows wonderfully the uncertain role that black crew had on slave ships. Bristol helped the seamen by revealing the plot and then assisted in suppressing the uprising. To the captives below decks, however, his actions were, naturally, anathema. They managed to grab him and tried to drag him below into their body in order to harm him for the betrayal of their plans. Meanwhile the seamen tried to haul him back on deck to save him. While this wonderfully metaphoric example of the

---

[33] Butterworth, *Three Years* 109–10, 425–7.
[34] Ibid, 109–10, 122.

role of a black crewmember was occurring, the black cook of the vessel was also desperately flaunting his separation from the captives. Faced with the rebels, he "d[amne]d their black souls, and fought furiously". Pouring a bucket of boiling water "over his much injured countrymen, whose naked bodies were ill calculated to endure the scalding fluid", Butterworth claimed that the cook was so vicious that his actions caused "pity" among his brothers-in-arms, the other seamen. But Butterworth was clearly wrong in deeming that the rebellious slaves were the cook's "countrymen", for evidently he did not see them as such. They were not from his ethnic group, and, like Bristol, he had allied himself firmly with the seamen.[35]

It is not hard to see how Bristol, and other African seamen, had a sense of identity and loyalty might have encompassed their fellow crewmembers more easily than those held captive below the decks of slave ships, especially for those of the merchant class. Even for those of more humble standing, there was reason to identify with the free crew rather than the captive cargo. Separated by ethnicity or tribal affiliation and lacking any sense of shared African unity – for it was the result of the slave trade which fermented solidarity through showing "otherness" – African seamen could and did occupy some fringe place at the edge of crew society. Eager to share the experiences of those free men above decks rather than express connection with those of similar skin colour to be sold as slaves, they certainly had reason to act as loyal employees and colleagues.

Quadgeo, listed as a "Negro cabin boy" on the *Mary* in 1795, was doubtless both doing his duty and saving his own life when he reported that a slave mutiny was planned. In so doing, a consequence was that he endeared himself to his white crewmates, unconsciously ingratiating himself into their pseudo kin network based on their shared work.[36] Yet this was not universal. Some African seaman hired by a British slave ship in the Gambia in 1773 passed tools to the captives below decks to assist them to revolt. During the ensuing rebellion the ship blew up, with the loss of everybody but the captain and a single slave.[37] These African sailors evidently felt unity with, and sympathy for, their human cargo, and did not ally themselves with the other crew, whatever the personal costs.[38]

---

[35] Ibid, 106–10.
[36] BT 98/56; Lorenzo J. Greene, "Mutiny on the Slave Ships" *Phylon* 5 (1944) 346–54.
[37] David Brion Davis, "Slavery – White, Black, Muslim, Christian" *New York Review of Books* (5 July 2001) 51–5.
[38] David Eltis, *The Rise of African Slavery in the Americas* (Cambridge: Cambridge University Press, 2000) 231–3.

In fact free African men on slave ships occupied an extremely ambiguous place within the hierarchy of the ship. Contingent upon far more than just the colour of their skin, such men's positions rested upon their skills, status within Africa and on the individual personalities involved. It would certainly be erroneous to suggest that Butterworth's loyalty to Bristol, or the allegiances formed in helping to suppress slave revolt, meant any kind of universal alliance between black and white shipmates. The issues at stake were far more convoluted, varied and varying than that.

Some black men who became part of the crew on slave ships were not part of the African maritime groups whose seafaring expertise captains were happy to utilize, but members of the merchant hierarchy involved in supplying slaves to Europeans. Perhaps those who made the ocean crossing with a slave ship and planned to return to Africa on a later voyage were learning skills that they hoped would serve thcm well in the future, just as African merchants sent their sons to school in England for this reason. They had more guarantees than most African seamen, as their associates on shore could retaliate by hindering trade if they did not return, or even pursuing them to the Americas, as in the case of Amissa. What this also meant, however, was that they often had more authority during the voyage than common sailors, partly because of their presumed ability to understand and intercede with the captives. These African men had a more variant situation on board than those who joined as lowly crewmembers, and consequently were treated differently by the rest of the crew.

The case of a man hired as an interpreter to the slave ship *Rainbow* illustrates this well. The African, known as Dick, was apparently taunted by some of his European colleagues that he would be sold as a slave when the ship reached the West Indies. As has been shown, this was a far from unlikely outcome, and one that fully reveals the divisions in potential experience between white and black crewmembers. All may have been whipped, tortured and half-starved, but none of the European men would face this particular fate. These men were clearly emphasizing, rather than downplaying, Dick's division from the rest of the crew, and were doing so by making an assertion based solely on his skin colour.[39]

Dick's plight, however, did not go unnoticed. When Captain Harrison "Observ'd an Alteration in Dick's behavior", he asked his interpreter what was wrong, and "with some reluctance" Dick told him what the seamen had alleged. Harrison investigated, and found that seaman Richard Comer had started the rumour. Dick "demanded Satisfaction of the Said Comer",

---

[39] Donnan, *Documents* IV 370–2.

presumably asking for some sort of revenge to be exacted upon him. Captain Harrison's reply was telling. He could not oblige, he told Dick, because he could not allow him to beat "any White Person on board". Dick, however, was "Dissatisfied, and stormed and Raged upon Deck". Eventually, fearing that this chaos would cause the slaves to revolt, he allowed "Dick to take Satisfaction". Dick tied up Richard Comer, and gave him "at two different times, about three or four and twenty lashes." Comer died, allegedly as a result of this whipping.[40]

This incident was clearly far more complex than a divide over skin colour. Dick's authority on board ship was based on his ability to communicate with the slaves, and indeed he had a status which set him apart from the body of tars. His position was very different to that of a black seaman or even a cook, for they potentially shared work duties, food, grievances, and other uniting factors with the non-black sailors. The reaction of Captain Harrison suggests that what Comer and the other seamen might have disliked about this situation was that Dick had a status superior to their own, based on his presumed ability to control the slaves. Yet in tormenting the man they felt to be above them, they resorted to invoking the racial make-up of the Americas. Dick should not forget, Comer implied, that while he might have had a superior status at that point, his black skin would ultimately make him eligible for enslavement when they reached the western side of the ocean. Dick's standing was based on the dangers of the trade in which they were engaged; Richard Comer was reminding him that when they reached South Carolina, that same trade, in its long history, had ensured his inferiority.[41]

There was a final twist in this tale, and one which shows again why black crewmembers had many reasons to firmly stake their allegiance with the seamen not the slaves. Dick's reputed ability to expose any planned slave revolts before they occurred proved to be erroneous. In fact when they rebelled, he was the only one of the crew to be murdered. Dick, like Richard Comer before him, was cast to a watery grave, the slaves obviously feeling particularly aggrieved about his role in their fate.[42] This was not a unique case. Shakoe, a black man who sailed to Suriname as part of the crew of a slave ship, met a similar fate. The ship was nine days out from the coast of Africa when the slaves attempted to revolt, and Shakoe was the prime focus of the captives' hatred. One

---

[40] Ibid.
[41] Ibid; Eltis, *CD-Rom*, 90467.
[42] Ibid.

morning one of them "struck him with his shackle and then jumped overboard". Caught by some other rebellious slaves, Shakoe was killed, "His head ... beaten to pieces – a ghastly sight". Tellingly, the whip which he had previously "plied ... until it became actually encrusted with blood" was torn to shreds.[43] Shakoe, like Dick, was fully part of the merchant class, Africans who grew wealthy from slave trading and had status based on their power to supply arriving ships. The captives hated them as slave traders, and because they were the men most likely, often because of a shared language, to reveal their plots to regain their freedom.

Dick, Shakoe and other members of African merchant groups who made the Atlantic crossing were not part of the central body of lowly crewmen who incorporated men of many colours into their ranks, and attempted to protect sailors of any ethnicity as their own. The fact that Joseph Harrison let Dick whip Richard Comer shows that he had a standing, in the eyes of the captain at least, that was possibly what the seamen most disliked. Never men to take kindly to perceived slights from authority, perhaps Comer and his allies felt indignant that a man with no seafaring skills, and an African, had such sway with their captain. Comer's retaliatory insult shows that when aggrieved by their lack of status, white seamen were certainly not above asserting their superiority based on the status their skin tone would convey when landfall was made at the slave markets of the Americas.

Despite the divisions based on rank, and the fact that black men might be enslaved in the Americas while white sailors could not, there is evidence to suggest that crews sometimes formed alliances across the colour line. Revealing that status was at least as divisive aboard a slave ship as colour, it seems that when black men were part of the main body of lowly seafarers – and particularly where they were considered to share grievances with their white counterparts against the ship's officers – they were often fully accepted as fellow crewmembers. Resisting the perceived abuses or over-zealous discipline of the captain and mates was a unifying experience when sailors of all racial origins stood shoulder to shoulder against a common enemy.

Events aboard the Bristol slave ship *Lovely Lass* illustrate well what could occur when seamen of varying origins felt that they were ill-treated. Arriving in Africa in 1792, Captain John Wade Robison decided to enlist three Africans to supplement his original crew of thirty-nine. Later jail

---

[43] Richard Drake, "Revelations of a Slave Smuggler: Being the Autobiography of Capt. Richard Drake, an African Trader for Fifty Years – from 1807 to 1857" George F. Dow, *Slave Ships and Slaving* (Westport, CT: Negro Universities Press, 1927) 207–8.

records would describe Cudjoe as around thirty years of age, 5'7" tall, and simply "black," while his colleague Joe was five years younger, had been born in the Anomabu area, and had "shock hair". The third African, known as Quow, did not live to have his physical appearance noted down by the Newgate jailer. Quow was employed as the ship's cook, and trouble brewed after he apparently answered only "yes" rather than "yes, sir" to one of Chief Mate Robert Milligan's orders. Milligan beat Quow for this supposed slight and cut him on the head with a cutlass. Heavily intoxicated, Milligan then ordered a white seaman named John Owen to flog Quow, and loaded a blunderbuss and threatened to shoot Owen when he refused. Quow was given a "very severe flogging" and manacled to the mast.[44]

Enraged at this treatment, revenge was sought on Milligan not just by Quow, but also Cudjoe, Joe, John Owen and a white boy named John Dixon. When Milligan subsequently died, all five were charged with murder. John Owen and Cudjoe were accused of being the ringleaders behind the plot. The five men were sent to England on *HMS Charon* to stand trial before the Admiralty Courts, although Quow died during the voyage and never reached London. In a somewhat ironic support of sailors' views on black seamen's right to equal treatment, there was apparently no question that the sentence Cudjoe, Quow and Joe would face was that of perpetual slavery, like those they would have helped ship to the Americas. This was doubtless due to their free status within Africa, as slave traders could not afford to override native attitudes regarding legitimate and illegitimate slaves. In fact after their acquittal due to lack of evidence, Cudjoe and Joe returned to Africa, so much pressure being exerted on Archibald Dalzel, governor of Cape Coast Castle, that he anticipated "a very serious Palaver" if they were not returned in haste.[45]

Unfortunately little is known of John Owen, but Cudjoe was truly an Atlantic African who was an experienced seaman, could speak English, and earned wages for his labour. Presumably of Akan origin, he had originally sailed on the slave ship *Mars* from Africa to Grenada where it delivered two hundred and thirteen slaves. He was discharged from this voyage in Liverpool where he would have mingled with the men of many nationalities who lived and roamed among the dockside communities, inveigled into life on the edge of the Atlantic along with the trading goods from around the world unloaded onto its quays. After his sojourn there,

---

[44] HO 26/3 20; HCA 1/25; HCA 1/64; Eltis, *CD-Rom* 18149.
[45] HCA 1/25; HCA 1/64; T 70/33: Letters from Archibald Dalzel to the African Committee dated 8 August 1795 and 30 August 1796.

Cudjoe returned to Anomabu in the *Jane* under Captain James Bachope, where he worked for a "Mr. Torrane" for two years until he joined the *Lovely Lass*. At sometime during his journeys he would seem to have become an integral part of the seafaring community, a man who John Owen could empathize with to such an extent that they were accused of plotting murder together. This is hardly surprising, for they evidently shared many of the same experiences as seafarers, creating a familiarity which transcended their different racial origins, regardless of the trade in which they were both engaged.[46]

In another case that bears some similarities, on board the *Wasp* in 1793 was an African seaman known as Jack who was accused of having united with some of the other crew, and some of the captive slaves, to throw the surgeon of the vessel overboard. There are parallels between Jack and Cudjoe, for after this revolt the *Pennsylvania Gazette* described Jack not only as "a yellow negro, of very stout make" but also pointed out specifically that he "spoke a good deal of English". He had "shipped himself at the [African] coast" possibly at the Old Calabar region where the ship had loaded its human cargo. Like the case of the *Lovely Lass*, the facts of the crime allegedly committed aboard the *Wasp* are hard to discern. Here it was alleged that Jack, along with the steward Joseph Nees who "appeared to be a man of color [with] curled black hair", and a white cabin boy named Thomas Beddo, joined with some of the captive slaves and "pelted the doctor with stones.... kept for scouring". Although it was Jack who apparently finally pushed the doctor overboard, an interesting component of this case is that one of the other crewmembers alleged that Nees and Beddo had been abusing the doctor from the time they left Bristol, the inference being that Jack and the accused slaves continued this work.[47]

While Africans held ambiguous places within a slave ship's crew, the position was somewhat more straightforward for black men who lived in and worked out of Britain's port cities, and joined slavers at their point of origin. Whatever their heritage – whether African, African-American, Caribbean or native-born Britons – they were all in a sense Atlantic citizens, occupying much the same space as white men of the same occupation. Like Cudjoe, who apparently learned the ethics of sailors as well as the work of a seaman during his voyages and stay in England, they were far more central to the seafaring body than Africans like Dick and Shakoe who, by contrast, were part of the slave merchant network. Men

---

[46] HCA 1/25; HCA 1/64.
[47] *Pennsylvania Gazette* 3 April 1793.

of African origin can be identified within the muster rolls of Liverpool slave ships which survive for the late eighteenth century, despite the fact that, unlike in North America, there was no obligation for captains to note the racial origin of their men on the muster. Some masters did so, but how many other African men went unrecorded is impossible to guess.

Despite the lack of quantifiable data, the Liverpool musters show the truly cosmopolitan nature of many Africans' life experiences, and the diverse ways that they interacted with the Atlantic world. African seamen were discharged from slave ships in Liverpool or London, and from there often joined other slaving vessels in order either to return home or to make another circuit in this most catastrophic of trades. Maintaining their own identity, however, or revealing how they were viewed as people apart by the ships' officers, many seem to have adopted place names as their own, or more likely been randomly assigned them by the person completing the required list. The *Ann,* captained by Reuben Wright had a seamen named on the muster roll as "Peter Coast Guinea". The huge ship *Kingsmill* had Peter Annabona from Africa among its eighty-two man crew in 1799, he most likely had been given this name by one of his previous employers. The *Amazon,* captained by James Coznahan, lists James Amacre from Africa having been on board when it departed from Liverpool, a name often used for the New Calabar area. The *Elizabeth* had a man named Joseph Samuel listed fourth on its muster roll as "Island Princes" – today called Príncipe – among lots of men all listed as being from Liverpool. He made the whole voyage with the ship.[48]

Other men took non-African place names as their own, such as the man called John Liverpool aboard the schooner *Goodrich* from an unnamed African place. He also had an African crewmate named John Sabally, possibly a play on the term "sable", just as a man named Peter Black from Annabon had presumably been given this rather crude descriptive surname by some captain he had come into contact with. Others from Africa are alone on the crew lists as having no surname listed at all, such as the men named Dick and Sam who worked on board the *Eclipse.*[49]

These men stand out among the Liverpool muster rolls because of their African names, but men from all over the globe can be found in these lists. In Britain's major port cities dwelled men who had been swept into a maritime life for a variety of reasons and from a wide spectrum of backgrounds. Britain's role as primary seafaring trader in the eighteenth

[48] BT 98/56 f.265; BT 98/59 f.162; BT 98/62 f.276; BT 98/63 f.284.
[49] BT 98/60 f.93; BT 98/64 f.29.

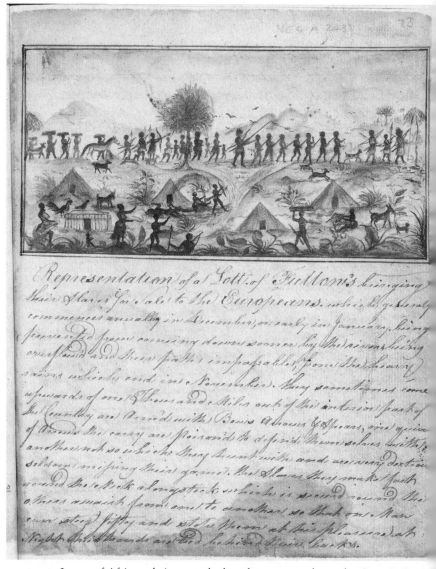

FIGURE 2. Image of Africans being marched to the coast, as drawn by Captain Samu Gamble of the *Sandown*.

From the log of the *Sandown*, held by the National Maritime Museum, London, a reprinted with their permission.

century meant that men from at least five of the seven continents lived and worked among its dockside communities. The crews of slave ships inevitably reflected this gathering of people from around the world, so while African seamen remained relatively unusual, they were only a section of a multiracial body of seamen by the later eighteenth century. If the slave trade was entered into only by the lowliest and desperate of seamen, the xenophobia of most of British society meant that this included those of non-British origin who searched for employment among Liverpool's wharves. To take one example, the crew of the slaver *John* included John Prussel from Jamaica; Joseph Rodrigues from the West Indies; Joseph Galley from Leghorn [Livorno]; Mich Gray from the Gambia; Barry Bollers from Norway; Golperce Charles from Copenhagen; Sven Nelson from Sweden; John Salvadore from Naples; Antonio Rodrique from Portugal; John Swift from Salem, Massachusetts; Edward Kitchen from Jersey and John Brown from New York. These men sailed with the ship to an unspecified African embarkation point, delivered two hundred and eighty slaves to Kingston, Jamaica, and then sailed back to Liverpool.[50]

While it is perhaps unsurprising that men from other slave trading nations were frequently employed on slavers leaving Britain, (and presumably the reverse was also true) it is over simplistic to see these men as Europeans unreceptive to their African colleagues. Just as there was little African unity in this period, Europeans too had their differences and were prepared to fight over them. Sailors, as men who were frequently impressed into Naval service to fight against the French, Dutch, Spanish, Americans or whoever was deemed the enemy, were most unlikely to have completely put aside these animosities. Relatively often men who served on board slave ships had previously been imprisoned by another European nation as a prisoner of war.[51]

What is more the Irish were a considerable percentage of all slaver seamen, though hard to identify on muster rolls because of their similar names to British men. As Nicholas Canny, Theodore Allen and others have shown, they had long been demeaned in English thought and literature.

[50] BT 98/63, f.63; Eltis, *CD-ROM*.

[51] T70/32; T70/34; Darold D. Wax, "The Browns of Providence and the Slaving Voyage of the Brig *Sally*, 1764–1765" *American Neptune* 32 (1972) 171–9; Liverpool RO 387 MD 45: The *Enterprize*; Birmingham City Archives, JWP C7/19; Dorothy S. Towle (ed.), *Records of the Vice-Admiralty Court of Rhode Island 1716–1752* (Washington D.C.: American Historical Association, 1936) 212–4; Joseph E. Inikori, "Measuring the Unmeasured Hazards of the Atlantic Slave Trade: Documents Relating to the British Trades" *Revue Français D'Histoire D'Outre-Mer* 83 (September 1996) 53–92.

Because of the necessity of justifying their "civilization" through colonization, the English conceived the Irish as being a separate, and darker skinned, race of mankind.[52] Irish seamen perhaps had more to gain than most through association with the single category of "free white man" in the Americas, but equally were themselves an oppressed group. It should not be assumed that English and Irish seamen were any more united than, for example, the Igbo and the Kru.

Beyond Europeans, men of other origins can certainly be identified among slaver crews. Despite the fact that until 1802 lascars, or Asian seamen, were not officially allowed to work on ships sailing west of the Cape of Good Hope, Asians can be found among the muster rolls. [53] Liverpool ships the *Crescent, Amacree, Hinde, Dart, Mary, Lord Nelson, Levant* and *Martha* all clearly had men of Asian origin aboard. Sailor William Butterworth wrote that one of his fellow tars on his voyage on the *Hudibras* was Antonio, a lascar, whom he described as "not of the cleanest sort".[54] Men from the Americas apparently worked alongside them – there was Simon Peters from Curaçao for example, and Peter Jordan from Quebec who was a sailor on the *Polly* in 1800.[55] Joseph Dornett from Cartagena was employed on the *Elizabeth* in 1799 that took 327 slaves to Barbados.[56]

A poem written by W. Clark Russell in this period, entitled "The Sailing Ship", expresses the international, racially mixed nature of men who worked at sea, and acknowledges too their rebellious image:

> The Dago and the Chaney Man,
> The Dutchman and Hindoo
> The Proosian and Hi-tal-ian'
> *Do form her measley crew.*
>
> They flies our red flag on such craft,
> And honours thus the rabble;
> No Anglees shoken fore or aft-
> *Nowt speech but gabble-babble.*[57]

---

[52] Nicholas Canny, "Identity Formation in Ireland: The Emergence of the Anglo-Irish" Nicholas Canny and Anthony Pagden (eds.) *Colonial Identity in the Atlantic World, 1500–1800* (New Jersey: Princeton University Press, 1987) 159–212; Jacobson, *Whiteness of a Different Color* 4–5, 48–55.

[53] Conrad Dixon, "Lascars: The Forgotten Seamen" Rosemary Ommer and Gerald Panting (eds.) *Working Men who Got Wet* (Newfoundland: Maritime History Group, 1980) 265–77.

[54] Butterworth, *Three Years* 14.

[55] HCA 1/58.

[56] BT 98/60 f.258.

[57] W. Clark Russell, *The Turnpike Sailor* (London: Skeffington and Sons, 1907).

Although the poem does not mention Africans, in these circumstances free black men felt themselves less conspicuously different working as seamen than in other occupations. For black men in Britain going to sea was a mixture of preference, survival and absence of other possibilities. By the days in which Britain was the primary slave trader of the world, many men and women of African origin had been taken to Britain not only as servants to wealthy families but large numbers of escaped or manumitted slaves had drifted there too.[58] The Royal Navy employed others in the Caribbean but discharged them in Britain.[59] At the time of Lord Chief Justice, the Earl of Mansfield's judgement on James Somerset's case in 1772, the total black population of Britain was calculated at 15,000. The war with America caused the black population to expand greatly as the army and navy discharged African-Americans in Britain. In 1786 Granville Sharp, an acquaintance of Olaudah Equiano and prosecutor in both the Somerset and *Zong* cases, established the "Committee for the Relief of the Black Poor" in London. Some of those whom the committee helped were those who would later settle in Sierra Leone.[60]

Because the British cities of London and Liverpool, were the centres of trade with the West Indies and North America, they became hubs where men of African origin often found themselves. Certainly after the Somerset decision, which made it unlawful for slaves to be shipped out of the country against their will, slavery in England became increasingly untenable, due mainly to the agency of the Afro-British themselves. Many escaped their bondage and took up residence in the newly expanding urban areas. As Peter Fryer writes, they "voted with their feet... [and] had largely freed themselves by the mid-1790s".[61] Because of this, Britain ended up as more of a sanctuary, however flimsy the freedom and insalubrious the living conditions, than either the Caribbean islands or the North American colonies/states. Just as runaways flocked to urban centres on the American mainland and islands because of their increased anonymity and chances for employment, so London and Liverpool offered more of both, being so much further away from their former masters and with livelier port communities.

---

[58] Norma Myers, *Reconstructing the Black Past: Blacks in Britain 1780–1830* (London: Frank Cass, 1996) 19–21; Folarin Shyllon, *Black People in Britain 1555–1833* (London: Oxford University Press, 1977) 101–2; Fryer, *Staying Power* 68.

[59] R. Pares, "The Manning of the Navy in the West Indies, 1702–63" *Transactions of the Royal Historical Society* 4th Series, 20 (1937) 31–60.

[60] Braidwood, *Black Poor* chapters 1 and 2.

[61] Fryer, *Staying Power* 132.

To get there African-American and Caribbean men, often runaway slaves, joined ships heading that way. Inevitably sometimes this meant joining slave ships, taking the place of European seamen who had deserted in the West Indies, as between approximately one eighth and one quarter of them did.[62] Robin Blackburn has called the "ports and ships engaged in the Atlantic trade" a "slave frontier", which, "given the slaves' powerful urge for freedom, [was] often a porous one".[63] In fact so widespread was this practice that laws had to be passed in some Caribbean islands cutting down on *grand marronage* at sea by making all potential black sailors have a pass and written permission to enlist on a ship.[64] But more furtive routes still remained, as slaves attempted to stow away, sometimes begging seamen to conceal them aboard. The men of the *Canterbury* had been entreated in this way in Puerto Rico in the late 1760s.[65]

Slave runaway advertisements in the West Indies worried especially that the men in question would escape by getting a berth working on a ship. A man called Durham was known to have already worked as the cook of the *Lady Juliana* at the time of his escape, so his owner warned in particular that "he may possibly pass for a free fellow, as he knows how to work in boats or craft". Twenty-three year old Hector was described by his owner as having "followed the sea, [so] it is probable he may attempt to pass for a free man, and endeavour to ship himself aboard some vessel". Another man, known as Gil Blas, was described as an "expert seaman".[66] Pompey had learned his seafaring skills when he "served on board a vessel for two years [in the] last war".[67] All of these men's owners implored ship captains not to employ these men and so remove them from the island and take them out of their grasp.

Some of these men had probably gained their seafaring skills within Africa or the Caribbean, but there is also a suggestion that some had

---

[62] Peter Earle, *Sailors: English Merchant Seamen, 1650–1775* (London: Methuen: 1998) 168.

[63] Robin Blackburn, *The Making of New World Slavery: From the Baroque to the Modern, 1492–1800* (London: Verso, 1997) 396.

[64] N.A.T. Hall, "Maritime Maroons: *Grand Marronage* in the Danish West Indies" *William and Mary Quarterly* 92 (October 1985) 476–98. Neither rules and regulations deterred runaways, of course. Captain Jacob Loran was to lament how a "Negro stowed himself away in my ship" and was not discovered until three days after they had sailed. Loran claimed that he took the man back to London with him and fed and clothed him, but he ran away four weeks later. Loran complained that he was forced to pay the man's calculated value, £84 pounds, to his dispossessed former master the next time he sailed to St. Kitts. ZHC 1/82 .

[65] Clarkson, *Substance of the Evidence* 3.

[66] *Cornwall Chronicle and General Advertiser* 22 February 1777, 12 April 1777.

[67] [Kingston, Jamaica] *Royal Gazette* 29 December 1792 – 5 January 1793.

learned this proficiency during the middle passage, while they were being transported as captives. Jeffrey Bolster writes "every new slave came face to face with European seafaring technology during the ordeal of the Middle Passage."[68] There are indeed many cases when captives had to help man a ship, often being put to the exceedingly arduous, repetitive work of assisting with the pumps if the ship was taking on water. Aboard the *Charlestown*, an American ship captained by Charles Harris, the crew took "some of the ablest men out of irons" when the ship "became so extremely leaky as to require constant exertion on the pumps". In this case the male slaves were "worked beyond their strength" at this grueling task".[69] In 1797 the crew of the *James* "determined to let a dozen of [the slaves] come on deck" after the ship grounded on the sandbar at Bonny. The Africans "went to work ... at the pumps".[70] Similarly, on the *Phoenix* in the early 1760s when the ship started leaking during a gale and a lightening storm, the crew was "under Necessity of letting all our slaves out of Irons, to assist in Pumping and Baling".[71] The crew of the *Mary* required the help of its captives when the "Ship sprung a Leake" and they were in a "very bad condition" struggling against the odds to "keep the Ship above Water". They, like the other ships, let some of the men out of their shackles to help at the pumps.[72] Aboard other slave ships captive Africans were used to man the guns to fight off enemy ships, an important task given the number lost to rival privateers.[73]

---

[68] Bolster, *Black Jacks* 57.

[69] Mungo Park, *Travels into the Interior of Africa* (London: Eland, 1983) 275–7; Eltis, CD-ROM 25406.

[70] Hugh Crow, *Memoirs of the Late Captain Hugh Crow, of Liverpool; Comprising a Narrative of His Life, Together with Descriptive Sketches of the Western Coast of Africa; Particularly of Bonny* (London: Frank Cass, 1970) 63–4; Eltis, CD-ROM, 81973.

[71] *Pennsylvania Gazette* 11 November 1762; *Gentleman's Magazine* January 1763.

[72] *Gentleman's Magazine* July 1737. Many other examples can also be found in the sources of captive Africans being worked as sailors on board slave ships. Robert Barker, *The Unfortunate Shipwright, or Cruel Captain, Being a Faithful Narrative of the Unparallel'd Sufferings of Robert Barker, Late Carpenter on Board the Thetis Snow, of Bristol, in a Voyage to the Coast of Guinea and Antigua* (London: Printed for, and sold by the Sufferer, 1760) 19–21; Darold D. Wax, "A Philadelphia Surgeon on a Slaving Voyage to Africa, 1749–1751" *Pennsylvania Magazine of History and Biography* 92 (1968) 465–93; Robinson, *Sailor Boy* 97–8; *Pennsylvania Gazette* 28 November 1765; Donnan, *Documents* III 213.

[73] One calculation suggests that about two thirds of all British slave ships that failed to return were lost as the result of capture by an enemy nation. Joseph E. Inikoiri "Measuring the unmeasured hazards of the Atlantic Slave Trade: Documents Relating to the British Trade" *Revue Français D'Histoire D'Outre Mer* 83 (September 1996) 53–92. For examples see BT 6/9; ZHC 1/90 38; Daniel P. Mannix and Malcolm Cowley, *Black Cargoes: A History of the Atlantic Slave Trade 1518–1865* (New York: Penguin, 1962) 131–2; Gomer Williams, *History of the Liverpool Privateers* (London: Heinemann, 1897)

Evidence suggests, however, that other African captives did assist more with the sailing of the ship than simply working the pumps or manning guns. Seaman James Stanfield recalled how as disease, mistreatment and death drastically reduced the crew of his ship, "all idea of keeping the slaves in chains were given up" and a large number of the captives "were therefore freed from their irons and they pulled and hauled as they were directed by the inefficient sailors".[74] In this case they were clearly being instructed in basic seafaring tasks. When the *Mermaid* approached Grenada in 1792 it was reported that "Capt. Taylor [had] lost all his Hands to four, & these together with himself, were in so weakly a state" that he only succeeded in getting the ship into port with "the assistance of a few Negro Boys, who the Capt. had wise precaution to train a little to the Business of working the Ship".[75] The *Benson* must have trained some of its captives as it had "only two white men upon her yards handling the sails, the rest were black boys, slaves".[76]

However runaway slaves had learned the skills that secured their position aboard a ship to England, most found when they arrived there that their options for future employment were severely curbed. For those not in servitude to a wealthy family, career choices were extremely limited – one recent writer has summed them up as "going to sea... begging and crime".[77] The lack of alternative employment can be seen in the fact that, as a rough estimate, more than one in twenty seamen working out of Britain was of African origin by the 1770s, and more than a quarter of all London's black men were seafarers compared with only 3.6 per cent of white men.[78] Many of these men in fact seem to have been reduced to both seafaring and petty crime, as seventeen of the fifty-two black men transported to Australia as convicts prior to 1830 listed

560–1, 564–5; Basil Lubbock, "Seamen" *The Trade Winds: A Study of British Overseas Trade during the French Wars 1793–1815* C. Northcote Parkinson (ed.) (London: George Allen and Unwin, 1948) 120; *Gore's General Advertiser* 17 April 1800.

[74] Quoted in Thomas Howard (ed.) *Black Voyage: Eyewitness Accounts of the Atlantic Slave Trade* (Boston: Little, Brown and Co., 1971) 65.

[75] C107/13: Letter from Munro MacFarlane to James Rogers, 18th November 1792.

[76] ZHC 1/85 521: Evidence of John Ashley Hall.

[77] Ty M. Reese, "Toiling in the Empire: Labor in Three Anglo-Atlantic Ports, London, Philadelphia and Cape Coast Castle" unpublished PhD Dissertation, University of Toledo (1999) 110. For the approximately twenty per cent of black people in Britain who were female, prostitution could more accurately be substituted for seafaring in this unholy list of choices.

[78] Shyllon, *Black People* 101–2; Norma Myers, "Servant, Sailor, Soldier, Tailor, Beggarman: Black Survival in White Society 1780–1830" *Immigrants and Minorities* 12:1 (March 1993) 47–74.

their occupation as seaman or ship's cook.[79] Moreover, fully twenty-six per cent of black men recorded in England's Old Bailey records in this period worked as seamen.[80] A committee founded to help Lascars in London found that in fact more black than Asian seamen were in desperate need. [81]

For many of Britain's black men the necessity of going back to sea was pressing, whatever the potential risks. This meant some had little choice but to sign aboard a slaving vessel. We can only surmise what led a man named James Blue, who presumably had found his way to the relative freedom of life as a seaman in Britain, to sign on the slave ship *Blanche* in 1802. Whatever his motivation he paid dearly for it, for his freedom was curtailed when he was "taken out of the ship 21st May 1803 by his Master at Barbados being a runaway negroe". (It is an interesting footnote that he would almost certainly have lost his freedom soon after even without this unfortunate circumstance, for the ship was captured on its way home by the French.)[82] Although it is perfectly possible that some men of African origin who joined slave ships as sailors did so because it was their only chance to see their home continent, or their ancestral homelands again, the majority doubtless made a pragmatic choice between a slaving voyage and penury. Others, forced onto ships just like their white counterparts by crimps or unholy alliances between unscrupulous publicans and jailers, had no choice at all. Many were forced to take employment with captains with whom they had already worked, so having enlisted when the ship was in ballast or carrying plantation produce, they found themselves on a slaving voyage.

Given the ethnically mixed nature of Britain's capital city it seems likely that among the 1120 slave ships that left from that port between 1750 and 1807 were found numbers of seamen of African origin.[83] Unfortunately muster rolls from this city have not survived for this period. There is, however, the case of Briton Hammon who signed onto a slave ship in London and who has left one of the only instances where a black man recorded the events which led him to sign on a slaving vessel. Hammon had

---

[79] Ian Duffield, "From Slave Colonies to Penal Colonies: The West Indian Convict Transportees to Australia" *Slavery and Abolition* 7 (1986) 25–45.

[80] Myers, *Black Past* 67.

[81] Braidwood, *Black Poor and White Philanthropists* 32–3; Alexander X. Byrd, "Captive and Voyagers: Black Migrants Across the Eighteenth Century World of Olaudah Equiano" unpublished PhD Dissertation, Duke University (2001) 141.

[82] BT 98/63 f.292.

[83] Eltis, *CD-ROM*.

been on board *HMS Hercules* in 1759, and had been wounded in the head and had his arm injured, leaving him unable to work and incarcerated in Greenwich hospital. After a short spell on a naval ship, Hammon, in his own words, "ship'd myself on board of a large ship bound to Guinea" from London. His feelings about this, and the morality of it, are not mentioned, but the economic necessity of his decision is clear. Similarly though Hammon never made this journey, choosing instead to return on another ship to Boston, he says nothing about this choice other than that he preferred to go with a captain he knew, and wished to return to his home.[84] Briton Hammon, like so many other African-American seafarers, had a "multi-dimensional sense of self" which was not solely reliant on his colour.[85]

England's premier slave trading port, Liverpool, may not have been the most cosmopolitan of cities compared to London, but its deep involvement in the slave trade meant that many of African origin either lived there, or passed through on their often tortured journeys. Alongside the shops selling shackles and thumbscrews, the black "trophy" servants, the crowded Goree docks and the wealthy merchants with plenty of blood-soaked guineas to spend, people of African origin were inevitably also to be found there. When William Butterworth joined the *Hudibras* in the 1780s as a young boy at that port, he found a city whose "commercial pursuits collected, as a focus, the diversified inhabitants of Asia, Africa and America". [86] Another who sailed on a slave ship as a young boy wrote in his memoirs that he "had seen black men in Liverpool" when he had travelled there to embark on his voyage.[87]

For ships that left from Liverpool, muster rolls exist from 1772 until the abolition of the legal trade (see appendix 1), but it is impossible to evaluate an accurate percentage of black crewmembers from these lists as the crew lists of English slave ships, as already noted, did not require physical characteristics of the men to be listed. Although "place of abode" had to be given, many captains wrote in either the place where the men joined the ship, or even used this space to list their men's rank. Thus many ships listed all of their seamen as being from Liverpool, or the majority from Liverpool, then some from Africa, and others from the port of slave

---

[84] Briton Hammon, *A Narrative of the Uncommon Sufferings and Surprising Deliverance of Briton Hammon, a Negro Man* reprinted in Dorothy Parker (ed.) *Early Negro Writing, 1760–1837* (Boston: Beacon Press, 1971) 522–8.

[85] Bolster, "An Inner Diaspora" 419–48.

[86] Butterworth, *Three Years* 4.

[87] Robinson, *Sailor Boy* 33.

disembarkation. Clearly it would seem more than likely that this is where men joined the ship than their actual place of origin. In addition, of course there were plenty of black seamen whose place of abode was Liverpool. The *Fisher* for example lists all its men as being from Liverpool, but one, George Williams, was a black man.[88] Similarly no residences are given for the crew of the *Betsey* which left in 1772 for Bonny and Jamaica, but the man listed right at the bottom of the muster roll and named only Cato was very probably of African origin.[89]

Occasionally Liverpool ships listed men as blacks, as if their skin colour held some inherent definition of status, as indeed it contemporaneously did. Captain Pratt of the *Hibernia* listed six of its crewmembers as "black sailors" in the "station" section of his muster list. Named as Thomas Tittle, Peter Tittle, Anthony Cacandia, Henry Caffrir, James Curtes and John Banks they were all discharged at Liverpool at the end of the voyage after selling their cargo of slaves. Another man on this same vessel, ranked as a "black ordinary seaman" and named Abraham Newland, is reported to have "ran at Cacandi 10 Jan. 1804", no doubt also telling us where the man named Anthony Cacandia had originated from. The brig *Mars* listed a man as simply "Alfred – a Black" at the very bottom of its muster roll. Definitely a seaman and not the cook, he made the entire voyage with the ship. In other cases it seems likely that some of these men listed as Africans were in fact African-American or Afro-Caribbean, but were listed as Africans either due to the registrar's ignorance or their own wish to be seen as inviolably free. The *Mercury* for example, captained by John Sillars, had a John Dido listed from Africa who shipped at Liverpool before the ship left. He died at Surinam on 12 July 1801.[90]

If the information in these muster rolls is taken at face value, then the percentages of black men who worked on Liverpool slaving vessels at the end of the eighteenth century and early nineteenth centuries were very small. In 1797, for example, only eight of the ninety-three slavers that departed from that port are listed as having black men aboard, although four of those eight had more than one black crewman. In 1803 nine captains, from the eighty-six slave ships which sailed from Liverpool for Africa, noted that they had black men among their crew. Of these nine ships, the *Minerva* had three black men and the *Hibernia* had the seven

---

[88] BT 98/58 f.203.
[89] BT 98/33 f.142.
[90] BT 98/64 f.215; BT 98/64 f.140; BT 98/61 f.220.

men mentioned above.[91] This would seem too vastly different from the approximately five percent of all seamen working out of Britain being black, however, even taking into account that many probably avoided slave ships, both for the same reasons as their white colleagues and from motives all their own.[92] It seems certain that many captains simply did not differentiate between black and white seamen when completing the muster.

This assertion is backed up by the fact that few British Navy captains noted black crewmembers on Admiralty muster rolls in this period.[93] It is also strengthened by the frequency with which black seamen are noted throughout scattered evidence from parliamentary papers to ships' logs, journals to newspaper reports. To give a few examples, aboard the *Lady Nelson* there was a "stout black man, an American" among the crew.[94] The list of men who had wages advanced to them before the sailing of the *Calveley* in 1757 contains one named "Coffee Black".[95] A sailor testified before the House of Commons commission into the slave trade that the *Black Joke* of Liverpool that sailed in 1764 was reduced by death during its passage to "the captain, 3 white men, and one black".[96] Thomas Lee, recorded as "a Black", testified to the Admiralty Court that he was an American and the cook on board the *Sarah* when it sailed from Liverpool to Bonny.[97] The brig *Sally* had a black steward named Adam Messoe on its slaving voyage that took the ship from Liverpool to the Rio Pongo.[98] Among those who were probably of African origin is a man named only as "black John" who was on the *Lyon* while it slaved at Angola, but who absconded when it reached Guadeloupe.[99]

For slave ships that departed from Bristol, where the high point of trade had been in the 1720s and '30s, some muster rolls survive but have similar problems to the Liverpool lists (see appendix 2). In some cases it is unclear whether men listed as black were actually of African origin or

---

[91] See appendix 1; Eltis, *CD-Rom.*
[92] Shyllon, *Black People* 101–2.
[93] The ADM 36 series contains thousands of Admiralty muster rolls, of which a lengthy, though far from comprehensive, check by the author, found that few captains noted the racial background of their crewmen prior to the nineteenth century. Pares, "The Manning of the Navy in the West Indies"; Vincent Caretta, "Naval Records and Eighteenth Century Black Biography, with particular reference to the case of Olaudah Equiano (Gustavus Vassa)" *Journal for Maritime Research* (November 2003).
[94] Robinson, *Sailor Boy* 52.
[95] Merseyside Maritime Museum, DX 169.
[96] ZHC 1/84 126: Evidence of Isaac Parker.
[97] HCA 1/61.
[98] C108/214: Papers of John Leigh.
[99] HCA 15/55.

simply had dark hair.[100] At other times it is evident that black men were not differentiated on the musters. Thomas Jupiter, for example, made at least three slaving voyages but was only noted as being black or African on two of them. What the lists do suggest, however, is that the number of black men on Bristol slave ships decreased during the 1770s and '80s, probably because the city sent far fewer ships to Africa in these years than it had in the late 1720s and '30s.[101]

Again there are also plenty of random examples of men of African origin working aboard Bristol slave ships. Like their counterparts working from other ports, they were employed in lowly positions as cooks, stewards and common seamen. On the *Ruby* from Bristol on its voyage that departed in August 1787, the cook was described as "a poor black Portuguese sailor".[102] The *Alexander* of Bristol had a cook who was a black man.[103] There was also a black cook on the *Juno*.[104] On its 1792-3 voyage the *Wasp* had a "man of colour" as the steward as it, delivered captives from New Calabar to Kingston, Jamaica.[105] Thomas Clarkson met a free black sailor at Bristol named John Dean, who had been one of the original crew of the slaver *Brothers* which had sailed for Africa in July 1785.[106] Captain Tucker on the *Royal* (or *Loyal*) *George* had a black cabin boy.[107] Free black sailors were also not unknown on the ships which left from smaller British ports in an earlier period: a black man named George Yorke was listed as a sailor on the *Daniel and Henry* which sailed from Dartmouth in 1700.[108]

In the American colonies/states as much as in Britain black men came to be engaged on slave ships. Runaway slaves, ex-slaves and free blacks had few other employment opportunities, saw the sea as a means of

---

[100] It is worth noting Captain Bligh's description of Fletcher Christian – a 'white' man from the Isle of Man off the NW coast of England – as having a "Blackish or very dark brown Complexion" immediately after his mutiny. Greg Dening, *Mr Bligh's Bad Language: Passion, Power and Theatre on the Bounty* (Cambridge: Cambridge University Press, 1992) 70.

[101] Bristol Muster Rolls, Merchant Venturers' Archives; Eltis, *CD-Rom*.

[102] BT 6/11.

[103] ZHC 1/85 631: Evidence of Alexander Falconbridge.

[104] Fryer, *Staying Power* 57.

[105] *Pennsylvania Gazette* 3 April 1793.

[106] Thomas Clarkson, *The History of the Rise, Progress, and Accomplishment of the Abolition of the African Slave-Trade by the British Parliament* (London: Longman and Co.,1808) 1 298–300.

[107] Silas Told, *Life of Mr Silas Told* (London: G. Whitfield, 1796) 18.

[108] Nigel Tattersfield, *The Forgotten Trade: Comprising the Log of the* Daniel and Henry *of 1700 and Accounts of the Slave Trade from the Minor Ports of England, 1698–1725* (Pimlico: London, 1998) 54.

escape and could mingle into multi-ethnic seafaring culture more easily than onshore society. America's ports as much as Britain's denoted
long distance trading routes, as men from far flung trading ports crowded
its dockside communities. Some of these men, just as in Britain, made
their way onto slaving vessels. There was the Chinese "caben Stewart"
and "Henry Sandwich Islander" aboard the *Resource* in 1805 as already
mentioned, while the *Adventure* during its slaving voyage of 1773–4 listed
"Indian" John Warwick as its cook.[109] It is unclear whether this man was
of East Indian or, in true *Moby Dick* style, Native American origin.

On the North American mainland the strengthening of racial divisions
cast more non-white men into the seafaring labour force as the eighteenth
century progressed. Reflecting both the pull of the sea and the lack of
other opportunities, by the post-revolutionary period black men are estimated to have totalled seventeen per cent of the seafaring labour force
in the North American Atlantic seaports.[110] It is certain, however, that
the numbers of black sailors working on slave ships were significantly
less than the percentages for maritime industries as a whole. Among so
many men who had suffered the horrors of slavery themselves, or had
ancestors who had done so, there was bound to be opposition to the slave
trade. Some black sailors were escaped slaves, who would doubtless wish
to remain as far away from plantation slavery as possible to protect their
freedom. Beyond this, black seafarers were also among the ranks of the
earliest and most virulent attackers of the institution of slavery and pro-
moters of black unity and honour, so they were hardly likely to join in the
process of enslavement if they had a choice.[111] The first black benevolent
society in Providence, Rhode Island voted that its members would vow
not to work on slave ships.[112]

Outside this principled resistance, however, was a real world of hard-
ship and poverty. Given the total numbers of black sailors, and the fact
that the slave trade represented potential employment, some would have
had little choice but to enlist on a slaving vessel. Certainly many of the

---

[109] Jay Coughtry (ed.) *Papers of the American Slave Trade* (Bethesda, MD: University Publications of America, 1996) A/2/19/968-20/107 and A/2/5/37.
[110] Ira Dye, "Early American Merchant Seafarers" *Proceedings of the American Philosophical Society* (1976) 331–60.
[111] Julius S. Scott, "Crisscrossing Empires: Ships, Sailors and Resistance in the Less Antilles
in the Eighteenth Century" in Robert L. Paquette and Stanley L. Engerman, *The Lesser
Antilles in the Age of European Expansion* (Gainsville: University of Florida Press, 1996)
130–1.
[112] Bolster, *Black Jacks* 160.

reasons that drove European-American sailors into the trade – debt, destitution or downright kidnapping – were not unknown, and may have been accentuated, among black sailors. While they probably understood the greater danger that they would face in the trade, and many no doubt had ideological objections, they too understood that the trade would provide them with rudimentary food, board, wages and maybe opportunities to better themselves.

From the crew lists of Rhode Island's ports – Newport, Providence and Bristol – which exist for the slave trade's final few years of legality, it is possible to locate a number of free black men (see appendix 3). Again, as with the Liverpool and Bristol muster rolls, the total number of black seamen, compared to the numbers involved in the slave trade as a whole, does not appear to be very substantial. As many Rhode Island ships were very small, however, even one black man among a crew would be a central part of a tiny workforce. The 1804 voyage of the *Rising Sun,* for example, had two black seamen and a black cook among a total crew of only eleven men.[113] In the same year the *Eagle* had a crew of only seven men, of whom one sailor and the cook were black.[114] The four black men aboard the *Hope* could have been a majority of the total crew on the tiny 87 ton vessel.[115]

Just like other black men aboard slave ships, African-Americans were overwhelmingly confined to the lowest positions aboard ship, most commonly filling the rank of cook, steward or common seaman. Many were apprenticed to the captain of the ship, and were often years older than would have been deemed acceptable for a white man holding this position. A mixture of racism, fear and bigotry severely limited black men's options, and many continued to go to sea, some confined to the position of apprentice, long after their European colleagues had settled down to a more secure life ashore.[116]

What is also clear is that free African-American sailors who signed on slave ships had completely different understandings of racial designations than free Africans they might have worked alongside. The case of a black sailor named Thomas Lee is instructive. Lee had completed his duties as cook of the slave ship *Sarah* and signed aboard the *Bacchus* when he testified before the Admiralty Courts, but he still "had upon his mind the

---

[113] See appendix 3; Eltis, *CD-Rom,* 36792.
[114] See appendix 3; Eltis, *CD-Rom,* 36794.
[115] See appendix 3; Eltis, *CD-Rom,* 36852.
[116] Bolster, "To Feel Like a Man" 1190.

bloody Murder he had seen committed" on board his former ship. It had already arrived in Jamaica, having sailed from Liverpool and Bonny, when sick slaves, Lee claimed, were dumped into Port Royal harbour from fear that they were too diseased to sell. Another of the *Sarah*'s crewmembers, a man named James Graham, backed Lee's assertions, reporting that he had seen a slave woman thrown overboard. Those guilty of this do not seem to have even made a clean job of the murder: the woman slave was not thrown directly into the sea but clung to the ship's side begging for assistance. Needless to say nobody helped her. Lee's conscience troubled him, however, and he remembered the act as "a Wicked thing" that "he was much shocked" by. Lee had not stepped forward to help the woman himself because he feared that he too would be thrown overboard if he did so. His fears were probably amply justified, for as a black American, Lee likely knew the dispensability of slaves from personal experience.[117]

A free black man born in the United States, Thomas Lee lived in a society in which the divisions were impermeable, and where the racial constructs of the age decreed that anybody with noticeable African heritage was "black", with all the negative implications that had. Lee was part of the maritime community in which racial lines could be blurred, and presumably he had some kind of co-worker relationship with white man James Graham, but nevertheless he came from a society in which lines were hardened. He undoubtedly felt loyalties to his fellow sailors, but he also understood the overriding loyalties to his race that belonged to the Americas. Free African seamen had their own realities dependent upon the categories of Igbo, Fante, Yoruba and all the other dispossessed ethnicities of Africa, but Lee knew that North America had a far less complex interpretation of race. He also knew which side of the divide he stood on, despite his free status and his employment aboard the ship. The ties of the job and to the seafaring lifestyle in general were critically at odds to the paramount racial identity that was so central to black life on the North American mainland.

Thomas Lee worked on the *Sarah* in the 1790s when racist attitudes towards black people were becoming inflexible, and North and South had ever more disparate attitudes towards slavery. Throughout the late eighteenth century race became increasingly divisive in American society. The term prejudice, chiefly pertaining to white people's attitudes to blacks, had come into wide circulation after about 1760 in the colonies,

---

[117] HCA 1/61.

and liberty had increasingly become coupled to white skin. After the Revolution, the constitution had enshrined the notion that a slave would count for three-fifths of a white man for tax and representation purposes, and in so doing had strongly implied a belief in his actual inferiority, being a fraction of an American of European origin.[118] Thomas Lee lived in this society, and he knew exactly what it meant to be a black man in America. He and his fellow seafarers had often been at the forefront of both pragmatic and principled resistance to slavery and racism.[119]

African-American slaves who were hired out to slave ships as workers were also familiar with America's uncompromising racial boundaries. Given that the realities of maritime work always unravelled the institution of slavery to some degree this might seem surprising, but in fact American slave ships occasionally had slave seamen throughout the eighteenth century and into the nineteenth. As early as 1736 a captain wrote to his financiers from Anomabu, reporting that he was "now very weke handed" having lost his "chefe mate" and another sailor, plus "the negro man Prymus and Adam" who had been lost overboard during the voyage to Africa.[120] Four years later Captain George Scott had his slave as a member of the crew of his ship in 1740, later writing home to the ship-owners to report that "My negro Bonner is ded".[121]

Into the Revolutionary era slave masters continued to hire out their bondsmen to ships to secure their wages. When Captain Thomas Rogers was recruiting crew for the *Adventure* which sailed from Rhode Island in the early 1770s, one of those he engaged was Prince Miller, the slave of John Miller, who was hired as a sailor for the entire voyage.[122] Slaveowner Samuel Freebody sent his slave Benjamin Freebody to sea on a slave ship in 1775 as "a new hand at about Six Dollars per month". "After One Voyage to the Coast of Guinea & back again he ought to have Sailors Wages which was Eight Dollars", he concluded.[123] Similarly, the slave Bristow Champlin was one of five sailors listed on the muster roll of the *Adventure* of Rhode Island – notably he was the most highly paid,

---

[118] Winthrop D. Jordan, *White over Black: American Attitudes Toward the Negro, 1550–1812* (New York: W.W. Norton and Sons, 1977) 276–87, 321–3.

[119] Scott, "Crisscrossing Empires"; Bolster, *Black Jacks* 60.

[120] Ibid.

[121] George C. Mason, "The African Slave Trade: In Colonial Times" *American Historical Record* 1 (1872) 311–19 cont. 338–45.

[122] Darold D. Wax, "Thomas Rogers and the Rhode Island Slave Trade" *American Neptune* 35 (1975) 289–310.

[123] Rhode Island Historical Society, MSS 9003, XVI 96–100.

reflecting that his wages would go straight to his owner.[124] As late as 1805 the *Resource* had the slave Sippeo among its crew – the man who had purchased trousers, shirts and knives totalling $7.55 from the ship's stores during the voyage.[125]

In fact American slave ships lagged far behind those of Brazil in their use of slaves as crew. Herbert Klein writes, "Unique to the Brazilian trade was the large number of American slaves who made up the crews of slave ships . . . 42 percent of the 350 slave ships arriving in Rio de Janeiro from Africa between 1795 and 1811 indicate slaves in their crew. The average number of Brazilian-owned slave sailors in the crew for the 148 vessels that had them on arrival was 14."[126] Although Klein's assertion that the use of slaves as crew was "unique" to Brazilian ships is obviously overstating the facts, there is no doubt that the numbers he gives are far above those found on US ships even in the last years of trading.

What is immediately apparent, however, is the strange position that they occupied, being neither one of the incarcerated captive Africans who comprised the ship's cargo, nor enjoying the freedom of the other sailors. Slave ships, as working environments, should be seen as societies with slaves rather than slaving societies (as ephemeral societies as they were), but slaves employed on ships nevertheless inhabited a uniquely marginal position.[127] Benjamin Freebody's life at sea is a wonderful example of this. Unusually, he was literate and after having been sent to sea by his owner he occasionally wrote letters to his master Samuel Freebody. When his ship captured a prize vessel while at sea, Benjamin clearly believed that he was entitled to the £90 that his crewmates had apparently received as each man's share of the profits. While positioning himself firmly among the other sailors in this regard, however, his different standing was also apparent. Not only did he not receive his share, he could not appeal for it either. Rather, he had to write to his master begging that he would claim the money on his own behalf. What Freebody's fellow sailors intended to

[124] Coughtry, *Papers* A/2/5/10. Black men could earn higher wages for their labour simply because they were more highly skilled, W. Jeffrey Bolster, "Every Inch a Man: Gender and the Lives of African American Seamen, 1800–1860" Margaret S. Creighton and Lisa Norling (eds.) *Iron Men, Wooden Women: Gender and Seafaring in the Atlantic World, 1700–1920* (Baltimore: Johns Hopkins Press, 1996) 148.

[125] Coughtry, *Papers* A/2/19/1004.

[126] *The Atlantic Slave Trade* (Cambridge: Cambridge University Press, 1999) 85–6.

[127] On the implications of these differences, see Philip D. Morgan, "British Encounters with Africans and African-Americans circa 1600–1780" Bernard Bailyn and Philip D. Morgan (eds.) *Strangers within the Realm: Cultural Margins of the First British Empire* (Williamsburg, VA: Institute of Early American History and Culture, 1991) 163–70.

spend their money on is not known, but tellingly the bondsman himself hoped beyond all hope that it would purchase his freedom. Benjamin's bizarre standing was similarly revealed in another instance when James Brattle, his captain, tried to charge Samuel Freebody insurance for him when the American Revolutionary War broke out. Samuel was angered, and asked "what right [he] had to Charge me a large premium for Insureing my servant against my own Countrymen".[128]

Caught between the worlds of slaver seamen and enslaved merchandise, or more accurately outside of both of these groups, slave seamen aboard slaving vessels almost certainly led a tortured existence. Ben Freebody's case is again revealing. In one of his letters to his owner he reported how badly Captain Brattle was treating him. "I have Sincerely wished I'd never had left you the Swill that was given to the hogs I have often wish'd for", he wrote.[129] In another instance, an eyewitness wrote of the treatment metered out to the slave cook on board an American ship when she dined with them off the coast of Sierra Leone in 1792. "Dressed in the noble Captain's dashing coat, hat, sword, &c" he was ordered to re-enact the firing of a gun with a "mop stick" to "shew with what expertness he could perform the manual exercise." He did it, claimed the observer, "to the ridicule of himself, and the great amusement of his colleagues and the ship's crew".[130] Figures of fun, objects of torment and alienated outsiders, slaves employed on slave ships as seamen were perhaps the most debased men who sailed the Atlantic oceans above decks.

Their lives were also fraught with danger. If the liberty of all free black sailors was at risk as the ship sailed into Caribbean waters, the predicament of those already enslaved was in some cases more hazardous still. Many must have been working desperately to exhibit their worth aboard ship in the hope of not being sold into plantation agriculture. Furthermore, many had families and other attachments to return home to. In some ways the lives of sailors who worked on ships were preferable to those bonded to plantation labour in terms of working conditions and relative freedom. The disadvantage of life at sea was the unpleasant proximity to slave markets – the dreaded scourge of every slave's life – if this ship was involved in slave trading. For slaves employed aboard slave ships

---

[128] Rhode Island Historical Society, MSS 9003, XVI 96–100.
[129] Ibid.
[130] Anna-Maria Falconbridge, *Two Voyages to Sierra Leone During the Years 1791–1793* (London, 1794) reprinted in Deirdre Coleman (ed.) *Maiden Voyages and Infant Colonies: Two Women's Travel Narratives of the 1790s* (London: Leicester University Press, 1999) 101–2.

there can have been little escaping the fact that they were people "with a price".[131] The uncertainty of life as the ship sailed into North American waters must have been palpable.

Although slavery was increasingly untenable in Britain, there surprisingly were some slaves (as opposed to the numerous runaways) employed as seamen on board slave ships. Archibald Dalzel, sometime governor of Cape Coast Castle, slave trader, historian and bankrupt, took a slave to England with him in the 1770s of whom he wrote, "this boy is a Cooper by trade & I brought him home to improve him, with a view to get him employed in a guinea ship".[132] A captain of a slave ship that was on its way to England called his slave seaman Boatswain, while slave ship captain Thomas Ralph advertised for the return a runaway who was both his slave and his apprentice in a Liverpool newspaper in 1780.[133] Another black man named Boatswain ran away in Jamaica rather than have to go to England without the other slaves who had been shipped from Africa.[134] Both campaigner Thomas Clarkson and seaman William Richardson encountered female slaves employed aboard slave ships.[135]

Ever shifting with the tides, late eighteenth-century maritime culture was a mixture of many land-based ones, yet with a singularity all its own. With each all too frequent death and personnel change, the culture aboard these floating microcosm societies subtly altered. Contingent upon those who lived and worked between bow and stern, sailors' identity was fluid, and their sense of self could change rapidly in the many different circumstances they encountered. It was partly this malleability which made seafaring more amenable to sailors of non-European origin than land-based ones. The wind which propelled the ships and their debased cargoes across the seas also carried with it ever-changing cultural understandings, not a small

---

[131] Walter Johnson, *Soul by Soul: Life Inside the Antebellum Slave Market* (Cambridge: Harvard University Press, 1999) 1–18.

[132] Archibald Dalzel's Letters, Sydney Jones Library, University of Liverpool MIC 740, Letter 31 (originals in Edinburgh University Library DK 7/52); I.A. Akinjogbin, "Archibald Dalzel: Slave Trader and Historian of Dahomey" *Journal of African History* 7 (1966) 67–78.

[133] Michael Mullin, *Africa in America: Slave Acculturation and Resistance in the American South and the British Caribbean, 1736–1831* (Urbana: University of Illinois Press, 1992) 35; *Williamson's Liverpool Advertiser* 4 May 1780.

[134] *Royal Gazette* [Kingston, Jamaica] 15–22 December 1781.

[135] Clarkson, *History of* I 399; William Richardson, *A Mariner of England: An Account of the Career of William Richardson from Cabin Boy in the Merchant Service to Warrant Officer in the Royal Navy, 1780–1817* Colonel Spencer Childers (ed.) (London: John Murray, 1908) 59–60.

part of which were from Africa. The numbers of Africans who worked on board slave ships as crewmembers may have been tiny compared to those who made the Atlantic crossing only once, but their experiences have much to reveal about the nature of race in this period.

Far away from men such as Afro-Brazilian Francisco "Cha Cha" da Souza who became wealthy trading slaves after having deserted the crew of a Brazilian slaver, men of African origin embroiled in the Anglo-American slave trades during the eighteenth and early nineteenth century joined slave ships for reasons of survival rather than riches.[136] Already marginalized by the extremely limited opportunities offered to black men in the North Atlantic, they did so as freemen, slaves and every permutation between. Africans travelled all ways across the Atlantic world. At the same time it was the conditions of the slave trade that made it impossible for those of European origin to be enslaved by other Europeans, as their racial identity solidified against this most racially divisive of backgrounds.

Therein lies the paradox, for the very fact of the "guinea trade" employing so many ships and sailors changed the maritime world by the later eighteenth century, with both Africans and African-Americans enlisting on ships. Seamen became more accepting of Africans as colleagues than other occupational groups at the time – at the same time sailors continued to be directly involved in the enslavement process which had resulted in such extreme racial inequality. European slaver sailors retained ambiguous sentiments towards Africans, pragmatically signing on slave ships if it would earn them wages, while also being renowned for treating people of African origin with egalitarianism unheard of among eighteenth century shore-based society. Put another way, seamen were an occupational group who paid less heed to colour lines than most; they also viciously quelled slave rebellion, raped enslaved women and committed many other untold atrocities against Africans. One young slave trade sailor recalled the time on his first voyage at which he first became "a young citizen of the world" who "looked on all mankind as my brethren".[137] Certainly this seems strange to those used to reading of sailors as the men who committed such horrendous deeds on board slave ships. It is stranger still to imagine that the trade in Africans contributed towards seafarers' unique nature, a uniqueness which, conversely, made it occasionally possible for men of African origin to integrate into maritime society as free men.

[136] Michael Cohn and Michael K.H. Platzer, *Black Men of the Sea* (New York: Dodd and Mead, 1978) 26.
[137] Butterworth, *Three Years* 72.

The *Amity* can stand as a potent example of this paradox, being a slave ship involved in the trade that had been the agitator behind this hardening of racial lines, while its crew apparently fermented inter-racial rebellion between its decks. This can only be understood by seeing it in a maritime context – the racial intermixing among slave trade seamen directly reflected the ports and regions the slaving vessels touched at, and so involved a "motley crew" of men from around the Atlantic littoral.[138] It is often noted that ships had specificity in terms of racial admixing, with Paul Gilroy citing "the image of a ship in motion" as a launching pad to explore his concept of a *Black Atlantic,* and Peter Linebaugh calling them "extraordinary forcing house[s] of internationalism.[139] What is less readily accepted, however, is that this refers to the slave trade not only in terms of those who began the creation of a unified African-American identity while crammed into the fetid holds, but also, albeit on a much smaller scale, with those who worked the ships.

What happened to the *Amity*'s rebels is not clear. The captain and mate definitely regained control of the ship, for around a year later it arrived at St. Kitts with a cargo of enslaved Africans ready for sale. Whether Richard Squire, John Mathew, Alexander Evans, John Boadman and Stuart made this voyage or were being tried for piracy at the time is not known. It is improbable that Dick and Will were facing the Admiralty Courts. Far too valuable in themselves to be removed from the voyage, they were almost certainly among the crew that went slave trading after the initial rebellion. Whoever their white colleagues were, they would have treated their captive passengers with little humanity, and little regard, for such was the nature of slave trading.

[138] Peter Linebaugh and Marcus Rediker, *The Many-Headed Hydra: Sailors, Slaves, Commoners, and the Hidden History of the Revolutionary Atlantic* (Boston: Beacon Press, 2000) 27–8.

[139] Paul Gilroy, *The Black Atlantic: Modernity and Double Consciousness* (London: Verso, 1993) 4; Peter Linebaugh, "All the Atlantic Mountains Shook" *Labour/Le Travailleur* 10 (1982) 87–121, quote 112. This same phrase is also used in Linebaugh and Rediker, *Many-Headed Hydra* 151.

3

The Bloody Rise of Western Freedom

In 1767 the *Gentleman's Magazine* published a short, fairly commonplace news article informing its readers that the crew of a British slave ship had "mutinied on the coast of Africa, and attacked their officers." It referred to the men of the *True Blue,* which had sailed from Liverpool earlier that year under the command of Joshua Hutton. Such a rebellion against a ship's officers was not an uncommon event. Far more remarkable than the scant details of the mutiny itself were the insightful, and quite sympathetic, words the magazine offered its readers about the incident. "Several attempts of the like have lately happened on board merchant ships", it noted, "where the petty officers are too apt to exercise cruel and wanton severity towards the common men, by which they are rendered desperate." Rather than condemning the men out of hand, it offered further explanation to its readers, stating, "the slave trade is in itself a brutal trade, by which the feelings of humanity are suppressed, and all tenderness towards fellow creatures totally obliterated."[1]

When abolitionism gained in strength and support towards the end of the eighteenth century, the plight of seamen in the slave trade was almost as common a cause of complaint as that of the slaves. Thomas Clarkson made many pleas for abolition based as much on the sufferings of seamen in the business of slaving as on its African victims. In fact his account of a dinner to discuss the founding of an abolitionist society states clearly that it was the "loss of seamen in the trade" that "greatly impressed" the attendees, who included both William Wilberforce and Sir Joshua

---

[1] *Gentleman's Magazine* 39 (1767) 265; Eltis, *CD-ROM*, 91087.

Reynolds.[2] Of course there was a good deal of racism inherent in this line of argument, for Clarkson judged that the British parliament would care more that numbers of British seamen were suffering and dying than that African slaves were.[3] It was symptomatic of the times for contemporary Britons were well aware of the value of their navy to the nation's security and to its pride and sense of glory. So the abolitionist movement brought the injustices endured by seamen to the public arena, empowering them by revealing to many the circumstances of their hard lives.

Arguments regarding the treatment of seamen in the slave trade touch upon a larger historiographic debate about the severity of punishment in the maritime world during the eighteenth century. The protagonists, at opposite extremes as it were, are N.A.M. Rodger who argues that discipline in the Royal Navy in this period was "enlightened" and based on Christian principles, and Marcus Rediker who argues for a far less optimistic picture. My intention is not to join in this increasingly unpleasant dispute.[4] While accepting, as Rediker does, that much of the evidence about violence and discipline aboard slave ships represents only the most extreme cases because these were the ones that ended up in front of the

---

[2] Thomas Clarkson, *The History of the Rise, Progress, and Accomplishment of the Abolition of the African Slave-Trade by the British Parliament* (London: Longman and Co., 1808) 252.

[3] Thomas Clarkson, *Grievances of Our Mercantile Seamen: A National and Crying Evil* (Ipswich, 1845) 4–5; Thomas Clarkson, *History of the Rise* especially 297–414.

[4] Marcus Rediker set the subject alight by describing punishments on board merchant ships in the early half of the eighteenth century as "sordid and vicious" and listing a large number of cases where seamen were cruelly treated by their officers, *Between the Devil and the Deep Blue Sea* (Cambridge: Cambridge University Press, 1987) 9 and chapter 5. In reviewing Rediker's work, Rodger accused him of being "burdened by serious professional disabilities" and of having produced "a mass of anecdote rather than a sustained argument." "Review of Between the Devil and the Deep Blue Sea" *Mariners Mirror* 74 (1988). The ideological and political differences between the two do, of course, range much further than the nature of authority and discipline aboard ships. This is, nevertheless, a central bone of their contention, as summed up by Peter Earle, along with other maritime historians' views on this issue, in *Sailors: English Merchant Seamen 1650–1775* (London: Methuen, 1998) 145–7. Rodger's analysis is central to the larger debate surrounds the issue of punishment on board Royal Navy ships. See N.A.M. Rodger, *The Wooden World: An Anatomy of the Georgian Navy* (London: Fontana, 1988) 211–7; Markus Eder, *Crime and Punishment in the Royal Navy of the Seven Years War, 1755–1763* (Aldershot: Ashgate Publishing, 2004) especially chapters 5 and 6; Alan G. Jamieson, "Tyranny of the Lash? Punishment and the Royal Navy during the American War, 1776–1783" *Northern Mariner* 9:1 (1999) 53–66; Jonathan Neale, *The Cutlass and the Lash: Mutiny and Discipline in Nelson's Navy* (London: Pluto, 1985); John D. Byrn, *Crime and Punishment in the Royal Navy: Discipline in the Leeward Islands Station, 1784–1812* (Aldershot, Hants: Scholar Press, 1989) 3–5, 64–88; Greg Dening, *Mr Bligh's Bad Language: Passion, Power and Theatre on the Bounty* (Cambridge: Cambridge University Press, 1992) 113–56.

Admiralty Courts, the crucial point is not the frequency or fairness of whipping. Rather, the additional severity of control and punishment in the slave trade is the starting point for exploring the paramount relevance freedom and justice came to have for seamen employed on slave ships. Slave trade seamen objected vehemently when they considered their treatment was parallel to, or even worse than, that of their captive cargo.

Just as the opposition to impressment into the Royal Navy gained ground during the 1770s when freedom took on a whole new connotation during the American Revolutionary conflict, so on each slave ship seamen loathed physical punishments and constraints not only in themselves, but because they were tainted by their association with slavery. Summing up his seminal argument about the concept of freedom and its peculiar place in western culture, Orlando Patterson writes, "freedom was generated from the experience of slavery. People came to value freedom, to construct it as a powerful shared vision of life, as a result of their experience of, and response to, slavery."[5] The small acts of this drama of reinterpretation were played out on board wooden slaving vessels.

It was not the actual nature of seamen's punishments that particularly provoked them, but what they implied. Some theoretical attachment to the notion of freedom was not what mattered to the average sailor, but that his condition as a free man should be fundamentally different to that of the captives he was paid to transport across the Atlantic. This was particularly pertinent in the case of men who had been crimped onto their vessel – where the divisions of free and non-free were blurred – because by the late eighteenth century society and culture in both Britain and America began to decree that the lines should be absolute. Seamen had first hand experience with slavery from which to construct their own ideas of liberty, and it is hardly surprising that it came to be crucially, vitally important to them.

Seamen rejected treatment they considered to be akin to that inflicted on slaves, and they did so by invoking long-established maritime methods of rebellion. Stealing food, deserting, votes of allegiance, and even the extreme action of taking over the ship and becoming pirates were old forms of protest reconceptualized to take into account the particular grievances of the era. Yet where freedom became a prized commodity because of the proximity of slavery, it grew to belong to one racial group more than any other in society at large. Protests could easily include black seamen, but often seamen's rejection of their status of slave encompassed

[5] *Freedom: The Making of Western Culture* (New York: Basic Books, 1991) xiii.

no empathy towards those they kept enslaved. The traditional maritime forms of rebellion were often used to protest the liberty of the crew, whatever the origins of its members, but this did not often extend to the captive cargo in the later eighteenth century. Moreover their own harsh treatment aboard slave ships led sailors to treat ever more brutally those over whom they held power. They asserted their own claims to liberty ever louder as the eighteenth century progressed, while holding the musket or whip of repression firmly in their hands.

The past was a harsher, crueller place than denizens of the twenty-first century would tolerate.[6] In eighteenth century Britain "convicted whores [were] stripped to the waist and whipped" in public, and a man who tired of his wife could still break his "wed-lock" by "selling" her. A healthy wife might fetch a nice ox. Mass crowds would turn out to enjoy the spectacle of a felon being hanged, and there was little outcry even when the crimes of which they had been convicted were incredibly minor, or the guilty very young. In Norwich, for example, a seven-year old girl was hanged for stealing a petticoat. In his wonderfully entertaining book *English Society in the Eighteenth Century*, Roy Porter takes his readers into a world in which gory fascination was considered normal. When a Bristol man poisoned himself after having been convicted of murdering his wife, a mob, cheated out of his hanging, dug up his body and mutilated it. Even the upper classes defecated in public. Porter says:

Life was raw. Practically all youngsters were thrashed at home, at school, at work – and child labour was universal. Blood sports such as cock-fighting were hailed as manly trials of skill and courage. Felons were publicly whipped, pilloried and hanged, traitors were drawn and quartered. Jacobites' heads were spiked on Temple Bar till 1777 . . . People were not squeamish about inflicting or bearing physical pain.[7]

---

[6] J.S. Cockburn, "Punishment and Brutalization in the English Enlightenment" *Law and History Society Review* 12:1 (Spring 1994) 155–79; J.S. Cockburn, *Crime in England, 1550–1800* (London: Methuen, 1977); J.A. Sharpe, *Crime and Early Modern England* (London: Longman, 1984); J.A. Sharpe, *Judicial Punishment in England* (London: Faber, 1990); Simon Devereux and Paul Griffiths, *Penal Practice and Culture, 1500–1900: Punishing the English* (London: Palgrave Macmillan, 2004); Lawrence Stone, *Honor, Morals, Religion and the Law: the action for criminal conversation in England, 1670–1857* Anthony Grafton and Ann Blair (eds.) *The Transmission of Culture in Early Modern Europe* (Philadelphia: University of Pennsylvania Press, 1990); Lawrence Stone, "Interpersonal Violence in English Society, 1300–1980" *Past and Present* 101 (1983) 22–33; Malcolm Gaskill, *Crime and Mentalities in Early Modern England* (Cambridge: Cambridge University Press, 2000).

[7] (London: Penguin, 1982) 17–18, 31.

Even though most people were free wage earners in this period, physical means of control remained quite standard. Nowhere was this truer than at sea, where the lash was the established punishment for any number of offences. Studies of discipline in the Royal Navy suggest that severity actually increased over the eighteenth century, with up to five hundred lashes being the designated sentence for a man convicted of theft by the later part of the period.[8] On board merchant vessels too, many seamen encountered the "cat" as they familiarly called the "instrument of torture" known as the cat-o'-nine-tails. One slave trade sailor remembered this as being "composed of nine pieces of whipcord, about eighteen inches long each, with nine knots on each strand."[9] Even in this world of ubiquitous bloodshed, seafaring and the lash – and the resulting welts in the flesh – were closely associated in the public conscience in both Britain and America. As late as the nineteenth century American planters fought abolitionists who decried the whipping of slaves as inhumane by pointing to the fact that men were regularly whipped in both the navy and merchant marine.[10]

Not unlike the way African-American slaves dealt with the brutality of the regime they found themselves in, seamen adopted the scars of the lash as proudly worn symbols of defiance. One early eighteenth-century sailor remembered, "many a tar was 'as proud of the Wales on his Back, as a *Holy-Land* Pilgrim is of a Jerusalem print.'"[11] It was a method by which the brutality of the system was turned to their own advantage, as attempts to discipline through the whip were subverted in the sailors' alternative honour system that deemed it a matter of esteem.

The precise number of whippings was not the crucial factor. As Marcus Rediker writes, defending his position that violence pervaded maritime life, "I wonder whether those who trivialize the use of violence in the eighteenth-century merchant shipping industry would also argue that since 99.9% of black folk in the post-Civil War American South were never lynched, the terror of lynching was not an important part of their experience. The point, of course, is not whether lynching (or flogging) was the exception or the rule, but rather that "rule" was organized through

---

[8] Earle, *Sailors* 145–6.
[9] Samuel Robinson, *A Sailor Boy's Experience Aboard a Slave Ship* (Wigtown: G.C. Book Publishers, 1996) 21.
[10] Eugene D. Genovese, *Roll, Jordan, Roll: The World the Slaves Made* (New York: Vintage, 1976) 63–4.
[11] Rediker, *Between the Devil* 211.

exceptional example."[12] Officers tried to enforce discipline through the threat of the whip as much as the use of it, and seamen conversely used any resulting marks on their skin as symbols of their own subversive anti-authoritarianism. Scars from flogging became the insignia of endurance and rebelliousness, and a component of the collective occupational identity of seafaring.

Part of the reason that the rule of a ship was often based on terror or the threat thereof, rather than more modern forms of control, was the circumstances that prevailed in deep-sea trades. Geographically distant from any other authority, while a ship was at sea a captain had practically absolute power. His word was law, and that law was to be upheld as he saw fit. Ships were "total institutions." Physical remoteness meant that they had to provide at least the minimum requirements of food and lodgings for those on board in return for which the inhabitants lived and worked in a manner that was totally dominated by the figures in authority.[13] A sailor's contract stated that he had to obey the officers' commands, and to not do so constituted behaving "in a riotous and disorderly manner."[14] The men of the slave ship *Fame*, for example, agreed "to behave with due Subordination and Respect, and to obey the lawful Commands of our Commander."[15]

This concentration of authority in one man's hands was in many ways a necessity of seafaring, for the lives of all those aboard could depend upon cohesion and co-operation. It also rendered the captain singularly powerful, the vessel being something of a kingdom of which they were king. Captain John Newton used this terminology in a letter home to his wife Mary in 1752, describing the *African* as "my peaceful kingdom."[16] William Butterworth wrote of Captain Evans of the *Hudibras*, "in him were blended the most discordant passions: this moment phlegmatic, the next choleric, in the extreme... an unlimited despot."[17] Speaking more generally, American seaman John Willock remembered, "The most absolute monarch on earth, has not his subject more completely in his power

---

[12] "The Common Seamen in the Histories of Capitalism and the Working Class" *International Journal of Maritime History* 1 (1989) 337–57, quote 342–3*n*.

[13] Vilhelm Aubert, *The Hidden Society* (Totowa, N.J.: Bedminster Press, 1965) 236–58.

[14] ZHC 1/82 99: Evidence of John Knox.

[15] C107/5; C107/6.

[16] John Newton, *The Journal of a Slave Trader, 1750–1754*. Bernard Martin and Mark Spurrell (eds.) (London: The Epworth Press, 1962) 9*n*.

[17] William Butterwoth, *Three Years Adventures of a Minor in England, Africa, the West Indies, South-Carolina, and Georgia* (Leeds: Edward Baines, 1822) 6.

than the captain of a vessel those under his command, when in his element: he can render them happy or miserable at please."[18]

While this may have been true of any ship involved in a long-distance trade in this era, in the slave trade this took on a new terror because this particular branch of maritime commerce seems to have employed some peculiarly sadistic men as captains. There were some humane masters who treated their men well, but on the whole it would seem to have been a profession that either attracted or bred cruel, violent men. The idea of mass inhumanity to the slaves they transported has of course become rather clichéd, fed in part by the claims of abolitionists. Roger Anstey alleges that the picture of immense cruelty related to the idea of enormous profits, which now, through the work of historians such as Anstey himself, David Eltis and David Richardson, have been proven to be exaggerated.[19] Nevertheless, it would be preposterous to argue that violence did not pervade the trade in slaves. The basis of all slave systems was power, and this proved especially true in slave trading. The transatlantic slave trade was only successfully executed through the frequent resort to stark force.

The coercion on which the trade was based was reflected in the way that the crewmembers as well as the shackled slaves were treated. Sailors testifying to Thomas Clarkson were unambiguous in declaring that slave vessels had more pitiless rule than ships engaged transporting inanimate cargo. One man who had sailed in both the British and French slave trades stated that he was "confident, that seamen are worse used in the English slave vessels, than in any other belonging to the same nation." Another who had been beaten by Captain Pollett of the *Pearl* on his first slave trading voyage reported that "the seamen in the slave trade are treated in general in a very barbarous manner." Even more revealingly, this man said that his treatment on his second slaving voyage aboard the *Cunliffe* was much better, a fact he ascribed to the fact that "the Captain had just left the West-India trade, to get into the African, and was therefore unacquainted with the practices of the latter." Captain Bowen of the *Russell* admitted that "the seamen in the slave trade are used worse beyond all comparison, than in any other."[20]

In the testimony before the parliamentary enquiry into the slave trade are countless examples of seamen alleging extraordinarily cruel treatment

---

[18] John Willock, *The Voyages and Adventures of John Willock, Mariner* (Philadelphia, 1789) 51.
[19] Roger Anstey, *The Atlantic Slave Trade and British Abolition, 1760–1810* (London: MacMillan, 1975) 403.
[20] Clarkson, *Substance of the Evidence* 67, 24–5, 47.

aboard slaving vessels. Just to take the allegations of brutality shown to cabin boys, there were examples of torture, maiming and even murder. The *Briton*'s cabin boy, Paddy, apparently jumped overboard after being "singularly oppressed" by Mr. Wilson the chief mate who "seemed to take a delight in persecuting him."[21] John Bromley, a boy on the *Africa* was thought to have died after frequent beatings from his captain.[22] Of another case a seaman observed, "The cabin boy...was kept in a state of perfect misery [and] made a perfect copping-block of by the miserable old man." Exhausted to "a state of delirium" he died soon after.[23] There was an element in all of this of hardening young boys for a life at sea, and the position of cabin boy was rarely an easy one. They were, self-evidently, just learning many of the skills of the men before the mast, and in so doing they often frustrated their elders with their ineptitude. The suffering of these young apprentices on slave ships, however, seems to have gone above and beyond that in other maritime trades. Suffused with a climate of fear, violence and cruelty, slaving vessels were not conducive environments in which to learn through trial and error.

The myth-making scale of the tyranny survived for decades after the slave trade was abolished, leaving tales of unparalleled rough treatment and violence towards the seafaring labour force circulating the oceans. Writing in the 1880s the anonymous author of *Liverpool and Slavery* wrote that a captain known as "Bully" Roberts had once been kind-hearted, but because of his work in the slave trade spent most of his time harrying his crew and would "shoot a man down like a dog, have him thrown overboard, and allow no questions to be asked."[24] By this time, of course, the abolitionist movement and changing ideologies had firmly condemned slavery in the realm of unspeakable injustice, but in England this still pertained to the treatment of sailors as well as Africans themselves. A "folklore of tyranny" about working on slave ships existed for decades after the trade was abolished, having been borne of tales of wrong done to lowly tars.[25]

---

[21] Clarkson, *Substance of the Evidence* 39.
[22] ZHC 1/84 370–1: Evidence of Henry Ellison; HCA 1/23 f.52; T70/30; Macaulay, 'Journal', file 22, 1 June 1797 – 17 January 1798.
[23] Robinson, *Sailor Boy* 68.
[24] Dickey Sam, *Liverpool and Slavery* 21–2.
[25] Rediker, *Between the Devil* 221–2; Jesse Lemisch, "Jack Tar vs. John Bull: The Role of New York's Seamen in Precipitating the Revolution" unpublished PhD Dissertation, Yale university (1962) 51, quoted in Rediker, ibid.

Whatever the disputes about the relative harshness of naval *vis-à-vis* merchant punishments of seamen, most maritime historians agree that sailors on slave ships suffered additionally to those on board ships involved in other trades. Peter Earle examined the logbooks of many merchant vessels and found that only those of East Indiamen and slavers recorded the flogging of seamen, and the latter had far more instances of this.[26] Rediker writes, "Seamen in the slave trade, themselves the captors of slaves, were at the same time the captives of their own merchants and captains."[27] Captains, whose recourse to violence had been encouraged by their rule over captive Africans, turned this onto the seamen over whose lives they also had considerable power.

Rediker's comment is insightful as the threat of violence aboard slave ships spread much wider than the actual event and created dread among the seafaring community, trepidation which ultimately infringed their liberties further as it increased the numbers of men who had to be trepanned or crimped onto slave ships. This affected both the industry as a whole, and individual masters who gained such a reputation for cruelty among seamen that they could not secure a crew by legal means. Such an outcome happened to the captain of the *Brothers* in the late 1780s, after having apparently lost thirty-two men on his previous voyage.[28] Seamen's yarning meant that the tales of such men were told and re-told around the harbours of the Atlantic, giving such a captain a fearsome status of legendary magnitude.

Reports of particularly sadistic officers continued to circulate between ships while the "triangular trade" was in progress. A young sailor on board the London ship *Spy* was warned by the men on other slave ships while stationed at Anomabu that the captain and second mate of his vessel were known as "sharp hand[s]" in the trade. The captain had apparently "paid some hundreds in the course of law for bad treatment to the men." The chief mate, "Thorsby alias Cummins" also had a dark past he was informed. This man had been chief mate of the *Gregson* and had been accused of having "thrown the ship's cook into the boiling coppers", a crime for which he had been sent to jail in Liverpool, but had escaped, changed his name, and gone to London to ship on board the *Spy*.[29] In the

---

[26] Earle, *Sailors* 154–8.
[27] Rediker, *Between the Devil* 50.
[28] Clarkson, *History of the Rise* 297.
[29] Richardson, *A Mariner of England* 45–6.

public houses of the Caribbean too word of cruel captains spread on the nautical grapevine, so that those who were accused of having ill treated their crew had difficulty hiring any additional men needed for the journey home. All around the ocean the slave trade's reputation for inhumanity to its workers as well as its victims was notorious.

The problem was that violence was not a by-product of the trade in human beings, but rather its founding principle. While it is worthwhile to point out that this was not genocide in the traditional meaning of the word – the purpose was to deliver the men, women and children for sale, and clearly for this they had to be alive – there are nevertheless lessons to be learned from other historical atrocities.[30] The insight that during the holocaust there was a "banality of evil" is certainly pertinent. The same kind of all-pervading inhumanity meant that rather than being exceptional, physical aggression was mundane in its regularity, and gained widespread acceptance simply by being the norm. Certainly it could be argued that the situation existing on slave ships was more complex because of the large financial value of those who were primary victims of the cruelty, but still this was a trade "founded in blood", which legitimized violence through making it a part of everyday life. Ultimately, those who inflicted the worst degradations were degraded themselves as normal ethics, even by eighteenth century standards, were thrown to the winds.

Men who had witnessed the running of slaving vessels concurred with the seamen's complaints while also showing how the debasement of the African captives had created this omnipresent callousness. Surgeon Alexander Falconbridge expressed his belief that, "the common practice of the officers in the Guinea trade…justify the assertion, that to harden the feelings, and to inspire *a delight in giving torture* to a fellow creature, is the natural tendency."[31] Captain Wilson, a naval mariner who often encountered slave ships in his work, said that slave traders were expected to "divest themselves even of the appearance of humanity, [for] as a garb [it was] useless not only to the natives, but among themselves."[32]

In a similar vein Reverend John Riland, who was a passenger on the slave ship *Liberty* in the early years of the nineteenth century, wrote "such

[30] Seymour Drescher, "The Atlantic Slave Trade and the Holocaust: A Comparative Analysis" Alan S. Rosenbaum (ed.) *Is the Holocaust Unique? Perspectives on Comparative Genocide* (New York: Westview Press, 1969) 65–85.

[31] Alexander Falconbridge, *An Account of the Slave Trade on the Coast of Africa* (London: James Phillips, 1788) 46.

[32] Clarkson, *Substance of the Evidence* 105.

was the influence of familiarity with scenes of oppression, cruelty and human wretchedness...that my own colour was contracting a darker hue." He continued, "the truth obviously is, that all evil is contagious; and especially in the absence of any counteracting influence."[33] Aside from the racial implications of evil as "a dark hue" – phraseology reminiscent of Winthrop Jordan's work – Riland's choice of words unambiguously reflects his belief that the trade in slaves spread iniquity among those involved in it.[34]

This "contagion" of cruelty affected seamen in two ways, a factor symptomatic of their role as both debasers and debased, abusers and abused. They, indisputably, shared in the general brutalizing. The cruelty exercised by captains on captive Africans, and the universal degradation of the trade as a whole, created an environment where stark violence appeared to have no consequences for the persecutor, and where the squandering of human life appeared mundane. In this situation many captains appear to have found it necessary, or at least acceptable, to exercise their ferocious authority over the ship's hands as well as its cargo. This created the slave trade's reputation for being especially murderous for seamen.

This is evidently only part of the picture, however. Not infrequently sailors turned the brutalizing back onto those whom they had in their power – the Africans who were to be sold as slaves. Patently, sailors were not just permitted to use violence against their captive cargoes, but at times actively encouraged to do so. Any activity which reduced the financial value of the men, women and children being transported for sale was restricted unless the safety of the ship was in question, but the seamen were goaded into developing the kind of furious passion which would keep them on their guard against possible threats. Slave ships carried crews around fifty percent larger than other merchant vessels to protect against slave revolt, and all members of the crew would have been required to keep on constant guard against the minutiae of a possible plot.[35] Ignorant of African languages, a captain and his crew were on the look out for insubordination, secret signs, or even just the look of hatred in a man's eyes. Slave ships operated in a climate of fear.

[33] John Riland, *Memoirs of a West India Planter* (London: Hamilton, Adams and Co., 1827) 48.
[34] Winthrop D. Jordan, *White Over Black: American Attitudes Towards the Negro, 1550–1812* (New York: W.W. Norton and Company, 1968) especially 7.
[35] David Richardson, "Shipboard Revolts, African Authority, and the Atlantic Slave Trade" *William and Mary Quarterly* 58:1 (2001) 69–92.

This necessity of provoking seamen to be at loggerheads with the slaves had strange causes, sometimes at variance with the popular image of racial divisions aboard a slave ship. A case that came before the courts in Charleston, South Carolina illustrates the rationale behind the especially harsh treatment of seamen on slave ships as it related to their relations with their unwilling migrants. The sailors of the *Cleopatra* of Liverpool claimed that their commander, John Butman, had killed three of their original crewmates, and the rest of them had been "miserably bruised and maimed". Butman's defense, which ultimately proved successful, was that "the assaults...were, in some measure, rendered necessary by the state of the slaves".[36] This could have simply been a reference to the fact that captains dreaded that slaves would exploit any rebellion among seamen to secure their own freedom. They had good reason for such fears, which were hardly unfounded. Newspaper reports of a 1793 incident, for example, stated, "the ship's crew had been weakened in consequence of a mutiny among the seamen, the slaves took advantage of that circumstance, and rose upon the crew".[37] In this sense Butman was quite right – violence spread violence in the transatlantic slave trade.

A divergent interpretation can also be argued for Butman's statement however, as implicit is the idea that the captain had to divide in order to rule. As improbable as it might be with our received ideas of the slave trade to think that sailors may have helped the slaves to revolt against their imprisonment, it is not clear whether the men whose money was invested in the slave trade considered this a totally unfeasible outcome. In the early 1750s, while on board the *African,* Captain John Newton worried not only that the divisions within his crew would lead to slave rebellion because they perceived their captors to be weak, but his worst fear, "had it ever come to extremity", was that the sailors and slaves might "have joyned hands" against him.[38] In 1790 a Bristol sailor was hanged for his part in a slave rebellion off the African coast.[39] Then, in 1803, *HMS Calcutta w*as hailed just south of the equator by the slave ship *Rio Nova,* whose officers wanted help with some rebellious seamen among its crew. The *Calcutta*'s third lieutenant, Nicholas Pateshall, rather ambiguously

[36] Elizabeth Donnan (ed.) *Documents Illustrative of the Slave Trade to America* (Washington D.C.: Carnegie Institute, 1931) IV 528–9.

[37] *The Star* [London] 4 April 1796.

[38] Newton, *Journal* 72.

[39] Peter Linebaugh and Marcus Rediker, *The Many-Headed Hydra: Sailors, Slaves, Commoners, and the Hidden History of the Revolutionary Atlantic* (London: Verso, 2000) 286–7.

wrote, "Ship's Company being in a state of mutiny with the Slaves we pressed three of the ring leaders."[40]

An earlier case, that of the *Wolf* in 1750, is most instructive of all in this context. This vessel's second mate, Thomas Gelston, was accused of having been the ringleader of a slave rebellion. The ship's officers could not "without the greatest reason be perswaded [sic] but that he is deep in the plot" despite the fact that an entirely other explanation of him having been seen in the women slaves' room might appear to be more likely. This example is particularly interesting because it illustrates well that Gelston was not thought to have provoked rebellion out of sympathy for the slaves' plight, but "in revenge to the usage he rec'd from the Capt, since the loss of the long boat". In other words, the disgruntled seaman saw the captives, and their propensity to rebellion, as the ultimate weapon with which to scupper the success – that is, the profitability – of the voyage. In the ensuing chaos he could then "turn pirate with the Vessel" and "procure the Gold dust to himself".[41] This, therefore, casts another light on the brutal way in which sailors were treated in the slave trade, for as Captain Butman insinuated, the crew had to be provoked into conflict with the captives. Captains could not risk sailors using the captive Africans on board their vessels in their own struggle against authority.[42]

In this climate of fear and hostility which existed aboard slave ships, it is little surprise that black seamen seem to have been considered particularly likely to assist the slaves to rebel. Their allegiance to the ship's officers was thought to be suspect above and beyond the way that all sailors' loyalty would at times be questioned. Of course, this may well have been so. Seamen of African origin could have felt more sympathy for the members of their shackled cargo than their crewmates who could not so closely envisage themselves or their family members in that situation. This was particularly relevant in the case of sailors who had themselves endured the middle passage as victim, or whose parents or ancestors had made that

---

[40] Nicholas Pateshall, *A Short Account of a Voyage Round the Globe in HMS Calcutta*, 1803–4 Marjorie Tippin (ed.) (Victoria: Queensbury Hill Press, 1980) 44; ADM 36/16071.

[41] Darold D. Wax, "A Philadelphia Surgeon on a Slaving Voyage to Africa 1749–1751" *Pennsylvania Magazine of History and Biography* 92 (1968) 485.

[42] David Eltis claims that there are no examples of slave-white sailor mutinies on board slave ships, which may be true in the sense that these cases – the case noted by Rediker and Linebaugh excepted, which I have not been able to trace – were supposition on the part of the ship's officers. What relation they had to reality is unknown. David Eltis, *The Rise of African Slavery in the Americas* (Cambridge: Cambridge University Press, 2000) 157n, 233.

tragic journey. Equally, however, these allegations that black seamen were more likely to have been involved in assisting the slaves to rebel can be seen as reflecting the racial attitudes of the Americas channelled through slave ship captains. Fearing the loyalty of all seamen and desperate for them not to see any common cause with the captive Africans, a black man among the crew could be seen as the most highly suspect of all his men.

In fact the only clear-cut case of crew members helping slaves to rebel aboard ship did involve African crewmembers. In 1773, a slaver captain had hired some African seamen in the Gambia region, who, after the ship sailed, passed some weapons to those imprisoned below decks. A revolt subsequently erupted and in the fracas the ship blew up, causing the deaths of all except the captain and one slave.[43] A similar situation occurred aboard the *Africa* of Bristol, when the ship's black cook was alleged to have given the captives the cooper's tools to knock off their shackles. Clearly horrified at this potential risk to security, the captain's response was swift and vindictive. The cook was chained up, put in a neck collar, and starved. He survived for five weeks before being "relieved by death" from the Captain's punishments. At the time of his death he was reported to be "a most shocking spectacle". "For three days before, he had been delirious" it was reported, "and had attempted to free himself from his fetters." In the process he had excoriated his skin to the bone.[44]

This kind of cruelty to black seamen and cooks seems to have been endemic on slave ships, and was perhaps linked to the fear that they were perceived to be potential security threats. This was certainly not its only cause, however. Engaged in an industry which relied on notions of white supremacy for self-justification, black sailors were obvious targets of cruelty on the part of a captain or his mates. What is more, singling a black seaman out for especially harsh treatment was a means of dividing to rule, seen as an important tactic as a crew's rebellion had potential consequences on a slave ship above and beyond those usually feared by ships' officers. Testifying at the parliamentary enquiry into the slave trade, surgeon's mate James Arnold made special mention of the treatment of the black cook of the *Ruby*. "It would be tedious to enumerate the many instances of barbarity wantonly exercised on the seamen by the captain and mates", he said, but felt that he had to speak of this case in particular.

[43] David Eltis, cited in David Brion Davis, "Slavery – White, Black, Muslim, Christian" *New York Review of Books* (5 July 2001) 51–5.

[44] David Eltis, *The Rise of African Slavery in the Americas* (Cambridge: Cambridge University Press, 2000) 231–3, 40.

He claimed that the captain and mates took a specific pleasure in torturing this man, and that the former "often amused himself by forcing the man to swallow cockroaches alive...and having beef brine rubbed into his wounds". While in Africa this man was tied up with a chain.[45]

Similarly, the surgeon of the *Alexander* recalled that when their black cook broke a plate by accident "he had a fish-gig darted at him, which could certainly have destroyed him, if he had not stooped or dropped down". On another occasion both he and the carpenter's mate were "tied up, stripped, and flogged, but the cook with the greatest severity". "After that the cook had salt water and cayenne pepper rubbed on his back."[46] The black cook of the *Juno* was equally badly treated. Captain Parnell and the surgeon of the ship, it was claimed, beat him with handspikes and the implement used to stir the slaves' rice, and made him work at the copper while chained.[47] Aboard the *Lord Stanley* in 1805 it was the black steward who particularly suffered. He reported that he had been chased overboard, given more than one thousand lashes all told until his back was "in a state of mortification" and had the lacerations rubbed with beef brine. "A large portion of the flesh came away over the surface of the back, sixteen inches square" under which "there was a prodigious accumulation of fungus."[48]

Ordinary black seamen were also picked out for atrocious treatment. On the *Brookes* one free black sailor from Philadelphia was said to have been lashed "to one of the topmast heads" for twelve days, a punishment the captain was later heard relating to some fellow ships' masters with "a degree of triumph and satisfaction that would have disgraced an Indian scalper". His audience "applauded his invention for the novelty of the punishment".[49] The captain of a Bristol slaver in the 1780s was reported to have treated a "black boy" so cruelly that he jumped overboard after having been "beaten daily".[50] John Dean, who sailed on the *Brothers* of Bristol in July 1785, was chained up by the captain who then "poured hot pitch upon his back, and made incisions in it with hot tongs".[51] Employed in a trade which fed the plantation slavery of the Americas, and which

---

[45] ZHC 1/85 631.
[46] BT 6/11.
[47] Clarkson, *Substance of the Evidence* 16.
[48] *The Star* [London] 11 July 1806. Potter sued for his mistreatment and was given 500 compensation.
[49] ZHC 1/84 88; ZHC 1/84 112.
[50] ZHC 1/85 598: Evidence of Alexander Falconbridge.
[51] Clarkson, *History of the Rise* 297–8.

increasingly relied on claims of black inferiority to attempt to validate its atrocities, black sailors seem to have been particularly susceptible to the all-pervading brutality.

It would be erroneous to suggest that it was only black sailors who were singled out by ships' captains for mistreatment however. As shown by the mistreatment of cabin boys already mentioned, the depravity of the slave trade could affect all those who sailed in its employ. Moreover men could be abused because of their ethnicity even if they were not black, thus in some ways running counter to the idea of a unified whiteness. Irishmen, Frenchmen, Italians and many other non-Anglo-Saxon groups were traditionally disparaged in English thought, and this did not totally disappear aboard ship. John Warren of the *Surry* of London was called "an Irish son of a Bitch" by his captain as he allegedly kicked the sailor to death.[52] No notion of a unified whiteness which included Irishmen was available to save Warren.

Thus the "dread Middle Passage [was] brutalizing to any man" and this violence, while not completely random, could strike anybody.[53] There is clearly evidence that those who were non-white were more harshly treated than those who were, their skin colour marking them out in officers' minds as suitable for belittling. Yet the bloodshed was all-pervading and seemingly infectious.[54] Although atypical, the cases brought before the Admiralty courts reveal that sadism could often result from the circumstances of slave trading. A man who had found that he suffered no dire consequence from the cruelty he inflicted on his captive cargo could beat his cabin boy to a point of incapacity, perhaps having got a taste for megalomania or the infliction of suffering. A black member of his crew might have seemed particularly suited to receive his cruelty in the environment the slave trade created. Sailors were provoked into active conflict in case of a slave revolt, while their own position was bounded by some of the same techniques of rule.

Beyond the ubiquitous associations of cruelty and the slave trade, the Admiralty court records from the traffic in human cargo also reveal the convoluted links between race, liberty and working-men's labour. Not only were slave ships likely scenes of violent rule, but when seamen from them protested they frequently did so by invoking comparisons of their

---

[52] HCA 1/24 f.57–59.

[53] Stanley Elkins, *Slavery: A Problem in American Institutional and Intellectual Life* (Chicago: University of Chicago Press, 1976) 100.

[54] HCA 1/22 ff.174–176 and f.195; HCA 1/25 f.147; JVA 101, Jamaica Archives, Spanish Town, Jamaica.

own situation with that of those they had carried as captive cargo. While this illustrates clearly that the treatment of slaves in the Anglo-Atlantic world had become a by-word for the ultimate in debasement by this period, it also reveals the growth in the importance of freedom as a concept, and the ever-hardening lines between free and non-free. "How can I, a free man, be treated as a slave" sailors seemed to be imploring. "How can I, a white man, be treated as a slave" was an implied angle to the issue. Freedom had noticeably taken on new significance when in such close contact with slavery, and those in possession of this uniquely acclaimed asset felt keenly any blurring of the lines between the two.

One case before the Admiralty Courts heard that Thomas Hall, surgeon of the *Nanny,* beat both a sailor and then a slave in quick succession. Seamen Michael Roach reported that he saw Hall "strike a Negroe Slave (who was then shitting upon the gratings and complaining of a Pain in the Bowells) several times about the head and Stomack and then laid hold of his Head and beat it against the gratings, until the Blood gushed out of his nose and Mouth, and that the said slave died within about ten minutes." A major part of the controversy of his case was not the cruelty towards the sick slave, however, but that it followed directly the beating of a sailor named Beith, who was being beaten by the captain when Hall shouted, "beat the son of a bitch more" and then joined in.[55]

Likewise, a key cause of the resentment towards Captain John Steele of the *Elizabeth* was that he had used the instruments of torture designed for use on the slaves on his cabin boy, Thomas Watson. While on the coast of Africa the captain had allegedly put Watson in thumb screws "which he screwed till the blood flowed from the ends of his thumbs & kept him in that pain & torture for about ten minutes at same time flogging him naked with a horse whip till his back was raw". He then ordered some other boys on the vessel to "rub him so raw & naked with a hard brush such as they clean decks with, & also salt water". Later other crewmembers were ordered to beat Watson, which they did, "one with a cat with nine tails and the other with a horse whip". He was also allegedly made to sing before the captain just like those who they would transport as slaves. It was said that Watson used to "frequently cry out murder, in Language of Negroes, & to Captain Steele don't kill me".[56]

Other seamen's comparisons to the treatment of slaves were subtler. One ship's carpenter related that he had been tied to a seaman "me by the right leg, and Richardson by the left, and to compleat [sic] the matter effectually, confined my right hand to his left, with a pair of handcuffs".[57] He did not expressly compare this to the way slaves were shackled, but anyone familiar with the way the trade was run could have identified with the descriptions of slaves chained "a right and a left leg, and a right and a left arm".[58] Although men on all sailing vessels of the era were shackled or chained if their disobedience was considered to be a serious enough menace to the safety of the ship, the implication aboard slavers was that their treatment had not been sufficiently dissimilar to that of the captives held below decks. Captain Coil of the *Lancashire Witch* used "an iron collar about his neck, shackled upon his right leg and arm, and then chained to a ring bolt on the deck" to secure one of his men while at the African coast.[59] Another captain chained a sailor by the neck for three months while they were at St. Vincent.[60] The inference was that they had been treated as slaves. Notably it was from an American ship, aboard which the crew probably had stronger associations of shackling with slavery, that the abused men did not wait to protest their mistreatment in the courts. While the ship was at Rio Pongo they deserted to protest that the irons and chains the captain had loaded for them were "heavy", and that they had been kept below, chained up, for six weeks.[61]

Such complaints, and the rhetoric of comparison with slaves, surfaced not only in relation to the seamen's punishments, but also about their general treatment on board ship. James Towne's protests about his treatment aboard the *Peggy* of Liverpool encompassed both the poor conditions, and the resort to the kind of torture and restrains associated with slavery. "[A]s soon as we were round the rock of Liverpool", he later claimed, "people were brought to an allowance of 4lb of bread per week; their chests brought on deck, and staved and burnt by the cook, and themselves turned out from lying below". "They were put in irons and chains and beaten if they complained." Towne also alleged that "when on the Coast of Guinea, if not released before their arrival there from their confinement, they were put into the boats, and made to row backwards and forwards, either with the captain from ship to ship, or on any other duty, still both legs in irons, and an iron collar about their necks, and with a chain locked to the boat." At night they were chained

[57] Barker, *Unfortunate Shipwright* 18.
[58] ZHC 1/82 85: Evidence of John Knox.
[59] ZHC 1/87 14: Evidence of Richard Storey.
[60] ZHC 1/87 102.
[61] Macaulay, "Journal" file 21, 7 June 1797.

to the deck he stated.[62] The assessment that they had been treated as slaves often extended to the conditions they had endured as well as the discipline.

The food and conditions on slaving vessels could, undoubtedly, be grim. Sailors often had to sleep on deck after their human cargo had been loaded, so exposing them to the heat, humidity, and rainfall of the African coast.[63] Drinking water, rank at the best of times, could be in fearfully short supply for the tropical climate in both Africa and the Caribbean. Food was monotonous. The articles of agreement between the investors of the voyage of the *Fame* in 1792 and the men they hired as crew guaranteed the following "good and wholesome victuals":

Sunday – One Pound and a half of Beef... and Half a Pint of Flour

Monday – One Pound of Pork... and Half a Pint of Pease

Tuesday – One Pint of Oatmeal, and Two Ounces of Butter, and Four Ounces of Cheese; or One Pound of Stock Fish, with One-Eighth of a Pint of Oil, and a Quarter of a Pint of Vinegar

Wednesday, the same as Monday – Thursday the same as Sunday – Friday, the same as Tuesday – Saturday the same as Monday. Each person also to have six pounds of bread per week, and a Quarter of a Pint of spirits.[64]

This example was probably as good as food got on British slave ships. Many fared much worse. If the voyage took longer than planned, food often ran short, so that by the time the Americas approached they could be "in great Distress for want of Provisions".[65] Such was the fate of an American brig which spent 100 days at sea in the middle passage during which it lost the captain, mate, and seventy slaves, and was found by another ship "destitute of almost every necessity of life".[66]

Such hardships, however, were certainly not exclusive to slaving vessels. The food of the working classes in Britain at this time was also deficient in both calories and nutrients, and seamen on any other kind of ship could equally suffer if food or water ran short. What was peculiar about complaints made by those employed on slave ships, though, was that they increasingly formulated their grievances in wording that compared their lot with that of their slaves. That their food and lodgings were as

---

[62] ZHC 1/87 27.
[63] Riland, *Memoirs* 56, 63.
[64] C107/6.
[65] *Pennsylvania Gazette* 7 November 1754.
[66] *Gentleman's Magazine* November 1786.

abysmal as, or even worse than, those of African captives, was a frequently heard protest. Their close proximity to the obscenity of Atlantic slavery meant that seamen could easily compare it to their own plight, and often considered themselves to be not much better off.

The harsh conditions and poor food, therefore, became symptomatic of a much larger issue, as sailors demanded better circumstances based on their different place in the economic system of the Atlantic world. Hard line discipline, rotten food, and appalling living conditions characterized much of working class British life, but when brought into close relief with the realities of African enslavement these things took on a new meaning. They were reviled not just in themselves, but because "freedom" was considered to equate to a materially better standard of life and work. The reality of their situation *a propos* that of the slaves was of course hugely different if viewed in wider perspective, but such considerations were beyond the average seaman's knowledge or interest. The seamen's perspective was that they were treated as slaves, and they fought their conditions with this particular injustice in mind.

William Butterworth complained that he and his fellow tars on board the *Hudibras* had been put on short rations during the six months they spent at the African coast. If a sailor became sick his food allowance was cut further. Although Butterworth and his crewmates ended up with very little personal clothing, having bartered away much of what they had for additional food, it was the fact that he considered the slaves to have been "infinitely better fed" that really seems to have galled him.[67] Richard Storey of the *Tyger* similarly complained before the parliamentary investigation into the slave trade that he had been "beat unmercifully . . . with a rope" because while "handing some rice forward to the slaves, I took a handful out of it for my own use". The crew had been put on short rations at the time.[68]

When Robert Barker, who had sailed on the *Thetis* as carpenter, having already made one slaving voyage on board the *Tryal*, published an account of his grievances entitled *The Unfortunate Shipwright, or Cruel Captain* the lack of food was central to his complaints. He wrote that by the time the ship was in Africa loading slaves his food allowance was so meagre that he had often finished the entire week's allotment by Monday, and then had to starve until the following Sunday. At Annobon he managed to trade the shirt off his back with an African who came to the ship in a canoe

---

[67] Butterworth, *Three Years* 40–1.
[68] ZHC 1/87 13: Evidence of Richard Storey.

in exchange for "two fowls, some caffavi bread, a few cocoa-nuts, and a quart of brandy" which he considered was "sufficient to have served me a week" if the first mate had not stolen any. Barker claimed his in publication that having traded what clothes he could for food, he was forced to sleep among the goats and hogs for warmth, and begged that he might be able to share the hogs' food but not allowed to do this. In common with other seamen who made slaving voyages, Barker recalled that the slaves had been moved by his plight, and had given him some of their own food.[69]

Similarly, among the long list of complaints of mistreatment endured by Thomas Watson, the boy on the *Elizabeth*, it was especially mentioned that his allowance had been cut so much that he "fed constantly with the hogs upon [illegible] rice, such as was tho[ught] too mean and bad for slaves to feed upon". His crewmate Richard Murphy claimed that Watson was so hungry that he would pick up the crumbs when he was sweeping steerage and eat them, while another, Robert Crosby, said that Watson was given only "burnt rice (which sticks to the bottom of the Copper in boyling Rice for slaves) such as they usually give to Hogs". This poor young boy did not even have clothes to barter, for he had possessed few when the ship sailed, and "was quite naked before they got to the Coast of Guinea".[70]

As Greg Dening has illustrated in *Mr. Bligh's Bad Language*, even small infractions on the standard system of punishment, respect and deference could have fatal consequences in the volatile environment of a sailing ship. Bligh, on the *Bounty*, actually whipped his seamen less than other naval men who ventured to the Pacific in the same era, but as the seamen were unable to read the nuances of his discipline he still lost his ship in the infamous mutiny. Seamen were often prepared to accept intense levels of violence, as long as its boundaries were defined and its purpose clear.[71] The additional problem for captains ruling over a slave ships was that punishment could not be considered by the men to seep into captivity. Just as sailors wanted a clear line of authority (and acceptance that trifling infringements would not be punished) so they wanted their own position to be firmly marked out from that of the slaves. Men who, in their working lives, saw the sufferings of those who were not free, placed fair treatment on a pedestal.

[69] 23–4.
[70] HCA 1/23 f.38 and f.40.
[71] Dening, *Mr Bligh's Bad Language* 61–3, 73–4, 119.

Unsurprisingly, seamen regularly sought to improve their lot through their own actions. Most benignly, they found ways to supplement their diet. On the *Lilly* the men caught and enjoyed a meal of catfish. On other vessels sharks, dolphins, and various kinds of fish were hooked, and the captain of the *Sandown*, Samuel Gamble, even found time to draw pictures of the latter in his logbook.[72] The crew of the *Florida* learned that it was easier to catch sharks when dead slaves had been thrown overboard, as they would follow the ship until the bodies were eaten.[73] While they were anchored off the Banana Islands the men of the *Rising Sun* had "a fine dinner" after having caught five turtles, and had several times before this acquired a quantity of "fine oysters".[74] The men on this ship seem to have fared better than most, as the ship's doctor even sent quarter of a goat to them so that they could celebrate Christmas Day. The *Rising Sun*, not co-incidentally, was a Rhode Island ship, and was therefore manned with seamen probably used to better quality food than their English colleagues. On other ships the men were reduced to less inventive methods of securing additional food. The crew of the *Pearl*, like Butterworth, Barker and doubtless many others, bartered articles of their clothing with free Africans for extra supplies.[75] The seamen of the *Gregson* frequently tried to beg food from the men of the *Warwick Castle* while they were on the African coast.[76]

Others, evidently believing that it was not the shortage of food on the whole ship that was the problem, but rather the inequality between captain and crew, merely helped themselves to the ship's stocks. There was indeed a major difference between some tragedy that caused food for all to be short, and incidences where seamen just felt that they were unfairly discriminated against in the allotment of what food was available. The former, which led to the incidences of cannibalism infamous in maritime lore, were an accepted risk of seafaring, and occasions when all the men suffered equally. The latter, however, were instructive of seamen's desires to improve their relations as a unified body. Robert Barker told his captain that if all the crewmembers were not equally treated with regard to food, they would be "obliged to go where we can to get provisions, and not

[72] ZHC 1/84 105: Evidence of William Dove; Barker, *Unfortunate Shipwright* 7; Butterworth, *Three Years Adventures* 24; Newton, *Journal* 10–11; Robinson, *Sailor Boy* 31; National Maritime Museum Log/M/21.
[73] British Library Add Mss 39946.
[74] Rhode Island Historical Society, Mss 828: Log of the *Dolphin*.
[75] C107/12.
[76] ZHC 1/87 123: Evidence of John Douglas.

be forcibly starved by you".[77] Here were the tenacious tentacles of class conflict, played out pragmatically over a piece of salt pork or a humble potato.

Faced with disobedient seamen, however, some captains utilized the most stinging insults of the era – invective based on racial stereotypes – to chastise their crews. A man who had protested that his food was too similar to a slave's might be abused for his insubordination through racial terminology, regardless of his own ethnicity. Edward Hilton was termed a "white negro" and left ashore after having complained that he was hungry.[78] On the *Lilly*, Captain John Scrogham allegedly took an even more extreme tactic. Initially having beaten a man for trying to get extra food, when the captain "was tired of flogging himself, and could not prevail on any of his officers to second him, he made the men Slaves come off the main deck, and flog him until such time as the man was dead".[79] For men who considered their situation to be close to enslavement and who were so eager to escape bondage, being flogged by one of their captive cargo must surely have provoked intense discontent. In the close confines of a wooden ship, thus could the seemingly small matter of food be inflated into a matter of ideological importance.

The way that common sailors fought against their other hardships reflected seamen's demands that their situation should be superior to that of slaves, while all the time their rebellions often mirrored those of bondsmen all around the Atlantic. The most common form of rebellion – desertion – was often a knee-jerk reaction to escape the privations of the ship, to withhold labour as the ultimate method of rejecting their conditions and treatment. It also, however, had relevance in the slave trade above and beyond removal of labour if seen in the context that it "affirmed the 'free' in free wage labor".[80] As men who protested about their meagre food allowances, appalling working conditions and physical punishments by contrasting their lot with that of slaves, desertion forcibly illustrated their rejection of such treatment. When a seaman ran from a slaving vessel, he was not only protesting his treatment, but was doing so in ways that showed his fundamentally different position in the economic system of the Atlantic world. Desertion was a way of asserting freedom. Ironically, however, it rejected his status as unfree labourer, the

[77] Barker, *Unfortunate Shipwright* 16.
[78] Clarkson, *Substance of the Evidence* 58.
[79] ZHC 1/87 29–30; Clarkson, *Substance of the Evidence* 59.
[80] Rediker, *Between the Devil* 105.

runaway sailor was acting out a form of resistance also commonly adopted by slaves.

The number of men who absconded from slave ships, and the manner in which they did so, is illustrative of both the harsh conditions that prevailed in the trade, and the growing anger at authority that it provoked among its lowly employees. Naval man Thomas Bolton Thompson reported that the sailors on the Liverpool slaver *Fisher* had been so badly treated by Captain Richard Kendal that they swam "between 2 and 3 cable lengths" in "shark filled waters" to protest their treatment to him.[81] The men on the *Liberty* were also so "eager to get from under [the captain's] power" that "eight of them swam on board a frigate, which lay in the harbour, at the risk of being devoured by sharks". They had previously mutinied.[82] These testimonies are particularly insightful because the Royal Navy was notoriously feared, and seamen, as has been mentioned, went to extreme lengths to avoid being pressed into service. Half of pressed men died in naval service, so these men must have been extremely fearful of their existing situations to have contemplated desertion into His Majesty's "care", even without the added hazard of shark filled waters.[83]

Indeed men ran from slave ships in huge numbers. Some, fearing what lay ahead, escaped even before the ship left its home port, regaining their freedom after having been crimped aboard. They did so on the inhospitable coast of Africa where opportunities to better themselves were certainly scarce, although they might have secured a berth with a more benevolent captain. Mostly they did so in the Caribbean and North American ports where they discharged the ship's load. Although it may be true that this was primarily an independent decision, it is problematical to ignore the larger significance in the setting of the slave trade.[84] The brutality that circulated created a situation where men were desperate enough to run even when no escape route was immediately obvious and in places which normally would have been considered extremely hostile by Europeans of the period.

More daring, threatening types of rebellion on slave ships similarly illustrated resistance to their exploitation in ways that placed the

---

[81] ZHC 1/84 168–9.
[82] Riland, *Memoirs* 62–3.
[83] Christopher Lloyd, *The British Seaman, 1200–1860: A Social Survey* (London: Paladin, 1970) 44–5.
[84] Daniel Vickers, "Reviews of Marcus Rediker's 'Between the Devil and the Deep Blue Sea'" *International Journal of Maritime History* 1 (1989) 311–36, see 313.

importance of not being treated like slaves at the fore.[85] In 1789, when Captain William Corren of the *Gregson* tried to quell a drunken rebellion amongst his men by placing five of them in irons in Dixcove fort, a slave trading garrison, he found that "they had signed a Note, to stick by one another, and that nobody should use them ill." This should not have come as a great surprise to Corren: on an earlier occasion when the captain had slapped a sailor named John Robinson, the latter had been heard to mutter "strike one and strike all". Now one of the men warned the captain that if he wanted peace on board his ship he should retrieve the men from the fort. Corren not only refused, he tried to place more under arrest there, escalating the problem so that "the Ship's Company, immediately begun to arm themselves" with "handspikes, marling Spikes, Scrapers, Iron Hoops, beat together, and made into a kind of Cutlass".

In large part the men's anger was plainly at Corren's decisions to imprison their colleagues in the slave trading fort. As one of the *Gregson*'s men would later claim, there had been "no dissatisfaction among the Crew till the Men were put in irons onshore".[86] The crew of the *Gregson* rejected being treated like slaves, but they did so in ways characteristic of maritime insurrection. In resisting they showed both reckless bravado and collective anti-authoritarianism. Yet in rejecting slavery, the *Gregson*'s revolt also showed the uncertain racial stratification of work in the slave trade, at least before the Américas hove into view, as the rebellion was eventually overcome not just with the help of the crew of another slave ship, but also with the assistance of some Africans who arrived from shore. In the wider context of Atlantic slavery it might seem that white seamen's complaints of themselves as being in positions akin to slavery was merely petty posturing, but that they themselves saw it that way is far from certain.

The collectivism the men of the *Gregson* displayed had been a central tactic of maritime rebellion for centuries before their revolt. Cooperative forms of protest against the captain's omnipotence were deeply entrenched in maritime tradition, and were still used among slave trade sailors in the late eighteenth century.[87] The Round Robin, for example, was a way for seamen to show their support for rebellion, but in a peculiarly egalitarian way so that none of them appeared to be the leader, and none to have been

---

[85] Williams, *Liverpool Privateers* 566; ADM 51/627.
[86] HCA 1/64; HCA 1/85 f.68.
[87] ZHC 1/84 87.

forced to join under coercion. Nathaniel Uring, a man who had experience of the slave trade, described them as a piece of paper on which the men drew two circles with their names signed around the outer one, and inside "they will write what they have a mind to have done".[88] This method was used by slave ship crews.[89] Yet as with so much concerning slave trade sailors the implications aboard slave ships were ambiguous. The egalitarianism of the round robin could easily include sailors of African origin, but it could also be used to foster revolts which further infringed the liberties of those they carried as cargo.

Seamen on British and American late eighteenth century slave ships had hundreds of years of maritime rebellion to build upon, which both promoted their own brand of egalitarianism while also at other times protecting the racial stratification of the eighteenth century. During the earlier upsurge in piracy potential rebels "had an alternative social order within living memory" to build their ideology upon, namely the buccaneers of the previous decades.[90] Their followers a half century later had the folkloric knowledge of their exploits, doubtless exaggerated among those that followed them as merchant mariners, as well as the ethics of the revolutions which circled the Atlantic world in this era.

Whatever the harsh realities that Black Bart Roberts, Blackbeard, Calico Jack and their ilk had wreaked upon those they had captured, to the men who sailed in their wake decades later they were undoubtedly heroes. They had, after all, defied a highly hierarchical age by allowing their captain few bonuses the rest did not enjoy, had divided their loot equally, and terrorized the merchants and captains who were the butt of many of the seamen's complaints. Aboard pirate vessels the captain was chosen by the men themselves, and could be removed from his position if they later did not support his rule. All hardships as well as food, alcohol and loot were shared in a far more equal way than on board an ordinary merchant ship. Pirates were free, and had lived by their own interpretation of "justice".

Part of the ethos of piracy had been its acceptance of sailors of African origin as equals under the pennant of skull and crossed bones. In the early years of the century "hundreds of people of African descent found places within the social order of the pirate ship," with the crews of Bartholomew Roberts, Edward Teach and Sam Bellamy all known to have included

---

[88] Quoted in Rediker, *Between the Devil* 234.
[89] Newton, *Journal* 70.
[90] Linebaugh and Rediker, *Many-Headed Hydra* 159.

black men. Other buccaneers went further. Pirate captain Mission was said to "abhor even the name of slavery", so that upon capturing African slaves he "humanely knocked off [the] chains of slaves [and] made them free men, and sharers of his fortune". Mission's onetime partner Thomas Tew was also said to have "treated on the foot of free people" slaves whom he captured. Pirates had many occasions to interact with those of African origin, for they settled all around the African coast, had strongholds on Madagascar and Anjouan in the Comoros Islands, and on the West African coast lived among the native inhabitants at Sierra Leone.[91]

Piracy and the trade in slaves had a long history. In the 1710s to 1720s men had rejected the harsh conditions on board ships, including slave ships, and had sailed instead under the black flag of piracy, swapping the omnipotent rule of a captain for their own brand of egalitarianism, characterized by Marcus Rediker and Peter Linebaugh as "hydrachy".[92] Some of William Snelgrave's slaving crew decided to leave him for life under the black flag after his ship was captured by pirates at Sierra Leone in 1719.[93] Other men in the golden era of piracy employed the more radical and treacherous method of taking over their own ships and raising the black flag. One infamous pirate captain, William Fly, had begun his years "on the account" by taking the slave ship *Elizabeth* of which he was the boatswain. This adventure would end with Fly swinging from the scaffold at Boston in 1726.[94]

Early in the century the Royal Navy had crushed gangs of pirates and hanged many by the neck as an example to others. Yet in spite of the fact that piracy was largely a spent force by the late eighteenth century, it would not die.[95] John Wynne (or Winn), who preferred to be known as "Captain Power the Brave", attempted to take control of his ship, the slaver *Polly* in the 1770s. On the pretext of chasing a pirate vessel, he endeavoured to leave the coast without giving the captain time to rejoin the ship. Seamen Jack Tomlyn, Robert Fitzgerald, Jack Hughes, Charles

[91] Anon, *History of the Pirates* 81–2; Rediker and Linebaugh, *Many-Headed Hydra* 165–7; H. Ross, "Some Notes on the Pirates and Slavers around Sierra Leone and the West Coast of Africa, 1680–1723" *Sierra Leone Studies* II (1928) 16–53. See also Rediker, *Between the Devil* chapter 6; Bryan D. Palmer, "Hydra's Materialist History" *Historical Materialism* 11:4 (2003) 383.

[92] Peter Linebaugh and Marcus Rediker, *Many-Headed Hydra* 143–73.

[93] William Snelgrave, *A New Account of Some Parts of Guinea and the Slave Trade* (London: Frank Cass and Co., 1971) 193–288.

[94] Anon, *The History of the Pirates, Containing the Lives of Those Noted Pirate Captains Misson, Bowen, Kidd, Tew, Halsey, White . . .* (Hartford: Henry Benton, 1829)133–42.

[95] *Pennsylvania Gazette* 6 October 1766; T 70/32.

Dee, Dick Thomas, and Jack Putt were also involved in the rebellion, and armed themselves with cutlasses and pistols. Wynne attempted to unify the crew by getting some liquor from the captain's cabin, and forced them to "take an Oath upon a Book to be true to Captain Power of the Bravo meaning him the said John Wynne". Wynne was thrown in the cabin by the other seamen for a while, supposedly while they discussed the merits of "turning pyrate" and whether the man who called himself Captain Power "had navigation enough to conduct the said Ship". They initially agreed to the plan, but Wynne was later betrayed by some of the men he then commanded, one of whom was "a mulatto". Wynne was returned to Britain where he was sentenced to death by hanging in 1776.[96]

As late as 1791 such activities continued aboard British slavers. In that year Captain Samuel Kitson was relieved of command of his ship as he traded at Anomabu and Tantumquerry. Later, at trial, the accused perpetrators, John Slack and Charles Berry, claimed that their reason for attempting to take the ship was that Kitson had used them ill. Berry, a twenty-seven year old Swede, had declared to Kitson that he was now the captain after an armed struggle. This was a short lived attempt at piracy as Kitson managed to get hold of Slack and threaten the crew that he would throw him overboard if they continued to resist. Briefly held at Tatumquerry fort, they were shipped back to England, found guilty, and sentenced to hang. They met their demise at "Execution Dock" in Wapping at the "time of the reflux of the sea" just as countless other mutineers had publicly been "hanged by the neck until dead".[97] Another slave ship rebel, George Hindmarsh, accused of having thrown an officer overboard from the *Fly* in 1790, swung alongside them.[98]

Rumours circulated that other seaman had got away with their crimes. The men who allegedly killed a notorious slaver captain named "Beau" Walker in the 1790s were "supposed . . . gone for the Brazils or the South Seas". The story was that Walker had apparently been "exercising his usual barbarities on his officers & crew" during his final voyage when the men conspired against him. A seaman hit him with a handspike, but the blow did not have the desired effect, leaving another to shoot him dead. "His body was immediately thrown overboard" and the ship quickly departed the African coast where the event had taken place and sailed far

[96] HCA 1/58 ff.106–110.
[97] HCA 1/25 f.191, 205; HCA 26/1; HCA 1/61; HCA 1/85 ff.69–71; Rediker, *Between the Devil* 24–7.
[98] HCA 1/25 ff.191, 205; HO 26/1.

away. "There could not possibly have been a more inhuman monster", commented one who had known him, "many a poor Seaman has been brought by him to an untimely end."[99]

Although many Africans and African-Americans – some of them former slaves – enjoyed relative equality among pirate crews even in the late eighteenth century, by this era those who were captured while being shipped as slaves rarely seem to have benefited when the crew took a ship. Sailors were used to working alongside men of different ethnicities and were happy to do so under a black flag as much as any other, but this impartiality often did not extend to chained captives being taken for sale. John Wynne and his fellow mutineer John Putt, for example, murdered a pawn named Bassam, presumably from the Grand Bassam area. They claimed that he had been encouraging the slaves to revolt. Wynne whipped the pawn and cut him with a cutlass, and then Putt allegedly decapitated him with an axe.[100]

More significantly, many latter-day Atlantic pirates did not hesitate to use slaves in the manner that their former captains had displayed. In other words, they saw them as disposable commodities. When John Fawcett of London "with force of arms did turn pirate" on the *Plumber* when it was off the coast of Guinea he took an African canoeman hostage. Fawcett tried to get to Suriname, but the winds and his navigation skills proving unequal to this task, after several weeks the mutineers agreed to go to São Tomé instead. There Fawcett went on land and sold the black man he had captured.[101] When John Richardson of the *Thetis* attempted to take the ship, his boast to those he wished to join him in rebellion was that he knew "where to carry the vessel and how to dispose of the slaves". The would-be pirate, "speaking to the people on board, said, lads, will you live or die?" and when one of them said "live", he said, "then cut the cables and slip the other, loose the top-sails, and hoist the Jolly Roger." This particular rebellion was short lived as the rebel was soon put in shackles, but undoubtedly his intention had been to sell the human beings imprisoned below decks for his own financial benefit.[102]

Similarly, a sailor named William Harry remembered that when the Bristol slave ship *William* had been taken by Stephen Porter and his accomplice Richard Hancock, the slaves were sold for the men's profit.

---

[99] Macaulay, "Journal" file 22, 1 June 1797 – 17 January 1798.
[100] HCA 1/58 ff.106–10.
[101] HCA 1/23 f.9; HCA 1/23 f.23; HCA 1/58 ff.114–24.
[102] Barker, *Unfortunate Shipwright* 14–15.

The rebels reportedly "murdered the Captain and Mate with a Broad Axe, when asleep, the former on the Round house, and the latter in the Cabbin". When, after this the men had succeeded in sailing the ship to St. Kitts, "the Slaves were sold to the Portugueze for 50 Dollars a Head".[103] The men of the *Clayton* of Liverpool apparently attempted a similar ruse, but with less success. They shot the captain and set him adrift in the long boat on their way across the Atlantic, with a view to sailing to Brazil to sell the slaves for their own enrichment. They were imprisoned by the Brazilian authorities before they could do so.[104]

All around the Atlantic littoral the association of blacks with inferiority was strengthening among the ruling white society, and for men as desperate and tumultuous as common sailors the temptation to use them to further their own aims sometimes proved too strong to resist. When Wynne killed the pawn named Bassam, and Fawsett captured and sold a man who came to trade, they repeated crimes committed many times throughout the history of the slave trade by those who were "legally" in charge of slaving vessels. Over three hundred years since Europeans took the first West African slaves away from their homelands, the association of black skin and saleable merchandise was deeply entrenched. Even those who did not enslave Africans directly regularly considered those they were shipping as cargo to be fair game as the spoils of piracy. African seafarers were well treated, but others of African origin were considered as expendable as coin, cloth, or any other kind of captured booty.

The slave trade denigrated seamen above and beyond the usual rather brutal conditions, especially at sea, which were common to the era. More importantly, sailors hated the particularly violent rule not only because of the pain and distress it caused, but because they associated it with slavery, having experienced the inhumanity of this in close relief. They protested their living conditions, treatment, and the severity of their punishment by invoking comparisons of their own situation with that of slaves. When they forwent protest and instead rebelled, they did so in ways that formulated their grievances in terms of class protest – they were free waged labourers, and demanded to be treated as such. Protests against employment in the slave trade built upon traditions of maritime rebellion, such as collectivism and egalitarianism, and co-opted them for their renewed

[103] *Pennsylvania Gazette* 2 April 1767.
[104] Zachary B. Friedenberg, *Medicine Under Sail* (Annapolis: Naval Institute Press, 2002.)

fight for freedom and justice. Rarely in the late eighteenth century did that egalitarianism extend to captive Africans however.

In a sense, the growth of freedom in the western world was therefore furthered by the gross sufferings of those who were forcibly transported across the sea and the resulting harshness of the conditions of those who were employed to take them. In seeking to explain why, in the late eighteenth century, slavery suddenly became an abhorrent institution in the western world, David Brion Davis concluded that it was because it was in direct contradiction to the powerful movement for personal liberty.[105] To those who worked aboard slave ships, and who in many ways had their own freedom impinged by their working conditions, this was not some remote ideology, but a tangible goal to be fought for. Liberty to the average tar was to be found in respite from floggings, better pay, sufficient food, and more control over their lives. It was this that they would fight for in port cities all around the edges of the ocean, and often on board their vessels too. They had been shown the importance of such benefits by their close contact with the unfortunate Africans who they were transporting for sale as chattels.

[105] David Brion Davis, *The Problem of Slavery in Western Culture* (Ithaca: Cornell University Press, 1966); Orlando Patterson, *Freedom: The Making of Western Culture* (New York: Basic Books, 1991) xiii.

PART TWO

THE SLAVING VOYAGE

Full fathom five thy father lies:
Of his bones are coral made:
Those are pearls that were his eyes:
Nothing of him that doth fade
But doth suffer a sea-change
Into something rich and strange.[1]

[1] William Shakespeare, *The Tempest* (London: Methuen, 1961) Act 1, scene II.

4

Life in the White Man's Grave

White men are gone & daily going to live among the Negroes.
Thomas Melvil, governor of Cape Coast Castle, July 1751

There are sometimes a Dozen of worthless Sailors living in this Town getting Drunk and abusing the Negroes, these fellows think themselves above all Law, if I restrain them, I should only get into the Hands of some Wapping Sollicitor, who in Guildhall would present me as the greatest tyrant that ever lived.
Thomas Melvil, December 26th 1751[1]

Among a trade littered with peculiar perversions, it is nevertheless a curious fact that slave trade seamen occasionally spent more time as incarcerated captives in forts such as Cape Coast Castle than did African slaves. To sailors accused of mutiny, piracy or some other transgression, the forts represented outposts of Britain's rule, places where the long arm of the law reached out and detained them until they could be sent back "home" to stand trial. Locked away in miasmal conditions – better than those of the Africans trapped in the dungeons though hardly humane – they were susceptible to malaria, yellow fever, dysentery and a host of other diseases to which they had little resistance. The reason their confinement could last longer than that of Africans reflected the vagaries of the slave trade's economic rule. Quite simply, British naval ships arrived to transport the temporary captives home far less frequently than predatory slave ships arrived hungering to purchase human cargo.

[1] T 70/29.

FIGURE 3. "A New Map of that part of Africa called Guinea".
Original in William Snelgrave, *A New Account of Some Parts of Guinea and the Slave Trade* (London, 1754). Reprinted by permission of New York Public Library.

Central as the coastal forts are to the history of the slave trade, holding in their dark past the final view that millions of Africans had of their home continent, to seamen they also functioned as outposts of the motherland's penal jurisdiction. This fact is symptomatic of a larger and often forgotten picture: to Jack Tar the harbours of the African seaboard simply represented ports of call on a long journey. Among the very valuable scholarship researching the various embarkation points of slaves, supply routes, prices and trading relations, it remains largely unnoted that numbers of seamen, principally of European origin, frequently spent considerable amounts of time along the African littoral. This omission mostly derives from the fact that works on the slave trade generally focus on either the merchants' economics – thereby citing the African coast as supply regions – or on the slaves' suffering, which of course places Africa as the violated homeland, dispossessed of millions of its citizens. That to seafaring men Africa was often merely yet another continent visited in a varied life is left unsaid, and thus, by implication at least, unimportant.

This oversight disregards the significance of the inter-racial contact that took place between the lowly seamen and Africans of all social stations.

The seamen who spent time anchored off the coast engaged in countless small acts of cross-cultural contact, so fashioning the ports and towns they frequented along the coast into a discrete part of the larger Atlantic frontier. The Africans they dealt with contributed immensely to the tapestry of relations created by slave trading. Philip Morgan is quite correct when he states "most Britons and Africans encountered one another, not in either of their respective homelands, but in the New World." The "approximately 333,000" sailors who visited West Africa while engaged in the slave trade from 1600 to 1800 were undoubtedly a tiny percentage of the overall flow, both forced and free, of people around the Atlantic world in this era.[2] Nonetheless, the way that those men acted and interacted while stationed on the African coast reveals an important, and variant, aspect of racial formation in the slave trade.

Seamen from slaving vessels used the towns that peppered the coast just as they did outlying ports associated with other long-distance trades, as places from which to procure extra food, alcohol, women and entertainment. Sometimes they were temporary homes as sailors deserted in search of a more amenable position, or were left on shore for a variety of reasons. The black skinned inhabitants of the "Dark Continent" were part of a large mosaic of races, ethnicities, cultures and skin colours with whom seamen came into contact on their voyages. Sailors were familiar with this array of different people, for maritime culture lived off its boundaries, drinking from all of its disparate elements, while all the time creating something of its own.

Contrary to the received image that eighteenth-century Europeans considered Africa inhospitable and populated by savages, desertion from slave ships all along the African coast was not rare at all. In fact it became one of the catastrophes that slaving merchants feared, another common reason that voyages could fail to ensure the hoped for profit. Before the *Bloom*'s 1787 voyage merchant Robert Bostock wrote to Captain Peter Burne warning him specifically of the danger of his men stealing one of the ship's boats in order to escape, a danger which, he claimed, had "overset" many slaving voyages.[3] Clearly for many sailors life among the Africans was considered infinitely preferable to subjection to the cruel whims of their captain, even if most later joined another slave ship to

---

[2] Philip D. Morgan, "British Encounters with Africans and African-Americans circa 1600–1780" Bernard Bailyn and Philip D. Morgan (eds.) *Strangers within the Realm: Cultural Margins of the First British Empire* (Williamsburg: Institute of Early American History and Culture, 1991) 160.

[3] Liverpool Records Office 387 MD 54: Letterbooks of Robert Bostock.

journey home. Sailors undoubtedly were sometimes dubious about the reception they would receive if they absconded ashore – and rightly so, given the trade they were employed in – but that sense of "justice" was evidently not dimmed by such fears. The beacon of maritime rebellion shone along the African shores.

A number of the crew, rather than an individual seaman, was often behind an escape attempt, but even when it was one lone man who fled there is evidence that the spirit of such action was well regarded by his colleagues. After John Hawkins attempted to desert, for example, he was caught and returned to the ship, whereupon he recorded that "the captain received me with great coolness, but the Doctor, the mate and sailors all with the greatest cordiality".[4] In 1750 three sailors named as Edward Shiddefield, Daniel Lake and Sampson Hardy ran away with a long boat belonging to the *Antelope* of Bristol, which as Captain Thomas Sanderson later lamented at the Admiralty courts, was never recaptured. Other crewmembers were evidently also disaffected on this vessel as they later usurped the captain's rule, ensuring that it never reached its American destination.[5]

Some groups of seamen who deserted in Africa comprised a significant proportion of their ship's crew, and acted as a unified company to make their escape. At least five men ran from the *Elizabeth,* captained by John Steel, while at its African slave embarkation port. On a 75 ton vessel this would have constituted a very severe loss of men.[6] On one of surgeon Alexander Falconbridge's voyages, eleven "of the best seamen deserted at Bonny from ill treatment" where most of them died. Falconbridge could remember the name of only one, a man named Surman from Bristol.[7] Nineteen men left an unnamed slave ship near the Rio Pongo and refused to rejoin until threatened with the press – five chose this option anyway.[8] Nine men ran from the *Bell* of Liverpool after their original captain died and they were harshly treated by his successor. They left aboard only three men and their officers, on a ship that already had two or three hundred slaves below decks.[9] Captain Daniel Darby's entire crew deserted him

4 John Hawkins, *A History of a Voyage to the Coast of Africa* (London: Frank Cass, 1970) 162–73.
5 HCA 1/58; Eltis, *CD-ROM,* 17198.
6 HCA 1/23 f.38; Eltis, *CD-ROM,* 24874.
7 Alexander Falconbridge, *An Account of the Slave Trade on the Coast of Africa* (London: James Phillips, 1788) 47; BT 6/9.
8 Hoffman, *A Sailor of King George* 196–8.
9 Macaulay, 'Journal' file 13, 26 July–26 September 1796.

when his ship was forced back to the Îsle de Los after a slave revolt
"thirty leagues out".[10]

The Irishman Nicolas Owen provided a first hand account of deserting on the African coast when employed aboard a slave ship from Rhode
Island. He later wrote that five of his crewmates who shared a watch were
"all of one mind" to regain the "liberty to which every Europain is inti-
tle to" after mistreatment. Leaving at four o'clock in the morning, Owen
and his co-conspirators left in the ship's longboat with some weapons they
had stolen from the captain and "stear'd W.N.W". They were followed
by an armed boat but managed to get away, and existed for some days
in the area around Cape Mount, occasionally putting into shore to trade
for food to supplement the exceedingly meagre amount they had appropriated from the ship. When Owen became ill, the men "call'd a counsele
of war ... [and] concluded that we should proceed to Sierelone and lay
ourselves at the mercy of the English governour of the factory". The men
must have been united in aims and the desire to escape, as to survive for
some time in these conditions at sea in a small boat was a feat of survival.
That the men were from a diverse area is suggested by Owen's comment
that the men would afterwards all go back to their own countries.[11]

While Owen mentions ill treatment as the motivation for running, other
seamen undoubtedly felt that their options were better in Africa. Isaac
Parker, who went capturing Africans with a trader's son after deserting,
almost certainly wielded more power during this phase of his life than
he had previously.[12] Likewise a young Irishman was persuaded to desert
at Bimbe Island by a countryman of his, known as Old Paddy, lured
by the possibility of taking part in the trade which the elder man had
built up in the area.[13] In his book *The Forgotten Trade* Nigel Tattersfield
conjectures that seaman William Hodge ran from the *Daniel and Henry*
at São Tomé because the island was exceedingly attractive, as were the
"mulatto Portuguese *senhoritas*".[14]

Some sailors, having decided to run away from their ships, found that
life in Africa was alien. Three men who were among the mutineers on
board the *Plumber* that sailed for Africa in 1765 worked on plantations at

[10] *Pennsylvania Gazette* 16 November 1774.
[11] Nicholas Owen, *Journal of a Slave Dealer* Eveline Martin (ed.) (London: George Routledge and Sons, 1930) 23–6.
[12] ZHC 1/84 123–5.
[13] Samuel Robinson, *A Sailor Boy's Experience Aboard a Slave Ship* (Wigtown: G.C. Book
Publishers, 1996) 46–7.
[14] (London: Pimlico, 1991) 117.

São Tomé after escaping first from the ship, and then from the main body of seditious sailors. Twenty-three year old John Quinn from Armagh tried to secure help from the resident Portuguese governor, a man of mixed-race, but the latter not sharing any common language with the seaman he "drove him away from his House as a Vagabond". Quinn then went with two of his crewmates, Jeffrey Sugworth of Lancashire and Abraham Berry of Stockholm to a plantation in the interior "to work for their subsistence". They later shipped on board the *Phoenix*.[15] Clearly in São Tomé in the 1760s, neither European origins nor white skin protected sailors from plantation labour or allegations of vagrancy.

John Newton, who later became a slave ship captain and then a zealous abolitionist, managed to encompass both the highs and lows of a white man working in Africa. After being threatened that he would be handed over to a naval ship because of his insubordination, he went ashore in Africa and worked on a lime-tree plantation. He bewailed his fate doing manual work in the tropics, but then afterwards found more lucrative work as a slave trader. Growing to like his newfound profession and the authority it conveyed, when a ship arrived to take him back to England he was "reluctant to give up his profitable job".[16]

These examples show that no easy formula can be advanced to explain seamen's fortunes in Africa, nor the extent to which those of European origin benefited or suffered because of their skin colour. For John Quinn, Jeffrey Sugworth and Abraham Berry at São Tomé there were clearly no "wages of whiteness" immediately on offer, not for an Englishman, a Swede or an Irishman. Outside of the Barbary Coast, however, seamen of European origin were safe from the fate of being rounded up by a slave trader and sold to a passing slave ship. Sailors' situations were very different depending on the part of the coast they were at, the local circumstances, recent events, and the people with whom they managed to ally themselves. A seaman might find himself attacked because of a slave ship's unacceptable treatment of the region's inhabitants, or discover that he was in danger because the area was seething with French or Dutchmen, and his own country was at war with them. There were few certainties to life ashore in Africa.

The situation was somewhat different after the British settlement at Sierra Leone was established in 1787. The settlement immediately caused

---

[15] HCA 1/58 ff.114–24.
[16] John Newton, *The Journal of a Slave Trader, 1750–1754* Bernard Martin and Mark Spurrell (eds.) (London: The Epworth Press, 1962) x–xi.

problems for the captains of slave ships in the area, and not only because of the founders' ideological objections to the trade. The majority of those who were the first settlers, both those who were members of the "black poor" and the smaller number of whites who had gone with them, came overwhelmingly from the same social groups that seamen occupied in England. Many of the men often had seafaring experience either on naval or merchant ships.[17] Faced with a town founded on values they recognized – at least in relation to other parts of the African coast – seamen from slave ships appear to have seen Sierra Leone as an outpost of welcome.

One visitor to the area wrote that they were "frequently much pestered by renegade seamen, quitting ships employed in the Slave Trade, and refuging here". While the writer was there, one ship, the *Fisher* of Liverpool, could not leave the coast because so many of its crew deserted to the settlement.[18] Nine seamen deserted from the *Bell* at Rio Pongo and took a boat to the settlement in search of sanctuary.[19] Governor Zachary Macaulay wrote that during 1796–7 they at times had as many as fifty or sixty "extremely dissolute" English seamen, mostly from slave ships, in the colony. Many had run to escape their harsh treatment aboard.[20] The two black men who ran from Captain Newell's ship at Sierra Leone show that black seamen also hoped that the settlement would be a haven for them.[21]

These deserting seamen revealed Britain's contradictory attitudes towards the slave trade, seamen and people of African origin in the 1780s and 90s. So many sailors deserted at Sierra Leone that Governor John Clarkson felt compelled to put up a notice warning sailors that they would not be given shelter. It was a decision that rather tormented Lieutenant Clarkson, for he had been instructed to "protect every man", and he felt that his pronouncement that this would not apply to slave trade sailors rather dented the ideology upon which Sierra Leone had been founded.[22]

[17] Stephen J. Braidwood, *Black Poor and White Philanthropists: London's Blacks and the Foundation of the Sierra Leone Settlement, 1786–1791* (Liverpool: Liverpool University Press, 1994).

[18] Anna-Maria Falconbridge, *Two Voyages to Sierra Leone* Deirdre Coleman (ed.) *Maiden Voyages and Infant Colonies: Two Women's Travel Narratives of the 1790s* (London: Leicester University Press, 1999) 110–11.

[19] Macaulay, 'Journal' file 13, 26 July–26 September 1796.

[20] Macaulay, 'Journal' file 21, 7 June 1797.

[21] Macaulay, 'Journal' file 3, 19 July–26 November 1794.

[22] Anna-Maria Falconbridge, *Two Voyages* 110–11; Christopher Fyfe, *A History of Sierra Leone* (Oxford: Oxford University Press, 1962) 53.

Engaged in a trade Britain would not outlaw for twenty years after the founding of the settlement, sailors from slave ships were not meant to take advantage of the liberty on offer in the "Province of Freedom".[23] That slave trade sailors were attracted to an African town founded for free blacks and based on notions of liberty, again emphasizes the peculiar, tangled relationship between race, slave trading and power in the Atlantic world of the late eighteenth century. It also shows that seamen had an ambiguous, multifaceted and changeable place in that world.

Many sailors just left their slave ships temporarily while in Africa, absconding in pursuit of things they were deprived of on board. The young, innocent ship's boy William Butterworth claimed to have eaten with Africans because he was "half-starved on his ship" and, while there, to have taught Africans to read and write, revealing his comparatively genteel upbringing before going to sea.[24] A small incident noted by another unnamed diarist writes of an African coming to him as he gutted fish to make an impromptu trade of the fish for a coconut.[25] Food was secured in less honest and affable ways too. Three seamen from the *African Queen* killed a duck onshore at Sierra Leone and provoked the ire of the inhabitants.[26] And obviously it was not just food that men went in search of. The crew of the *Duke of Argyle* "got drunk; [and] afterwards went on shoar to fight".[27] A slave ship surgeon wrote that at Princes Island [Príncipe] the sailors got free of their captain and proceeded to go around "pilfering the Negroes, and debauching their Wives".[28]

The temptation of the proximity of women on the coast did, of course, provide a potent reason for a seaman to desert at least temporarily from his berth. Jack Tar was infamous for having women in every port of call, and one maritime historian has even claimed that such forays ashore were necessary to reinforce masculinity in the traditional woman-less nautical

---

[23] Braidwood, *Black Poor and White Philanthropists* 185.
[24] William Butterworth, *Three Years Adventures of a Minor in England, Africa, the West Indies, South-Carolina, and Georgia* (Leeds: Edward Baines, 1822) 32–4.
[25] British Library Add Mss 39964.
[26] Falconbridge, *Two Voyages* 129–31. A similar story is told by Bryan Edwards. He reported that in 1788 two seamen from a Liverpool slaver killed a "guana" while at Bonny and so enraged the inhabitants that they were first sentenced to death. Eventually, after their captain interceded on their behalf, the punishment was apparently commuted to "700 bars" and enslavement to the king. Unwilling to pay this fee, Edwards reports that their captain left the unfortunate sailors to their fate. *The History, Civil and Commercial, of the British West Indies* (New York: AMS Press, 1996) II 91n.
[27] Newton, *Journal* 14.
[28] John Atkins, "Observations on the Coast of Guinea" John Atkins (ed.) *The Navy-Surgeon: Or, a Practical System of Surgery* (London, 1734) 8.

setting.[29] In Africa, just as elsewhere, men left their ships to go ashore to look for prostitutes and other willing – or not so willing – women. It was a practice shared by both crew and officers. One man named only as Captain Corbett enters the historical record because instead of arriving at Cape Coast Castle to meet his interpreter as arranged, he went on shore with the ship's surgeon "one in pursuit of Game & the other of a Doxey". We know that it was the captain who was searching for a woman because the doctor lost himself in the woods and missed his ship sailing.[30] While it was clearly commonplace for seamen to look for available women at all ports of call, something can be gleaned from their descriptions of African women which reveal an aspect of their attitudes towards race, at least here where it intersected with gender.

Not conforming to European models of monogamy, African marriages were often supposed spurious by visitors arriving on British and North American slave ships. For seamen this meant that most African women were considered to be potentially available sexual partners. Coupled with the centuries old European belief that Africans were strangely libidinous, this created a myth which circulated among seamen that African women were generally willing and rapacious sexual partners, who knew little of the contemporary middle class English ideal of women as prudish and sexually submissive. This, of course, was a trait that seamen believed, or at least fervently chose to believe, to be true about women of various nationalities they came into contact with. The Polynesian women that Captain James Cook's men encountered are perhaps the best-known example. In Africa part of this image was born of occasions when African traders offered ships' captains and other European traders women for the evening or the duration of their stay as a means of showing good faith and securing a good deal.[31] Sailors spent many, many hours at sea without the company of women, and doubtless tales of welcoming foreign damsels spread rapidly among them taking on ever-greater connotations as they circulated the oceans.[32]

---

[29] Bryan Nolan, "A possible perspective on Deprivations" Peter H. Fricke (ed.) *Seafarer and Community: Towards a Social Understanding of Seafaring* (London: Croom Helm, 1973) 91.

[30] T 70/30.

[31] Nathaniel Uring, *The Voyages and Travels of Captain Nathaniel Uring* (London: Cassell and Co., 1726) 29.

[32] For an example of a slaver captain having his wife on board, see *Gentleman's Magazine* July 1737. It is interesting that few clear examples of Captains' or officers' wives being on slave ships have been found, as they were at sea on ships in other trades in this period. This could be because the added dangers of slave trading, and possibly the

That such attributes were accredited to African women of some regions by seamen is clear from the writings of John McLeod. He professed to be knowledgeable about such matters when he sailed on a slave ship in the final years of lawful British trading. He was disappointed, however, for he found that in Dahomey the "mutinous wives" or "vixens" he expected – "the treasure and delight of an Englishman . . . the safeguard of his *ennui*" – were not forthcoming. McLeod, lamenting the absence of female company during his coastal stay regretted the dearth of "that noble spirit which animates the happier dames" on other parts of the coast. Or so the lonely man imagined.[33]

Perhaps the written works of men such as William Smith, who had been an employee of the Royal African Company in the 1720s, and Nathaniel Uring, a slave ship captain in the first years of the eighteenth century, had helped promote this image of African women. Uring recalled in his *Voyages and Travels* that while he and a fellow captain were lodged with an African merchant, "a young Woman was sent to each of us, who came and whisper'd softly, and offer'd themselves to us".[34] William Smith wrote that he at first protested to the African King who offered him a woman for the night, saying that it would be a sin to sleep with a woman unless married to her. The king, however, then asked Smith whether he had never "lain" with a woman to whom he was not married "in his own country". Smith, acknowledging his hypocrisy, accepted the woman.

Smith's account is not just the story of being offered a woman as part of a deal. He also had plenty to impart to his readers about the attractiveness and compliance of the woman. Although most seamen were not literate, such an account, published in London as early as 1744 can only have helped spread ideas about African women as sexually available. In Smith's words, he found attractive the "natural, pleasant and inartificial Method of her Behaviour" which he described as "not forward, yet not coy" and

---

proximity of so many African men, made it a trade considered especially unsuitable for mariners' wives. It is probable, however, that some white women ventured to sea aboard slave ships nonetheless and that have just not been located in the available sources. Lisa Norling, *Captain Ahab had a Wife: New England Women and the Whalefishery, 1720–1870* (Chapel Hill: University of North Carolina Press, 2000); Joan Druett, *Hen Frigates: the Wives of Merchant Captains under Sail* (New York: Simon and Schuster, 1998); Joan Druett, *Petticoat Whalers: Whaling Wives at Sea, 1820–1920* (Auckland: Collins New Zealand, 1991); David Cordingly, *Women Sailors and Sailors' Women: an Untold Maritime History* (New York: Random, 2001).

[33] John McLeod, *A Voyage to Africa, with some account of the manners and customs of the Dahomian people* (London: John Murray, 1820) 51.

[34] Uring, *Voyages and Travels* 97.

seemed surprised that she responded to him with "equal Ardour and Fervency". Smith was obviously pondering on the difference with women he had encountered in England when he felt the need to explain to his readers that "the Ladies of this Country imagine it no Fault to be free, nor to be fond of a Man; their Notion is that they were made for their Diversion as well as Use". Smith, nonetheless, remained uncertain of the attractiveness of the woman he had been offered, a fact that he directly linked to her skin colour. The fact that she was dark skinned was a "fault" that had to be "recompenc'd" in Smith's mind by "the Softness of her Skin" and "the beautiful Proportion and exact Symmetry of each part of her Body". Nevertheless, he confessed that later, in bed, he was able to "forget the Complexion of [his] bedfellow" in order that he could "obey the Dictates of all-powerful Nature".[35]

Sexual licentiousness was one of the central tenets of stereotypes of savage foreigners with darker skin, and undoubtedly in the seamen's writings of African women there is part of this fiction. There was certainly some false piety in their claimed surprise that women could be sexual predators, for these were men who frequented prostitutes in many of their ports of call, and whose wives and girlfriends in Britain were sometimes engaged in this occupation. It is easier to believe from the young William Butterworth than from others, who was certainly still "a minor" when he was apparently "led away by two African women" along with a fellow tar.[36] What can be read into other, less innocent seamen's remarks are both the comparison between African sexuality and the more repressed ideals of British middle-class womanhood, and an affirmation of the savagery myth Europeans had long held with regard to Africans.

There was, however, another aspect of the myth of dusky scandalous females that appears to have been played out in the setting of the slave trade. In this most antagonistic of port situations the fear arose among sailors that treacherous seductive women might inveigle them into paying fines for adultery. The subsequent fine might be not money, but the return of a pawn held aboard ship. Fiction or not, it was fear, akin to that of Africans' special skills at poisoning, that continued to spread among sailors stationed on the coast they considered so inhospitable. The fourth mate of one British slave ship was allegedly tricked by an African woman

---

[35] William Smith, *A New Voyage to Guinea: Describing the Customs, Manners, Soil, Climate, Habits, Buildings, Education, Manual Arts, Agriculture, Trade, Employments, Languages, Ranks of Distinction, Habitations, Diversions, Marriages, and Whatever Else is Memorable among the Inhabitants* (London, 1744) 251–4.

[36] Butterworth, *Three Years Adventures* 74.

in this way, for she apparently made him think she was free, but later he was forced to pay a fine to her husband for his adultery with her.[37] If this artifice was indeed used, it is unlikely many were as scrupulous as the deeply religious John Newton who fervently rejected any possibility that he could be misled in this way.[38]

However often seamen were tricked into paying fines of this kind, there were many more occasions on which they took advantage of women, sometimes even taking their "temporary wives" into a life of perpetual bondage. Joseph Hawkins was rebuked by the other officers on his ship for not having brought the "wives" he had acquired when trading inland back to the ship with him, as they had done. They would have brought "a good price when we arrived in America", he was told.[39] Others were apparently not as scrupulous as Hawkins in this regard, taking away the women who had been offered to them by African chiefs for the purpose of sealing a deal as if they had been purchased as slaves.[40]

Some sailors did seek to have relationships with African women which were, to their eyes, more legitimate, although this was rare. Richard Drake, the young orphan boy who also shipped aboard Rhode Island slavers "became a husband at the age of seventeen years" when he married "Soolah", the daughter of "King Mammee" with whom he was trading. Initially Drake's comments about Soolah were ambiguous at best, noting in his remembrances that his "vanity was touched by this mark of royal favor", especially as he "was not averse to the princess who was the handsomest young negress". Later, however, when he was taken on another slaving raid and was separated from his wife, Drake lamented her loss.[41] What Soolah made of the arrangement and of Drake can only be imagined.

Sailors who spent extended periods in Africa sometimes formed longer-term relationships with African women. Nicholas Owen, the Irishman who made several voyages on Rhode Island slave ships and did not hesitate to refer to himself as "a common jack tar" later in his life lived in Africa

---

[37] ZHC 1/84 81: Evidence of Thomas Trotter.
[38] Newton, *Journal* 76.
[39] Hawkins, *A History* 150.
[40] Anonymous, *An Account of the Evidence Delivered before a Select Committee of the House of Commons in the years 1790–1791* (Edinburgh, 1791) 18.
[41] Richard Drake, "Revelations of a Slave Smuggler: Being the Autobiography of Capt. Richard Drake, an African Trader for Fifty Years – from 1807 to 1857" George F. Dow (ed.) *Slave Ships and Slaving* (Westport, CT: Negro Universities Press, 1927) 200.

and mentioned "my woman" in his journal.[42] As with other types of relationships the emotions involved in such matters are impossible to assess. Captain Thomas Rogers evidently felt loyalty, responsibility and/or affection towards an African woman and a child he called "his blak boy" as he left them some cloth and other items in his will when he died in 1773. Having made seven slaving voyages, beginning on the *Titt Bitt* in June 1756 and continuing until his death near Anomabu on board the *Polly*, there is the possibility that this was a long-term relationship, renewed on his previous visits.[43]

An even more intriguing fragment of information comes from the story of Cudjoe and Quow, recorded in chapter two. Robert Milligan, second mate of the *Lovely Lass*, and the man who they were accused of murdering, apparently had a free African woman named Eccauh (or Ecour) who was interchangeably termed his "wife" or his "wench". After Milligan's death John Owen, the other accused ringleader, "slept with the deceased's Wench every night from the time of the Murder". The longevity of Milligan's relationship with Eccauh is unknown, nor how willingly and freely she had entered into it, but nevertheless the image of an abused, totally subjected African woman is brought into question by the fact that Owen was known to have shared his loot from the ship with her. Whether he was trying to secure her favours, assure her loyalty, assuage his own guilt, or whether there was an entirely different explanation for these events is hard to unravel.[44]

Seamen's sexual interaction with African women encompassed every conceivable permutation from outright rape to long standing relationships into which both parties had entered freely for their own individual reasons. These affairs had slightly different implications depending upon the origins of the sailors themselves, as of course they also had divergent meaning to the women involved contingent upon their various cultural mores, social standing and personal agency. A white man from the American South would be more accustomed to seeing black women as sexual beings, but also came from a society in which miscegenation was taboo as well as being commonplace.[45] A white British sailor would have been

---

[42] Owen, *Journal* 63, 85.
[43] Darold D. Wax, "Thomas Rogers and the Rhode Island Slave Trade" *American Neptune* 35 (1975) 289–301, quote 301.
[44] HCA 1/64.
[45] Winthrop Jordan, *White over Black: American Attitudes Toward the Negro, 1550–1812* (New York: W.W. Norton, 1968) 144–50; Edward E. Baptist, "'Cuffy,' 'Fancy Maids,'

more likely to view sexual conquest in Africa in the context of similar activities in other parts of the world with women of many nationalities. For African seamen the situation was evidently very different. For African Americans, themselves far more likely to have wives and families back home and knowing the degradation of black women in the Americas only too well, the picture changed again.[46]

As sailors seem to have found a variety of reasons to desert their ships in Africa, it is perhaps surprising that being put ashore was considered a punishment. While sailors were often put off a ship to stop their mutinous tendencies spreading, in this situation it also reflected the beliefs pervading the trade's command, for life among the Africans was considered to be an exceedingly sorry fate. There are plenty of examples of seamen being left in Africa. From the ship *Nile*, commanded by John Gwin, five men including the second mate were "left on shore in Africa".[47] From the *Otter* sailors John Darlington and John Smith were "discharged at Gaboon" [sic] for mutiny.[48] From the small crew of the schooner *Venus* John Robinson was "discharged on the Coast for bad conduct".[49] In a similar case, a twenty-one year old sailor named Thomas Powell was put ashore from his ship the *Pearl Galley* with only "a shirt, wastcoate, a cap, a hat, a pair of trousers, a pair of shoes, and a pair of buckles".[50] The subsequent fate of all is unknown.

The fate of seven men left ashore from the *Roebuck* and its tenders in 1797 "at Bassaw a very uncivilized part of the grain Coast" for disobedience to their master shows just how hard life could be for sailors abandoned in Africa. They had apparently tried to take the captain's weapons from him during his daily drunken rampages on deck during which he "wantonly wounded his people". Alleging mutiny, he "flogged them severely, put irons upon them, [and] with nothing but a shirt & a pair of trowsers, & no provisions, sent them ashore". These men faired badly, four dying at Bassau, probably from the disease environment to which they had little resistance. Another man managed to make his way

---

and 'One-Eyed Men': Rape, Commodification, and the Domestic Slave Trade in the United States" *American Historical Review* 106:5 (December 2001) 1619–50.

[46] W. Jeffrey Bolster, "Every Inch a Man: Gender and the Lives of African American Seamen, 1800–1860" Margaret S. Creighton and Lisa Norling (eds.) *Iron Men and Wooden Women: Gender and Seafaring in the Atlantic World, 1700–1920* (Baltimore: Johns Hopkins Press, 1996) 162–4.

[47] BT 98/65 f.365.

[48] BT 98/68 f.127.

[49] BT 98/63 f.224.

[50] Peter Earle, *Sailors: English Merchant Seamen 1650–1775* (London: Methuen, 1998) 59.

to Cape Mesurado and to the house of a trader named Mr. Graham, where he arrived starving, covered in ulcers and dressed only in rags. When the captain coincidentally arrived at Graham's house he showed no remorse for the suffering he had caused, but declared in revealing language that "the Man was his & he was determined to have him". Graham refused, but the argument was only settled the following day when the seaman died.[51]

The punishment value in leaving other sailors ashore was less clear. On the *Africa,* indisputably a ship of horror, the fate of one sailor, Thomas Carlos, was to be punished by being put onshore "among the Negroes" after having allegedly been forced to sign for wages he had not received. The penalty intended was clearly linked to the supposed savagery of the local inhabitants at the place Carlos was abandoned. The rumour that circulated was of a British slave ship having been "cut off" in that area just a short while before, and all except one sailor and one boy killed. The warped rationale of this decree was brought into focus by the events that followed, however. Carlos was not present at the trial to state whether in fact he considered his "punishment" to have been providential. He certainly might have believed so if he had bumped into his fellow tars from the *Africa* at a later date, as they could have told him that the sole survivor from the vessel previously "cut off" was taken aboard the *Africa* as his replacement, where he died under the merciless rule.[52]

Thus Africa was all things to seamen – the scene of desertion and rebellion, a trove of unrequited fantasies, the setting for seamen's tall stories and a place of punishment – just as other ports along long-distance trade routes. To crews of men closely confined within the boundaries of a wooden ship for around a year, foreign lands inevitably came to have a dreamlike quality, a whimsical location where untold luxuries and welcomes could be found. Aboard ship, land became a place of opportunity and potential, crowded with things he was deprived of at sea, a refuge from the captain's command and the sea's dangers and respite from hard work. Consequently, in the all too frequent event of disease attacking a ship, seamen, accustomed to a mishmash of folklore and broadcast fable, were more eager to try out native cures than might be imagined. An African woman nursed several of the *Pilgrim's* men for three months after they fell ill.[53] The English doctor's son, Silas Told,

---

[51] Macaulay, 'Journal', file 19, 18 January–20 May 1797; Eltis, *CD-Rom,* 84108.
[52] HCA 1/24.
[53] Macaulay, 'Journal' file 28, 15 July 1798–21 May 1799.

who sailed on the slaver *Royal George*, spent six weeks onshore in the care of a man he named as "Prince Arigo", where he was treated with what he considered to be typical African treatments, including animal sacrifice.[54]

Some places came to be celebrated in seafaring lore for having curative qualities. As the West African coastline was regarded by most Europeans as one of the least healthy places on earth, in the transatlantic slave trade this generally alluded to the islands off the coast where the ships sometimes weighed anchor for short periods. Although nowhere was reputed to have the panacean qualities ascribed to St. Helena, the islands of São Tomé, Príncipe, Annobon and Fernando Po, as well as the Banana Islands off Sierra Leone, were all considered to be places that white men could recuperate from the mysterious dangers of African diseases. In some ways such assumptions were correct, for the breezes that refreshed the offshore islands were partially effective in keeping mosquitoes away. Many seamen, however, were suffering as much from the effects of scurvy, venereal diseases, poor diet and floggings as from malaria or yellow fever. The ubiquitous "flux", as dysentery was commonly known, could strike anywhere.

Many captains sent sick sailors ashore not so they could convalesce, but rather to abandon them. They were disembarked in Africa because they were already too sick to continue the voyage, and were simply left to survive as best they could. Naval man John Simpson would later report before Parliament that a slaver seaman had begged him to be taken home to England after having been abandoned on the African coast because of his "ulcerated legs".[55] In April 1789 the *Manchester Mercury* printed a letter from a seaman who had sailed with Captain Hewitt for Africa, but who had been forced to leave the ship while there because he had "frequent eruptions breaking out on his Legs and Thighs". By the time he was lucky enough to get home to Liverpool he had "blotches all over his body".[56]

From the ship *Jemmy*, under the command of Richard Pearson, James Colen was "left at a factory in Africa" after he had "lost his leg by a Shark 12th April". Also disembarked with him was James Chambers who left "by his own request to take care of J. Colen".[57] Sailor Francis Myers of

---

[54] Silas Told, *The Life of Mr. Silas Told, Written by Himself* (London: G. Whitfield, 1796) 16.

[55] ZHC 1/87 42.

[56] *Manchester Mercury* 14 April 1789.

[57] BT 98/56 f.148.

the *Fanny* was "Left on the Coast Oct. 18. 1800 by accident".[58] The fate of being abandoned in Africa was not restricted to the white members of the crew. The slave ship *Dart* discharged its steward, a man from Calcutta called Antonio Rosario, while at the African coast.[59] Jack Williams, the African cook of the *Otter* was "sent on shore at Congo – 9 Mar. 1803 – by his own consent being lame".[60] If this was Williams' home region, then undoubtedly he had better survival chances than most.

Other seamen were left on the African coast en masse if a privateer took their ship. The French abandoned men from many captured slave ships at Sierra Leone in the 1790s. The crews from four or five ships were left there in 1794, and then two years later the men from several more ships were put ashore at Freetown after being made prisoners of war. Among the latter group were those employed on the *Speedwell* of Liverpool which had been trading for slaves at Cape Mount when taken. These men caused trouble in the nascent colony, behaving in a "noisy and riotous" manner. Offered work until they had a chance to leave, hardly any took this opportunity, choosing instead to live off what little money they had and bartering their clothes for rum. Zachary Macaulay believed that few would survive for more than a few weeks. Typically, they elected a "captain" from among themselves, and when this man was sentenced to be whipped in order to try and instil good behaviour in the whole gang, the men grouped together to oppose his punishment.[61]

Aside from all these reasons a seaman could also end up spending time on the African coast (as opposed to anchored off it) because of shipwreck or the not unlikely event of the ship being declared "unseaworthy".[62] Ships did not have a long life in the slave trade, and on occasion they were found to be so rotten they could not be used, sometimes at the instigation of the crew who refused to travel further in it. The *Lumbey* was found to be so eaten away by worms while in Africa in September 1793 that it was riddled with "holes so large as to receive your finger".[63] In 1796 the Rhode Island vessel *Rising Sun* was the subject of a joint decision by "all the white men on the island" that it was unseaworthy having being

[58] BT 98/61 f.347.
[59] BT 98/64 f.175.
[60] BT 98/64 f.100.
[61] Macaulay, 'Journal' file 3, 19 July–26 November 1794; file 13, 26 July–26 September 1796.
[62] House of Lords Records 1791; Bank of England: Humphrey Morice papers VIII; T70/31; T70/33; Coughtry A/2/28/176; Anna-Maria Falconbridge, *Two Voyages* 99.
[63] *The Star* [London], 4 April 1796.

damaged in a tornado the year before. For that year the unnamed seaman who wrote a diary of the occurrences had been stranded at the Île de Los, presumably with his crewmates.[64] Such events were common aspects of maritime life and trade.

Another ship was similarly condemned at Cape Coast Castle, "she being so eaten with worms for want of sheathing that by the time he came in our Road his pumps would scare keep her above water and his people were so jaded with pumping they refused to proceed any further." A delegation of captains and carpenters from other ships lying at Cape Coast gathered and "unanimously condemned her to be hauled ashore, because they found her plank so hollow that it was not capable of holding a nail or bear sheathing or doubling". At the time the letter was written the captain and his crew were lodged at the castle looking for further employment or transportation "home".[65] Despite the fact that Cape Coast Castle was a less salubrious setting than São Tomé, these men were more fortunate than the crew of the brig *John Bull* of Liverpool which was wrecked at the latter. This body of men were found "wandering about the island in a destitute and deplorable condition...emaciated by famine and sickness".[66]

That sailors were generally not hesitant to go ashore in Africa in many differing circumstances was a manifestation of both their cosmopolitan and rebellious nature, as well as a reflection on the strictures of maritime life. Sailors used the landmass of Africa as a place of relaxation just as they did all other locales, and the multiracial nature of seafaring, combined with the myriad cultural forms it embraced, meant that the stereotypes most Englishmen had about Africans were somewhat broken down through familiarity. Both of these factors were ultimately affected by the agency of the Africans with whom the seamen came into contact. It was these men and women whose employment created an important aspect of the multiculturalism of maritime life, and whose own resistance to the situation they found themselves in occasionally provided the backdrop for the unruliness of seamen.

When ships arrived at the coast to purchase slaves they employed a wide variety of African workers to supplement the labour provided by the

---

[64] Coughtry, *Papers* A/2/28/166–78.
[65] Bank of England: Humphrey Morice Papers, M8/4.
[66] Hugh Crow, *Memoirs of the late Captain Hugh Crow, of Liverpool; comprising a narrative of his life, together with descriptive sketches of the western coast of Africa; particularly of Bonny* (London: Frank Cass, 1970) 80.

seamen. Porters, cooks, washerwomen, canoemen, pilots and translators were all hired on a regular basis by visiting ships, producing groups of African men (and smaller numbers of women) who survived at least in part by earning wages from Europeans. Some of these men were slaves, commonly belonging to the European forts along the Gold Coast, but unlike those traded into the transatlantic market they were paid wages and could be sold only in most unusual circumstances. Just like the free waged seamen, the labour of non-free Africans who worked in the companies' forts "underlay the mercantile relations that bought and then transported 'chained slaves' to the American plantations". "In this sense", notes Ray Kea, "they were part of the Atlantic world's working class."[67]

The necessity of Africans to slave ships is illustrated fully by the log-book of the *Sandown* that sailed for Africa in 1793. The incapacity of its crew had already been exacerbated by the fact that some of the men were impressed onto *HMS Iris* in the dead of night before the vessel had even left Gravesend. The following excerpts reveal what happened on the African coast:

Monday 5th August 1793: Departed this Life Thomas Rawsley Aged 18 and at 3PM Departed this Life Humphrey Sullivan Seaman Aged 23 Years. Interr'd.

Wednesday 7th August 1793: Departed this Life Charles McLean Aged 25 Years.

Friday 9th: Ships company very Sickly. All hands sick but me and the Doctor and he complains very much. Got some of the Natives onboard and employ'd Men in Cleaning making fires and smoking the Ship between Decks fore and aft with Tobacco. All hands in a very bad situation.

Monday 30th: Got 2 White and 2 Black Carpenters to come & do the Necessary duty. Ships Carpenter very ill. 3 Grometas on board.

Thursday 3rd: 3 Carpenters 3 Grometas, Cooper and what are able employ'd at sundry necessary duty. One of the White Carpenters taken ill and gone.

Saturday 5th: Carpenters & Grometas at work . . . only 2 Seamen able to do Duty.

Saturday 12th October '93: Departed this Life, after a tedious illness of eleven Weeks, Marshal Fair Carpenter Aged 32 Years interr'd him.

Monday 14th: Grometas getting Ballast for the Ship.

[67] Ray Kea, ' "But I know what I shall do': Agency, Belief & the Social Imaginary in Eighteenth-Century Gold Coast Towns" David M. Anderson and Richard Rathbone (eds.) *Africa's Urban Past* (Oxford: James Currey, 2000) 169. Kea is referring specifically to the Danish companies, as described by Ferdinand Rømer, but his comments could equally apply to the labour of other European company slaves in the region.

Thursday 29th October 93: Employ'd a Black Cooper to trim the Casks.

Thursday 30th October: At 2AM Departed this Life John Rutherford Seaman Aged 32 Years. Interr'd him, paid the River Custom, and sold his Cloaths by Auction.[68]

Grumetes or "grometas" as the *Sandown*'s log named them were African seamen. By the later eighteenth century they had become familiar with European ways, and had often partially assimilated the visitors' culture as their own. Most spoke a hybrid form of a European language. The extent to which they were controlled by Europeans varied significantly along the coast – the most well known group, the Kru, were able to use their seafaring skills to largely protect themselves from becoming as subservient as other groups. Their maritime skills in most cases, although not always, saved them from the fate of the millions of Africans who were transported to the Americas to be sold as slaves.[69] In other locations Europeans controlled the *grumetes* more directly.[70] The African man John Newton hired in this role, "to go in the yaul, at 3 bars per month, if he behaves well" would seem to have had at least nominal freedom and negotiating powers over his labour.[71] The men from Bassam who helped a Liverpool ship fight a French privateer showed that they were not cowed, powerless workers. Having been offered "a considerable reward" by the captain if they would assist him, they retaliated and stole goods from the ship when the payment was reneged upon.[72]

African seamen could, and did, have an important part to play in the lives of English and North American seamen. Joseph Banfield, who would eventually make many slave trading voyages, owed his life to an African colleague. Banfield found himself stranded ashore on one of his first trips to Africa when the boat he was in overset, with the loss of one of his crewmates. Banfield and the black sailor managed to get to shore, but once there they realized that they "knew not wheare to go for Nothing but the wild wilderness was Exposed to our Vew, wheare the wild beasts Is Innumerable". They had, he lamented, "Not Even One Ragg Left to Cover Our

---

[68] National Maritime Museum, Log/M/21.

[69] Donald Wood, "Kru Migration to the West Indies" *Journal of Caribbean Studies* 26 (1981) 266–282. For the case of an African sailor, possibly Kru, who killed himself rather than be enslaved by his captain, see Macaulay, 'Journal' file 2, 5 October–12 December 1793.

[70] W. Jeffrey Bolster, *Black Jacks: African American Seamen in the Age of Sail* (Cambridge: Harvard University Press, 1997) 50.

[71] Newton, *Journal* 24.

[72] Macaulay, 'Journal' file 2, 5 October–12 December 1793.

Nakedness". When they were challenged by some armed men, the black sailor interceded and saved the situation, as well as both of their lives.[73]

Nicholas Owen, on his third slaving voyage, utilized *grumetes* as a means of escape from other Africans. After having been captured by some men at Sierra Leone in retaliation against a Dutch ship that had carried off some free people as slaves, Owen and his fellow crewmembers were held as prisoners. Doubtless showing symmetry between crime and punishment not shared by the Europeans, they were "secur'd by the natives, put in irons, and hove down on the ground in a barbarous manner" as well as being stripped of all their clothing. The men were "detained in irons for 4 or 5 days" before being freed by a European named Mr. Hall. Yet while it was a white man who had secured their freedom, Owen, his brother and his captain utilized free African seamen to make their escape. They put distance between themselves and their attackers by voyaging from Sierra Leone to the Cape Verdean island of Brava, with a crew that comprised of "10 or 12 black saylors, commonly known as gremetoes" who agreed to go with the white men for "a small demand of wages, not above 2 crowns pr. Month".[74]

Linguists, or translators, who were sometimes known as "gold takers" around the Anomabu area, were also crucial to vessels employed in the slave trade, and few British or North American slave ships spent their time on the coast without hiring at least one man in this role. Others hired several, or at least one at each of their major ports of call. William Snelgrave, for example, hired two linguists at wages of twelve "barrs" per month each, for a period of five months.[75] Some linguists, like the man known as Dick, made the Atlantic crossing with the ship, but most were simply employed by the ship for the duration of its stay.[76] Their role was multifaceted, as was their relationship with both the captive Africans and the foreign crewmembers. One slave merchant, who specifically mentioned to his chosen captain that he had to treat his translator "with familiarity and good nature", implicitly acknowledged their importance to the success of a slaving voyage.[77] The truth was that many were from the merchant hierarchy along the coast, and could be very influential. John McLeod, the surgeon of the *Trusty* in 1803, wrote in his account of the voyage that the

---

[73] Joseph Banfield, 'Journal of a Life at Sea', Huntington Library MS 57345.

[74] Owen, *Journal* 37–9.

[75] Bank of England: Humphrey Morice Papers, M7/11.

[76] Elizabeth Donnan, *Documents Illustrative of the Slave Trade to America* (Washington D.C.: Carnegie Institute, 1932) IV 370–2.

[77] Liverpool RO 380 TUO 4/7.

chief African merchant of Ouidah at that time had worked as a linguist in his youth.[78]

What is notable from the few accounts lowly seamen have left of their interaction with translators is that Africans holding this position sometimes had more power than the average tar. Peter Green, steward on the *Alfred,* was furiously beaten by his captain after he argued with the ship's translator, who was "A black woman, of the name of Rodney". The captain beat him, "using the lashes of the cat-of-nine-tails on his back at one time, and the double walled knot at the end of it upon his head at another". The captain wore out one whip in the process and had to replace it with another, and it was two and a half hours before the captain allowed the man to be taken down. He was later discovered to have died. One of Green's crewmates testified that "If Peter Green was not murdered, no man ever was".[79] Why Green was treated in this way is unknown, but as in the tale of Dick aboard the *Rainbow* in Chapter 2, it is clear that this linguist was considered particularly crucial to the security of a ship. It was supposed translators they could control the slaves and, in the last resort, to report on any planned uprising.

They could also try to arbitrate with the management of the sailors. One linguist, for example, stood by a cabin boy on board the *Africa* who was severely beaten after having been accused of stealing. This boy had been tormented all the way to Africa by the captain who told him that he was going to be given to the Africans as a sacrifice when the ship reached the River Gambia. The rest of the seamen apparently feared the captain's rule too much to protest the boy's treatment, but the linguist was prepared to do so. It was not enough to save the boy's life, however; he was sacrificed to the captain's sadism, the moral support of the African linguist unable to save him.[80] How ever atypical these stories may be, they reveal nonetheless that status and power aboard a slave ship did not always follow racial divisions.

---

[78] McLeod, *A Voyage to Africa* 35–6. Conversely, the *Pilgrim* was apparently loaned a young boy and girl from an African trader "to attend him in his Cabbin, and to act as interpreters". These were clearly not imbued with high status, and in fact were stolen away by Captain Prince to be sold for slaves. Macaulay, 'Journal' file 28, 15 July 1798–21 May 1799.

[79] Clarkson, *History of the Rise* 396–407.

[80] HCA 1/23. Another linguist, known as Acra, was interviewed in Africa in 1776 over the allegation that he had murdered two seamen, and was later sent to England to be tried for this offence. Acra stated that he had merely been part of a number of Africans who nailed a sailor "dead of the flux" into a coffin to be thrown overboard at Dixcove. HCA 1/58 f.118, see also f.112.

While translators often worked individually aboard ships, and could be said to have represented something of a labour aristocracy whose skills were held in high regard, potentially more significant to the success of a voyage, because of the sheer numbers required, were the canoemen employed by European ships. On the Gold Coast, where more than 300,000 African slaves were loaded onto British ships in the course of the eighteenth century, these men formed a distinctive and voluble part of the workforce. By 1790 there were between 800 and 1000 men who worked as canoemen in this region. Some were enslaved to the coastal forts but most were free.[81] There is no doubt that these men were an essential part of the European slave trade, and as such the visitors had in some ways moulded the labour market to their own requirements. Hugh Crow, for example, was approached by a canoeman brandishing certificates from other European captains testifying to his good character and hard work.[82] Others were recommended by word of mouth to other captains if they proved honest and industrious.[83]

Canoemen, as with other African maritime workers, became part of the larger picture of Atlantic citizens upon whose nominally free, paid labour, the slave trade's profits depended. Alexander Falconbridge recalled that the canoemen as well as the linguists often spoke English.[84] In addition, they formed a unique part of the trading network, for they often journeyed a short way down the coast aboard slave ships. The Slave Coast had impressively rough surf pounding its shores which European boats could not cross, so ships regularly hired skilled canoemen at the Gold Coast. Formed into crews of between fifteen and thirty men, they and their dugout canoes went on the slave ship to Dahomey and the surrounding areas, where they were used to transport goods and captive Africans between shore and ship in the hazardous conditions.[85] John

---

[81] Peter C. W. Gutkind, "Trade and Labor in Early Precolonial African History: The Canoemen of Southern Ghana" in Catherine Coquery-Vidrovitch and Paul E. Lovejoy (eds.) *The Workers of African Trade* (Beverly Hills, CA: Sage Publications, 1985) 25–49; Robert Smith, "The Canoe in West African History" *Journal of African History* XI:4 (1970) 515–33.

[82] Crow, *Memoirs* 78.

[83] Bank of England, Humphrey Morice Papers 7/9.

[84] ZHC 1/85 617.

[85] Robin Law, "Between the Sea and the Lagoons" *Cahiers D'Etudes Africaines* 29 (1989) 209–37; for examples see T70/30, where both Captain Benjamin Ashbrooke of the *Nancy*, and Captain Andrew Lesley of the *Bassnett* were both mentioned getting canoemen from Cape Coast Castle to take to Ouidah, and T70/30, which mentions Captain Chambers of the *Gascoyne* doing the same.

Adams chronicled that canoes and canoemen brought down from Cape Coast were "indispensable" to the slave trade between the ports of Ouidah and Lagos because the Africans native to that region "never passed the heavy surf".[86] Robert Norris wrote that European ships could not manage without the Fante canoemen they took to Ouidah to shuttle goods and people between ship and shore.[87]

Canoemen were crucial to slaving voyage throughout the eighteenth and into the nineteenth century. Captain Nathaniel Uring, who sailed in the reign of Queen Anne, praised the skill of the canoemen, noting that they "manage their Canows very dextrously". He had ventured to shore in one of their craft, crewed by eight men who had assured Uring and a fellow captain that "there was no Danger", and illustrated their skill in going close to the breakers, where they "laid still and watched for a Smooth, and then push'd forward with all their Force, paddling the Canow forward or backward . . . often lying between the Breakers" then "paddled with all their Might towards the shore".[88] Almost a century later surgeon John McLeod wrote a similar description, paying compliments to the canoemen's "skill in swimming and diving" by describing them as "literally amphibious". His main addition to Uring's description was in adding that the men sang or shouted a song as they went about the dangerous task of landing. McLeod explained his ship's decision to take canoemen and canoes from Cape Coast down to Benin by stating that in the latter area the sea was very rough, with such "tremendous surf" that "no European boat can live".[89]

While the African canoemen's skills were essential to slave ships, and their seafaring skills were acknowledged by many European observers, some were taken to the New World as slaves, after having been tricked or simply overpowered. [90] Such was the reprehensible duplicity upon which

---

[86] John Adams, *Remarks on the Country Extending from Cape Palmas to the River Congo* (London: Frank Cass, 1966) 238–40.

[87] Robert Norris, *Memoirs of the Reign of Bossa Ahaádee, King of Dahomy . . .* To which are added, the author's journey to Abomey the capital and a short account of the African Slave Trade (London: W. Lowndes, 1789) 61–2.

[88] Uring, *Voyages and Travels* 95–6.

[89] McLeod, *Voyage to Africa* 6–9.

[90] Despite the centrality of canoemen to the "success" of the voyage (that is, from the perspective of the investing merchant) there were many times at which free African canoemen were carried off by slave ships as captives, ZHC 1/84; ZHC 1/85; T 70/31. Prince Davie of Badagry, wrote to David Mill, governor of Cape Coast Castle, in May 1776 protesting that his canoemen were "thought carried off the Coast by one Johnson, who succeeded to the Command of the *Sneau Patty* of Liverpool", T 70/32. Duke Ephraim of Old Calabar forwent the appeal to the closest British rule when some of his canoemen were taken, but rather wrote straight to the owner of the guilty ship, James Rogers. "Sir, I

the slave trade functioned. A more salient question, however, than how captains and surgeons dealt with and perceived canoemen is how the common British or North American sailors interacted with them. As in all cases with the largely illiterate seamen, hard evidence is rarely to be found. However, the educated boy Samuel Robinson who went to sea on the slaver *Lady Nelson* in 1800 wrote an evocative memoir of going to shore with the African canoemen. "I liked it very much," he recalled. "It was very exciting to be perched on a puncheon of rum, or a bale of goods, while twelve naked savages were driving the canoe along like a weaver's shuttle – keeping time with their paddles to a chant struck up by the steersman, in which, at intervals, all hands would join." Robinson, who like many seamen could not swim, feared the landing as the canoe was overturned on the breakers approaching the beach, but soon came to like the excitement of it.[91]

Other seamen seem to have worked more closely with canoemen. Edward Rushton, who had joined a slave ship's crew at the age of eleven and later would become a prominent abolitionist, claimed that he taught one of his boatmen, Quamina, to read. The African is reported to have repaid this favour with his life when their boat overturned, saving Rushton at the cost of his own demise.[92] William Richardson termed one of his canoemen, known as Jack, "his right-hand man". Jack's fellow workers, too, Richardson noted were "a set of willing fellows" but Jack was the most useful because he had learned to speak some English. These men got their rations from Richardson's ship just like the rest of the crew, though what they made of the English ship's food can only be imagined. William Richardson wrote of these men throwing a libation of brandy into the sea at a piece of land known as "ju' ju' creek", and while he clearly thought this outlandish he still found the people "civil and obliging".

On the other hand the sailor's comment that he found the canoemen to be "harmless" is also telling, implying that he had been primed to find them just the opposite.[93] Similarly, Samuel Robinson's mention of Africans as "twelve naked savages" invokes the rhetoric of brutality,

been very good friend for that Ships [the *Jupiter*] and I have settle all my Debt & Family – I go for Corrott Island with Ships and Come Back for friend – So two my Cannow Man go aboard him to Sell Som Yams – he Carry of for nothing and Supose sold my people." C107/12.

[91] Robinson, *Sailor Boy* 76–7.

[92] Gomer Williams, *The Liverpool Privateers with an Account of the Liverpool Slave Trade* (London: Heinemann, 1897) 571.

[93] William Richardson, *A Mariner of England: An Account of the Career of William Richardson from Cabin Boy in the Merchant Service to Warrant Officer in the Royal Navy, 1780–1817* Colonel Spencer Childers (ed.) (London: John Murray, 1908) 53–4.

FIGURE 4. Canoes at Elmina.
From John Barbot, *A Description of the Coasts of North and South Guinea* in
Awnsham and Churchill, *Collection of Voyages and Travels* (London, 1752) vol. 5.
Reprinted by permission of New York Public Library.

primitiveness and incivility that Englishmen so frequently used to describe
Africans. The complexity and conflict of the two seamen's viewpoints
is clear, for Richardson referred to the Africans that he worked with
as his "motley crew".[94] In this most amoral of settings manifold ten-
sions and dimensions grew in such relationships, and developed in ways
which both bred personal tolerance and created hostility in the wider
setting.

   As Peter Gutkind's research shows, the attitudes of the high ranking
Englishmen stationed on the coast was highly ambivalent to the canoemen, with words such as "'rascally' 'impudent' 'ruffians' 'outcasts' and
'vagabondss'" frequently used to describe them. Such words, it will be
noted, are analogous to those the same men used to describe the European
lowly workers on slave ships. And the similarities do not end there, for
the canoemen of the Gold Coast were renowned for being peculiarly

[94] Robinson, *Sailor Boy* 77.

rebellious, a group of workers who early took on a self-conscious identity bounded by their job and the status it brought. Canoemen became notorious for being frequent protestors in both political and economic disputes. They, like their European and North American fellow maritime workers, were regarded as men likely to be protestors, known as *agyesemfo*, in disturbances along the African littoral. They rebelled in smaller less cohesive ways too, such as stealing and ruining goods by exposure to the seawater. Most commonly they rejected terms by withholding their labour, striking just like their English visitors in an attempt to secure better pay or conditions.

Living in an era of embryonic class-consciousness just as European mariners were, canoemen rejected being "abused, beaten or starved" because they were freemen, and demanded better wages as a primary condition of making freedom tenable. Like their paler skinned fellow seafarers, they too were at the forefront of labour protest.[95] In fact an early "strike" can be found in the annals of West African maritime labour history that pre-dates the radicalism of European and North American sailors mentioned in the first chapter. In January 1753 Fante canoemen ceased work for several days during the British building of Anomabu fort. It was the final stage of a labour protest in which the people of Anomabu had tried to make their British employers raise the wages they paid for the building of the fort. Even the resort to striking did not prove successful, however, as the British brought in workers from Cape Coast, so eventually forcing the Fante to work at the old wage or not at all.[96]

In the following decades revolutionary ideals circulating the Atlantic Ocean also spread to African workers. A crew of *grumetes*, for example, deserted at Sierra Leone after hearing of John Clarkson's declaration that any man who went there would be free, and "absolved from all obligation to serve his master". They also, as Zachary Macaulay noted in his journal, thought that in the colony they would be paid for their labour, and had run "to quit a situation when they earned nothing but their Clothes & victuals". They were sheltered, and armed, by the settlers. Macaulay was appalled, fearing that all other *grumetes* on the coast might fellow suit, and wrote, "I tremble at the consequence which may flow from this

---

[95] Gutkind, "Trade and Labor" 25–49; Peter C. W. Gutkind, "The Boatmen of Ghana: The Possibilities of a Pre-Colonial African Labor History" in Michael Hanagan and Charles Stephenson (eds.) *Confrontation, Class Consciousness and the Labor Process* (New York: Greenwood Press, 1986) 123–66.

[96] Margaret Priestley, "An Early Strike in Ghana" *Ghana Notes and Queries* 7 (1965) 25.

incident".[97] Here then were Africans who rebelled using the ideologies of the British settlement and the sympathy of the settlers, some of whom had been maritime workers, as the means by which to do so. The settlement of Sierra Leone had effects on the local Africans that the British government had not wholly intended.

The effects of interaction between black and white seamen and their shared ideologies was again shown in the settlement in the 1790s, when privateers captured numbers of African men, mostly free maritime workers. Macaulay's objection to these men being shipped to the Caribbean to be sold at slaves was not only because of his abolitionist beliefs. He wrote to Governor Rickets of Barbados warning him that it would be very dangerous to the island, in his opinion, to "import" "such a mass of jacobinical infection" as the slave ships' carried. "The free Blacks at Goree", he wrote, "by all accounts are become down right Democrats, and they therefore seem of all Men the least likely to submit to the yoke without wincing." The radicalism of the French and Haitian revolutions was clearly present on the coast of Africa, and in this case could have been shipped back across the Atlantic to the British West Indies.[98] Black seaman have left little knowledge of how these ideologies were assimilated into their own, but these historical fragments suggest that African seamen were very much part of the Atlantic working class by the 1780s and '90s.

African maritime workers were also, however, like their white counterparts, engaged in a trade in which the removal of the freedom of countless Africans was a requirement of their employment. Another time at which slave ships employed African workers was to prevent or suppress a slave revolt. The crew of the *Upton* was intensely grateful when a canoeman who could speak English warned them of an imminent revolt.[99] After a revolt on board the *Nightingale,* Henry Ellison recorded that the leaders were flogged by both, "the African's people and our boat's crew till we were all tired".[100] On the *Mermaid* in 1792 the captain and crew had already taken extreme measures before begging the assistance of the local Africans when their slaves attempted revolt. First they fired upon the slaves as they tried to break through the hatchings, and when that failed they twice tried to blow the slaves up by dropping lit gunpowder

---

[97] Zachary Macaulay, 'Journal', Henry E. Huntington Library, San Marino, California, MSS MY 418 file 1, 16 June–15 October 1793.

[98] Macaulay, 'Journal', file 25, 19 January–May 22 1798.

[99] ZHC 1/84 370.

[100] ZHC 1/84 369.

down into the hold. Only then did they send "Six of the Natives down with Cutlasses" and so secured the rebels' surrender.[101]

On the Rhode Island ship *Royal Charlotte*, about sixty of the captives on board rebelled after having been allowed on deck while the ship was in the Gabon River delta. Captain Frost was thrown overboard and then killed by a lance "which penetrated his Body" as he tried to climb back aboard. The first mate, who was sick in his cabin, had his throat cut, while an African "who belonged to the ship" was thrown overboard but swam ashore. Whether he alerted those on land as to what was happening, or whether it was apparent from the noise and confusion is not known, but soon after "some Blacks coming off in Canoes to retake the Vessels" caused the rebellious captives to fire at the canoes with the arms they had on the captured ship. Like most slave revolts this one did not end happily from the rebels' point of view. Around thirty of them were killed when the gunpowder on the ship caught fire and exploded. It was several days later before the surviving crewmembers and their African allies could retake the ship.[102]

At other times Africans were engaged to assist with subduing the revolts of seamen. Samuel Kitson later recalled before the High Court of the Admiralty that when he was captain of the *Fairy* in the early 1790s he had been forced to leave several of his men on the coast after they had taken the ship from him. He recalled that he had been woken one night by a noise on deck, and upon going up to see what was happening, was met by "[John] Slack with a pistol & saw [Charles] Berry with a Cutlass". He claimed, "they both told me not to come any further or I was a dead man." Kitson asked Berry if they had taken the vessel from him, and while confirming that he was indeed the captain now, he refused to answer Kitson's question regarding their intentions. Kitson attacked John Slack in an attempt to quash the insurrection, but it was only when some Africans arrived in a boat to assist that the rebels were overcome.[103] A similar case occurred on the *Gregson*, captained by William Corren, while it was anchored at Dixcove. When the sailors revolted they were only overcome with the help of "blacks and mulattoes" who came off from the shore to aid Corren.[104]

[101] C107/13.
[102] *Pennsylvania Gazette* 16 June 1763.
[103] HCA 1/61.
[104] HCA 1/64.

Captains evidently expected this kind of assistance from the free blacks and fort slaves, as the letter of William Buncombe, captain of the *Commerce* in 1783 testifies. In an urgent appeal to Richard Miles, governor of Cape Coast Castle, he was "sorry to write" that "my People has mutinied . . . they hove my Chief mate over board, and would myself and every Officer have they had it in their power". Buncombe had managed to overcome them, but asked Miles to immediately "send off a Canoe for three of these mutinous Rascalls [sic], with proper Blacks to take care of them, likewise send off half a dozen leg and hand Irons with Rivetts [sic]". As the ship successfully delivered slaves to St. Vincent's presumably Buscombe's petition was met with, and the mutineers removed from the vessel.[105]

Likewise, in the case of the runaway sailors that began this chapter, free Africans returned many to their billets. The peculiar mixture of race and class stratification on the African coast ensured the ransom of many to the profit of the few. African merchants, embroiled in the trade just as their European and North American customers were, would often help to regain crewmembers who had deserted. Many captains gratefully accepted this deal, as Africans were better acquainted with the terrain and possible places to hide, and in contrast to the Caribbean, where sailor desertion was actively encouraged, in Africa these men were still badly needed for the major purpose for which they had been employed. The six crewmembers of the *Phoenix* of Bristol, for example, who tried to escape in the ship's yawl were "taken up by Africans". Captain George Bishop apparently ordered them to be kept on shore chained by the neck, legs and hands, and to have only one plantain a day to eat. They all died there, the boatswain, Tom Jones, having become "raving mad".[106]

Similarly, from the *Thomas* in 1785 the boatswain and others from the crew tried to escape while on the coast of Africa, but were "brought back by the Black people". They allegedly had been very badly treated by the second mate of the ship, James Lavender, and ran to escape his reign of terror. After being returned to the ship by Africans they were put in irons and flogged.[107] William Snelgrave hired canoemen to look for a boy who ran away with his yawl. He noted in his accounts that he paid four shillings for their services in this matter, money that no doubt

[105] T 70/1549 part 1; Eltis, *CD-ROM*, 80883.
[106] Anon, *Extract* 95–6; Clarkson, *Substance of the Evidence* 39.
[107] HCA 1/25 f.147–9.

came out of the errant crewmember's wages if he was indeed caught.[108] John Newton likewise had two sailors, named as John Wilkinson and Richard Griffiths, who ran away with his yawl "tho chained" while they were anchored off the windward coast. Newton saw the boat lying on the shore and managed to reclaim it, but the men who had taken it were not so easily retaken, and Newton was forced to tell the local King that he would offer a reward to any men who captured them.[109]

From one of Alexander Falconbridge's ships "near a dozen" of the crew deserted in one of the boats with the intention of heading to Old Calabar. Taking with them what food they could from the ship and water, they "made a sail of a hammock and erected one of the boat's oars as a mast". When the captain returned from an evening of drinking onshore with some African traders and discovered them gone, he set off in search of the men. He did not find them. Later they were captured by some Africans, stripped, and marched across country from Bonny, where they had landed, to Old Calabar. While making their intended destination, the result was certainly not what they anticipated, for upon arrival at Old Calabar they were "sold" to Captain John Burrows of the *Lion*. Three of the men died on the march, while another five would be dead before the *Lion* delivered 315 slaves to Grenada. Another dying in the West Indies, only two of the runaways would ever make it back to Britain to explain why they had run. The list of corrections inflicted upon them was long according to their surgeon, Falconbridge. One would always bare the scars from where Captain McTaggert had set his dog on him.[110]

At other times both the ruling Europeans and the local African chiefs worked to returned escaped sailors to their ships. Some Africans were given a gallon of brandy for the capture of seaman William Lees who tried to desert from the *Duke of Argyle* at the Banana Islands [Sierra Leone]. Yet while the captain needed their services in this matter, it was fully his decision to look for a naval ship to send Lees home in.[111] The crew of the brig *Garland* were captured after Captain McQuoid "ordered the Gentleman in Charge of Annamaboe to catch the Sailors [and] put them in irons". Nine of the sailors were caught, whereupon McQuoid desired

[108] Bank of England: Humphrey Morice Papers, M7/6.
[109] Newton, *Journal* 68.
[110] Falconbridge, *Account* 44–5; Daniel P. Mannix and Malcolm Cowley, *Black Cargoes: A History of the Atlantic Slave Trade 1518–1865* (New York: Penguin, 1962) 149; Eltis, CD-ROM, 82258.
[111] Newton, *Journal* 17.

that they be held in Cape Coast Castle until they could be sent home on a man-of-war.[112]

The rule over seamen on the African coast thus involved both Europeans, and the Africans it bound up in its pressure for profit. The two worked hand in hand in governing the seamen, Africans often being used to capture the men, whose fate and punishment was then left to their compatriots. It is notable that it is from the diary of an African trader known as Duke Ephraim that we know of another case where Africans returned Englishmen who had deserted from a slaving vessel. Probably from the *Gascoyne*, they had run by taking a boat from the mate and had made off with "goods for fifteen slaves". There were certainly enough of them to warrant being termed the captain's "people", and enough to need a whole party of men to go in search of them.[113]

This need for the assistance of local Africans in running the slave trade was symptomatic of trading relations on the coast, for try as they might Europeans never succeeded in dominating the local Africans to the degree they wished. European command on the coast was always a series of negotiations, albeit bolstered by all too frequent recourse to the musket, because they needed African merchants in order to fulfil their main purpose. Without the cooperation of local sellers the trade in slaves ground to a halt. In fact it is notable that when the British did try and take control of part of the coast – in the form of the black settlement at Sierra Leone – this led to problems with returning runaway seamen to their ships. Zachary Macaulay wrote that seamen who had previously been captured and returned by Africans in exchange for a few gallons of rum now had a place to hide. To this fact Macaulay attributed slaver captains' hatred of the new settlement. The arrangement also proved unpopular with local Africans who were deprived of their usual bounty.[114]

The African limits to European power on the coast varied greatly over time and location, but were disregarded only at the outsiders' peril. Despite Walter Rodney's influential work suggesting that the Europeans always held sway – an appealing theory certainly, given the havoc the trade wreaked on the continent – it is clear that prominent Africans retained considerable influence. They stopped trade if they disliked the

[112] T 70/33.
[113] *The Diary of Antera Duke 1785–8* Daryll Forde (ed.) *Efik Traders of Old Calabar* (London: Oxford University Press, 1956) 38. Duke named the captain of the men who escaped as "Comesboch", probably referring to Peter Comberbach of the *Gascoyne* which sailed from Liverpool in 1785, Eltis, *CD-ROM*, 81559.
[114] Macaulay, 'Journal' file 1; file 21, 7 June 1797.

terms offered and played off the European powers against one another, just as the Europeans tried to rule by dividing the African groups. Just like the Europeans, they also resorted to more bloody and direct tactics, notwithstanding the settlers' powerful guns. Even on the Gold Coast where European dominance was most entrenched, the Africans were certainly not too cowed to protest their case.[115] Local Africans beat the Governor of Tatumquerry Fort in 1786, for example, after he had tried to levy a fine on them.[116] They also attached a British Army captain who stole their fish for his troops.[117]

Despite the African involvement in governing seamen in the event of them deserting, the judicial iron fist that controlled their behaviour on the coast was indisputably European. Violent domination could come from any quarter, but only the power of the British Navy to return seamen home to face the Admiralty courts constituted "real" authority as they saw it. This is not to suggest, of course, that they always accepted the courts' rule. Nevertheless it was considered to have a substance seamen certainly did not imbue the Africans' power with. In this respect then, final authority over the behaviour of the seamen employed on British slaving vessels resided in the hands of the highest-ranking man at the place the misdemeanour was alleged to have been committed. Commensurate with British influence, this control had a much firmer grip on the Gold Coast than elsewhere, supported as it was by the eight forts that stretched from Dixcove in the west to James Fort [Accra] and Prampram in the east. The hub of this dominance was Cape Coast Castle. The slave trade denigrated both the captives it was to sell as slaves and its lowly employees, and both were, to vastly different degrees to be sure, held ransom to profitability within the walls of the Gold Coast forts.

In the annals of Atlantic history the European forts along the West African coast represented an early incursion into the continent, and one that attempted to secure the interests of capitalism a place on Africa's accessible coast. This same system worked as a restraint on the activities, and freedom, of sailors. Although the forts were satellites of the home

---

[115] Walter Rodney, *How Europe Underdeveloped Africa* (Nairobi: East African Educational Publishers Ltd., 1972); Robin Law, " 'Here is No Resisting the Country': The Realities of Power in Afro-European Relations on the West African 'Slave Coast' " *Itinerario* 18 (1994) 50–64; Robin Law, *The Slave Coast of West Africa 1550–1750: the Impact of the Atlantic Slave Trade on an African society* (Oxford: Clarendon Press, 1991).

[116] Eveline C. Martin, *The British West African Settlements, 1750–1821* (London: Longmans, 1927) 51.

[117] T 70/33; TS 11/892.

nation's labour ethics, and this, theoretically at least, should have equated to free labour, in the late eighteenth century the issue was far murkier than that. British pressgangs found men not just for the ships that plied the Atlantic route in human beings, but also for the forts that administered the African end of the commerce. Masons, soldiers and carpenters were taken from the streets of London to toil at Britain's African coast forts just as men were crimped onto slaving vessels.[118] Even convict labour was temporarily toyed with as a possibility.[119] To some degree, therefore, the rulers of the forts attempted to reconstruct Britain's class structure in the heat and humidity of the tropics.

In this context then it is clear that the men who imprisoned sailors within the walls of Europe's coastal forts saw nothing ironic in this act. Archibald Dalzel, governor of Cape Coast Castle for a decade from 1792, wrote that seamen were sometimes held there for up to a year awaiting a ship to take them home to stand trial.[120] Given the seamen's rebellious nature, and the harsh conditions of slave trading, such occurrences were not isolated events. It was a regular responsibility of the coastal forts to function as temporary prisons for sailors, and many instances can be found in the historical record. In April 1771 Governor David Mill took two seamen from Captain Parkinson of Liverpool, and held them under the piracy act. They were taken back to England on *HMS Weazel* to stand trial.[121] Captain Arnold of the *Hannah* left a sailor named Darcy as a prisoner at Cape Coast Castle on 26 October 1800.[122] On the 10 September 1803 the captain of the *Sally* wrote in his logbook that he had "deliver[ed] the Boatswain Thomas Loren up to the Governor of Cape Coast Castle concerning a very serious case of Mutiny".[123] More unusually it was the first mate of the *Lady Nelson* who was put ashore at Winneba Fort for alleged insubordination.[124]

---

[118] Ty M. Reese, "Toiling in the Empire: Labor in Three Anglo-Atlantic Ports, London, Philadelphia and Cape Coast Castle, 1750–1783" unpublished PhD Dissertation, University of Toledo (1999) 79, 134.

[119] T 70/33; A. G. L. Shaw, *Convicts and the Colonies: A Study of Penal Transportation from Great Britain and Ireland to Australia and Other Parts of the Empire* (London: Faber and Faber, 1966) 43.

[120] I. A. Akinjogbin, "Archibald Dalzel: Slave Trader and Historian of Dahomey" *Journal of African History* vii:1 (1966) 67–78; T 70/33.

[121] BT 6/1.

[122] BT 98/62 f.195.

[123] C108/214.

[124] Robinson, *Sailor Boy* 53.

In some cases the crimes these men were accused of seem flimsy pretences, or at least within the usual range of behaviour at sea. Captain Corren sent some of his sailors, who were later taken home on HMS *Adventure,* to be imprisoned at Dixcove merely for the crime of drunkenness.[125] Others showed more propensities to real rebellion. The ten seamen from the *Antelope* of Bristol who were imprisoned in Cape Coast Castle later succeeded in escaping from Newgate jail in London while awaiting trial.[126] Captain William Sims of the *Hawk* took three seamen to Cape Coast Castle in 1781 to be imprisoned on the charge of "piracy" and "plotting to steal his ship away", but was later persuaded by the governor to take them back aboard his vessel. Other sources reveal, however, that the *Hawk* was captured by the crew and failed to make what its owners would have considered to be a successful voyage.[127]

This case clearly reveals the vastly superior range of freedom that seamen enjoyed over those to be shipped as slaves even while both were incarcerated in the coastal forts. Sailors might be considered to be mutinous and piratical with little evidence, but they had recompense to protest their innocence, and on occasion, as on the *Hawk,* took advantage of this leeway for their own gain. Incarcerated seamen had infinitely more hope for liberation than the African men, women and children packed into the stifling dungeons. The men imprisoned by Captain McQuoid of the brig *Garland,* for example, were freed by the fort governor because he feared that the sailors would come after him for wrongful imprisonment if they were later cleared of the charges by the Admiralty courts.[128]

Yet while the seamen enjoyed privileges that were undoubtedly dependent upon the fact that the majority of them were of European origin, the stereotype of their profession as rebellious still mattered to those who managed the forts. In 1788 so many seamen were held in Cape Coast Castle that governor Thomas Norris feared for the safety of the employees there, and hastened to send the prisoners home. "Accounts of their crimes attested on oath go with them", he wrote, which "will be sufficient to detain them in Prison untill the arrival of the Masters and Officers of the different Ships."[129] It seems most unlikely that Norris would have feared other groups of his fellow Englishmen in the same way that he feared the

---

[125] HCA 1/64; T70/33.
[126] HCA 1/20 f.35; HCA 1/55.
[127] BT 6/6; T70/32; Eltis, *CD-ROM,* 17900.
[128] T70/33.
[129] T 70/33.

rebelliousness of the seamen. Additionally, it is worth remembering that African seamen employed in the slave trade, if accused of mutiny, were held in the forts as prisoners not as captive slaves, as the case of Cudjoe, Quow and Joe revealed.[130] If race was the dominant factor deciding the freedom and treatment allowed those incarcerated in Britain's African coastal forts, its divisions were not absolute.

At other places along the coast British authority lacked the focal point that Cape Coast Castle, looming on the rocks, so obviously provided on the Gold Coast. The web of fiscal allegiances, however, extended much further. Along the Slave Coast, around the English fort at Ouidah (of which, incidentally, Archibald Dalzel was also the director in the late 1770s) lay numerous small factories built and sometimes fortified to protect their interests in the area.[131] The fort on James Island in the Gambia River remained the centre of British influence in that region, while all along the coast between Senegambia and the Gold Coast were dotted small British concerns. At some places the representative of English trade was merely a lone man who had settled in the area with aspirations to a fortune. In the Rio Pongo area, for example, a man from Liverpool named John Ormond was the dominant slave trader during the later decades of the eighteenth century.[132] Although these outposts lacked the powers of the major forts, nonetheless they were a part of the slave trade's network of influence, and as such helped reinforce the structures necessary for its successful fulfilment. That task included seeing that sailors remained in their billets on board ship, and subservient to the captain's regime. Where there was insufficient established British power, ships' captains and officers from other vessels acted to try and control seamen. As has been shown, sometimes this necessitated asking local Africans for help.

To sailors, therefore, the class and race-based aspects to their situation while they were in Africa definitively intersected, rather than the colour of their skin always being the decisive factor in their treatment and fate. English seamen did not shelter behind the privileges of European origin that the slave trade fashioned in the New World while they were at the African coast. Indeed they could not, for not only was overt racial stratification untenable in such an environment, the English merchants on the coast felt strongly that the class structure they had been born and bred

---

[130] See chapter 2.
[131] Law, "Here is no resisting" 55–6; Akinjogbin, "Dalzel" 70.
[132] Boubacar Barry, *Senegambia and the Atlantic Slave Trade* (Cambridge: Cambridge University Press, 1998) 78.

into should be upheld. For the majority of seamen who were of European origin, their ethnicity labelled them as foreigners in Africa, and in all probability as slave traders, with all the negative connotations this had inevitably come to have. To the European factors, merchants and captains who they came into contact with, however, their position was linked tenably to their lowly social status. Seamen, as has been argued, generally fell far outside the realm of respectable gentlemen. A certain dignity and respect had to be accorded the captain of a vessel, but for Jack, perceived as rowdy, intemperate and of humble birth, there was rarely such honour.

Rather than dining in ceremonious isolation in the closed apartments of the European castles, seamen of many nationalities interacted with African labourers, both slave and free, while they waited for their ship to be loaded with its wretched human cargo. Some found temporary homes with Africans, others just wanted to escape the rule of a callous captain and sought refuge among them. Doubtless each of the estimated 300,000 to 350,000 men who sailed to Africa as employees of slave ships had slightly different perspectives on their experiences there, and on the inhabitants of their ports of call.[133] This contact had some notable results, though. From it developed the habit of employing free African seamen on slave ships. It also imparted facets of African culture to the larger maritime understandings of the world.[134] The African seaboard was the scene of many distinct relationships and interactions which shaped part of the Atlantic frontier. They were infinitesimal aspects of the nature and meaning of race that the slave trade made, and constantly remade.

Many seamen, needless to say, were hardly sorry to leave the African coast with its strange diseases, threats of violence and misunderstood customs. As they were largely illiterate, we will in this case let an American

---

[133] Eltis, *CD-ROM.*

[134] See Peter Linebaugh and Marcus Rediker, *The Many-Headed Hydra: Sailors, Slaves, Commoners, and the Hidden History of the Revolutionary Atlantic* (London: Verso, 2000); Bolster, *Black Jacks*; Julius S. Scott, "Crisscrossing Empires: Ships, Sailors and Resistance in the Lesser Antilles in the Eighteenth Century" Robert L. Paquette and Stanley L. Engerman (eds.) *The Lesser Antilles in the Age of European Expansion* (Gainsville: University of Florida Press, 1996); Julius S. Scott, "Afro-American Sailors and the International Communication Network: The Case of Newport Bowers" Richard Twomey and Colin Howell (eds.) *Jack Tar in History: Essays in the History of Maritime Life and Labor* (New Brunswick: Acadiensis Press, 1991); and Julius S. Scott, "The Common Wind: Currents of Afro-American Communication in the era of the Haitian Revolution" unpublished PhD Dissertation, Duke University, 1986.

slave ship surgeon speak for them. He was so moved by his finally leaving the coast that he felt composed the following verse:

> Safely departed Afric's shore at last,
> I feel nor think on Dangers I have past,
> And hope in time, to reach my native shore,
> And never think of these dread voyages more.
>> William Chancellor, on board the 'Wolf',
>> January 1751.[135]

[135] Darold D. Wax, "A Philadelphia Surgeon on a Slaving Voyage to Africa 1749–1751" *Pennsylvania Magazine of History and Biography* 92 (1968) 465–93, quote 490.

5

Sea Changes

In 1805 Abubakr al-Siddiq, an educated Muslim boy born in Timbuktu, was captured during an African conflict, marched to the coast and sold to an English slave ship. Almost thirty years later, after having been freed from his bondage, he used the following words to describe his experience:

On that very day they made me captive. They tore off my clothes, bound me with ropes, gave me a heavy load to carry, and led me to the town of Bonduku, and from there to the town of Kumasi, where the king of Ashanti reigned, whose name is Osei. From there through Akisuma and Ajumako, in the land of Fanti, to the town of Lago, near the salt sea (all the way on foot, and well loaded.)

There they sold me to the Christians, and I was bought by a certain captain of a ship at that time. He sent me to a boat, and delivered me over to one of his sailors. The boat immediately pushed off, and I was carried on board of the ship. We continued onboard ship, at sea, for three months, and then came on shore in the land of Jamaica. This was the beginning of my slavery until this day. I tasted the bitterness of slavery from them, and its oppressiveness.[1]

It is uncertain whether Abubakr al-Siddiq meant that he had first experienced slavery from the men aboard the slave ship, or that he had first been a slave upon landing in Jamaica, but one thing is clear from this narrative: he did not regard his time as a captive in Africa to have been enslavement in the same way. When he was first taken on board the ship that would carry him far away, Abubakr al-Siddiq considered himself

[1] Ivor Wilks, "Abū Bakr Al-Siddīq of Timbuktu" Philip D. Curtin (ed.), *Africa Remembered: Narratives from West Africa from the era of the Slave Trade* (Madison: University of Wisconsin Press, 1967) 154–69, quote 162; I would like to thank Paul Lovejoy for the information regarding the more accurate spelling of his name.

FIGURE 5. Scene aboard a slave ship.
Reprinted by permission of New York Public Library.

to be an African man who just happened to have been captured. And so he was.

By the time he was offered for sale in Jamaica, however, as he himself implied, other forces had come into play. Those who crowded the docks of the New World eager to purchase workers saw the Africans who disembarked from the ship as already enslaved, with all the associations of both racial inferiority and ultimate possession that this state involved. They saw the men, women and children whom they purchased as ready-made slaves, separated from the people they had once been by the fact that they had arrived on their shores already reduced to the status of chattels. This was a device with which planters distanced themselves from the injustice of the system, as it allowed them to reconcile their notion of themselves as humane with their ownership of slaves. Somewhere in the Atlantic crossing captive had become slave. In the larger picture of transatlantic slaving, governed as it was by the "silver coins multiplying on the sold horizon", imprisonment became enslavement as it traversed the ocean.[2]

[2] Derek Walcott, *Omeros* (New York: Farrar, 1990) 149.

This fact is central to understanding the role of seamen in the middle passage, because conversion of African captive into slave required more than simply time spent below decks and transfer across the Atlantic: it also involved the preparation of sovereign people for sale at market as chattels. To the men and women chained below decks many of the acts of this conversion were simply stark, horrific terror, but they also formed part of the larger panorama that attempted to alter human being to thing. Sailors were employed not only to ensure that the ship crossed the ocean as safely and quickly as possible, as also intertwined in the fabric of their daily tasks was involvement in this process.

It was partially these trade-specific jobs that led seamen to loathe employment on slave ships, and to take a berth in any other trade in preference. Cleaning up after the human cargo, force-feeding those who had lost the will to eat, and controlling African men and women while they were washed and exercised were all tasks that seamen hated. Adding to the normal transportation aspect of seamen's work, this participation in production meant that tars were more deeply involved in this trade than in others in which they might find a berth. Even in the first and final legs of a triangular slaving voyage, cotton goods, guns, rum and sugar had simply to be packed onto the vessel, safely transported, and then off-loaded when they reached their destination. It was only in the middle passage that they were required to change the form of the "merchandise" as it crossed the seas.

Such work fundamentally changed the nature of seafaring by altering seamen's place in the economic scheme. One of the only other long distance trades where this occurred was whaling, which according to C.L.R. James gave whaleships a specific character. They were, he has written, "the modern world – the world we live in … industrial civilization on fire and plunging blindly into darkness".[3] According to James, therefore, sailors' involvement in production as well as transportation furthered their proletarianization. Slave production did not require additional skills or machinery, however, as whaling did; the additional work was guarding, punishing, quelling and generally trying to break a captive's spirit. The creation of slaves was not an industrial process but one of unmitigated, vehement coercion. Innate to the reduction of human to possession, and therefore in a sailor's labour, was the squandering of normal limits on

---

[3] C.L.R. James, *Mariners, Renegades and Castaways: The Story of Herman Melville and the World we Live in* (London: Allison and Busby, 1985) 51.

human behaviour. Aggression, violence, cruelty, and sometimes sadism were institutionalized in the trade's ethos.

A seaman's work drew him into the modern world through his employment in capitalist long distance trade, but at the same time it revealed to him in close relief what slavery – in its New World, chattel variant – entailed. In such circumstances these already brutalized men increasingly acknowledged that their own harsh treatment was unacceptable in terms of the new focus on free waged labour, under which they should theoretically have been controlled solely through payment or the withholding thereof. Violent subjugation was central to the system of slavery, as it had been since biblical times. Seamen came to question how, in this age of newly defined freedom, it could also be acceptable for them, as paid employees, to be treated in the same way. It is hardly surprising that sailors were at the forefront of battles for liberty – in its various guises – in this era, as their lowly paid employ had engaged them in the production of non-freedom.

While this understanding of slavery and freedom affected seamen's antiauthoritarianism in the long term, their immediate, knee-jerk reaction to the conditions of the slave trade often led them to abuse the captives over whom they had some authority. They took the violence demanded by their work as *carte blanche* to take out their pent up frustration on their captive cargo. The debasement value of the slaving merchants' economic demands regularly slipped into anarchic cruelty out on the open seas. In fact seamen (and captains for that matter) often took the violence mandated by the fiscal necessity of making human into slave and expanded it to a point at which it actually detrimentally affected the merchants' potential profits. Many of the ignominies heaped upon those who were forcibly transported across the Atlantic were not so much part of the attempted commoditization of mankind, but rather individual acts of callousness by sailors.

As Claude Meillasoux and Orlando Patterson among others have argued, slavery is, at base, a process. An essential element of the first stage of enslavement is that "the slave is violently uprooted from his milieu."[4] Thus part of the attempted reduction of human being to slave was inherent in the work of seamen, for it was their tending of the sails to catch the prevailing winds that took their African cargo into societies in which

---

[4] Orlando Patterson, *Slavery and Social Death: A Comparative Study* (Cambridge: Harvard University Press, 1982) 38.

they would be perpetual outsiders. Their "liminality" increased with each
nautical mile traversed. Their marginality grew in direct relation to the
distance from their homes until the final rupture of sale. Alexander X.
Byrd writes that "the men and women who set off from one side of the
Atlantic were not the same men and women who arrived at the other".[5]
Just so, for somewhere between "home" and "exile" the status of the men
and women changed.

There was more to the first stage of enslavement than simply transfer
to the enslaving region. Captives had to be rendered "socially dead". For
this to occur they needed not only to be separated from all that they knew,
but also to be stripped off their power and personal honour.[6] What was
significant about these tasks was that while the "natal alienation" of the
captives was contained in a sailor's usual terms of employment, the ritual
disempowerment and dishonouring went well beyond what was generally
required of a tar employed in any other trade. It is in understanding this
that insight can be gained into why sailors loathed the slave trade above
all others: they simply reviled the additional and very unpleasant tasks
required by the business of "making" slaves. The removal of a human
being's honour and power, moreover, encapsulated the truth of all slave
regimes: violence was their central tenet, the only way that the state of
slavery could be sustained.

In the eighteenth century British transatlantic trade the transformation
of person to slave was couched in the rhetoric of economics, but its over-
arching consequence was the same as in other slave systems. Ankles were
shackled and hands bound to stop a valuable article of trade from escaping, but the loss of personal power and self-will was evidenced in every
bolted limb. The shaving of heads and removal of any clothing may have
been considered necessary for health reasons, but these acts nevertheless
signified loss of independence just as surely as those things do today upon
entry into the army, prison, or a host of other institutions where indi-
viduality is not prized. The next stage of slavery, the introduction of the
slave to the enslavers' community, took place off the ships and after sale,
and thus beyond the duties of the seamen. It was in this period "between
capture or first sale and the acquisition of a new social identity" that "the

---

[5] Alexander X. Byrd, "Captives and Voyagers: Black Migrants Across the Eighteenth
Century World of Olaudah Equiano" unpublished PhD Dissertation, Duke University
(2001) 131.

[6] Patterson, *Slavery and Social Death* especially 38–51; Emma Christopher, "The Slave Trade
and Social Death" unpublished MA Dissertation, University College London (1995).

slave was unambiguously a commodity".[7] A sailor's task, therefore, was to render them socially dead without worrying about the intricacies of re-socializing them.

Being reduced to the state of a possession had a whole new horror in the transatlantic trade because commodities have relevance in capitalist society with which they are not otherwise imbued. At other times and places in history to be alien, an outsider, was enough to make a person a slave, but in the plantation economy of the Americas, allied as it was to capitalism, slaves had to be exhibited at market as desirable possessions. This was a world in which there was fetishism about owning commodities. It is not co-incidental that one of the major differences between autochthonous West African slavery and its New World counterpart was in the prevalence, and ease, with which masters sold their bondsmen. As Walter Johnson has illustrated wonderfully in *Soul By Soul: Life inside the Antebellum Slave Market* a central feature of slave life in the American South was the close proximity of the slave market. Slaves in the plantation South were "people with a price".[8] American slavery was chattel slavery, and in their reduction to possessions, slaves suffered the indignity of being merchandise in a society obsessed by the ownership of commodities.

Thus when Olaudah Equiano wrote of captive slaves aboard slave ships asking each other "if we were not to be eaten by those white men with horrible looks, red faces and long hair", he may have been wrong about the nature of abhorrence he was to face, but not necessarily in the scale of it. Johnson's thesis that "the slave trade was understood by slaves as threatening literal death" as well as social death is relevant in the Atlantic setting. In the traditional sense, clearly the primary purpose of slave trading was not cannibalism. Indeed, the valuable African human merchandise, variously known as black ivory or black gold, was far too prized and profitable to be eaten by men for whom salt pork and ships' biscuit were the normal fare, even if they had so desired. Although in times of dire necessity cannibalism was resorted to at sea, the type of "consuming" to which Stephan Palmié refers in his work is that of the voracious appetite New World planters came to have for slaves. Perhaps Mungo Park chose a better phrase than Equiano when he spoke of the fear among Africans that Europeans purchased them "for the purpose of

---

[7] Igor Kopytoff, "The cultural biography of things: commoditization as process" Arjun Appadurai (ed.) *The Social Life of Things: Commodities in Cultural Perspective* (Cambridge: Cambridge University Press, 1986) 65.

[8] (Cambridge: Harvard University Press, 1999) esp. 1–18.

devouring them", for that is exactly what the plantations of the Americas did. They devoured men, women and children as labourers, their demand not sated as profits grew and mortality rates remained high.[9]

Employed in the (attempted) reduction of men, women and children into these fetishist products, seamen, themselves suffering as the result of the same economic forces, hated this additional and particularly unpleasant labour. It is rather ironic that William Littleton, who had worked as the mate of a slave ship in the 1760s, in an attempt to justify the trade before the Houses of Parliament, stated "the sails requiring but little attendance – therefore the sailors are wholly employed in their attention to the slaves".[10] Aside from the fact that the rigors of the job in times of severe weather or crisis could be extreme, Littleton's point is in some ways very revealing. Sailors were aggrieved and hated the slave trade partly because many of the tasks they had to perform were not related to a seafaring life. In fact in some ways the basic circumstances of seafaring were antithetical to slave trading. On the *Andrews*'s voyage from Gambia to Charleston there was a gale so severe that they were "Obliged to Batten down Our grateings [sic] fore and aft". Engaged in saving the ship and the normal activities of sailing during trying conditions, they could pay none of the usual attentions to the slaves. Twenty suffocated during the crisis, and the chief mate reported that the "Remainder [were] mutch Impeaired, so that wee Came to A Very bad markett".[11]

In order to secure a healthy profit for their employers, therefore, seamen had to act as warder or guard as much as skilled mariner, and as the overseers of the transformation into a slave ready for market. "I considered myself as a sort of jailer" wrote one slave ship captain.[12] Sailors were indubitably tough salts, often ready with their fists and partial to the bottle, but they were also by all accounts proud of their seafaring skills. To have the kind of duties that Littleton stated, and which the *Andrews*'s voyage was so tragically lacking, can hardly have been popular, especially not when those duties were so execrable.

A good example of the process of commoditization was central to the running of the slave trade. Male slaves' movement was severely restricted

---

[9] Stephan Palmié, "A Taste for Human Commodities: Experiencing the Atlantic System" Stephan Palmié (ed.) *Slave Cultures and the Cultures of Slavery* (Knoxville: University of Tennessee Press, 1995) 40–54; Mungo Park, *Travels in the Interior of Africa* (London: Eland, 1983) 244, quoted also in Palmié "A Taste" 48.

[10] ZHC 1/82 182.

[11] Banfield, "Journal".

[12] John Newton, *Out of the Depths* (Grand Rapids, MI: Kregel Publications, 1990) 115.

by the iron fetters bolted around their ankles, and sometimes their wrists and necks, ostensibly because of the threat of revolt. In thus chaining them, however, they were also often forced to wallow in their own excrement because they could not reach the buckets provided as toilets. In the interest of security basic human dignity was denied them. Those who experienced slave ships as both free and white used the noxious smell, moreover, to imply that the captives were "beast-like" in some way. The surgeon of the *Brookes,* for example, stated that the air was so stale below decks that the prisoners gasped for breath like "expiring animals".[13] The only halter on their degradation was that they had to be kept alive, and thus seamen had to descend into the malodorous hellholes to clean. One man who had worked as a sailor before the mast remembered that "the floor of their rooms, was so covered with blood and mucus which had proceeded from them having flux, that it resembled a slaughter-house... I was so overcome by the heat, stench and foul air that I nearly fainted".[14]

Merchants and ship-owners demanded some of the work that implicitly enshrined this reduction – explicitly it was purely for the sake of profits – in the instructions they issued to their chosen captain. They wrote of the standards they expected of cleanliness, and of the necessity of washing the slaves. Such work, of course, was not performed by the captain himself but passed onto lowly crewmembers. Captain Edward Williams was ordered by the merchant/owner of his voyages, Robert Bostock, in 1787 and 1788 to "take care to have them [the slaves] well cleaned".[15] David Tuohy issued more specific instructions to one of his captains, William Spurs of the brig *Ranger.* Tuohy ordered Spurs to supervise "washing the beams and over the slaves heads with vinegar three times a week... while the slaves are twined up".[16] While at sea, sailors were employed in "scraping the slave rooms, smoking with tar, tobacco and brimstone for two hours, afterwards washed with vinegar".[17] On the *Britannia* in 1768 it would later be reported that the slaves were so crushed in their hold that "the chief mate, boatswain, and an active young man, were employed in stowing or packing them together; such as adjusting their arms and legs".[18]

---

[13] ZHC 1/84 84.
[14] ZHC 1/84 368.
[15] Liverpool RO 387 MD 54: Letter book of Robert Bostock.
[16] Liverpool RO 380 TUO 4/2: Papers of the *Ranger.*
[17] Quoted in Peter Earle, *Sailors: English Merchant Seamen 1650–1775* (London: Methuen, 1998) 78.
[18] Clarkson, *Substance of the Evidence* 14.

Similarly when a ship neared its American destination the sailors were employed in cleaning the slaves and getting them ready for sale. As the ship approached land Alexander Falconbridge recounted, "care is taken to polish [the slaves] for sale, by an application of the lunar caustic [silver nitrate]".[19] Captain Bowen of the *Russell* said that slaves were "prepared for sale" by mixing gunpowder with sulfur and lime juice and then this was "rubbed hard into the parts of the skin that are affected [by craws] by an iron hoop. Caustick [sic] is also applied to the yaw spots, to burn them off".[20] Captain Bowen evidently sought to get the best price by making his "cargo" appear healthier than they were.

In the detailed log of the ship *Mary* there are numerous repetitive entries to show that the crew was busy with tasks that were peculiar to the slave trade. On Wednesday, 3 February 1796 the sailors were "Claring [the] Mens room out" after eleven slaves had been purchased in a day of "Brisk Trade". The following Tuesday they were employed "tending Slaves". Three days later, as the ship was travelling down the Gold Coast, they were again cleaning the men slaves' room. The following week as the carpenter made gratings for the men's and women's rooms they were still "Imployd in tending Slaves". This was followed by a day where they were busy "overhauling... potatoes and cleaning out the Womens Slave room". Tellingly, the next week as the number of slaves increased, they were "Imployd onbord in tending Slaves and Over hauling our Arms". And so it goes on, with frequent entries such as "Cleaned out the Slave rooms fore and aft" and "Emp[loye]d Cleaning Slave Rooms and tending Slaves".[21] Given that the average length of stay on the African coast was seven months, seamen doubtless regarded this work as monotonous and odious.[22]

Many seamen considered their skills and no doubt their macho bravery to be insulted by the rather effeminate task of cleaning up after slaves, but such precautions were essential to the lowering of the mortality rate among slaves in the eighteenth century British trade. As such, therefore, they were also a vital factor in ensuring the merchants' profits. Two historians recently noted that in the British slave trade "Cleanliness was

[19] Alexander Falconbridge, *An Account of the Slave Trade on the Coast of Africa* (London: James Phillips, 1788) 29.
[20] Clarkson, *Substance of the Evidence* 45.
[21] Elizabeth Donnan, *Documents Illustrative of the Slave Trade to America* (Washington D.C.: Carnegie Institute, 1932) III 360–78.
[22] Stephen D. Behrendt, "Crew Mortality in the Transatlantic Slave Trade in the Eighteenth Century" *Slavery and Abolition* 18 (1997) 49–71.

FIGURE 6. "Scene of the Blood Stained Gloria". From Richard Drake, *Revelations of a Slave Smuggler* (New York, 1860). Reprinted by permission of New York Public Library.

not only next to godliness, it was the handmaiden of commerce; it was worth pursuing for its own sake".[23] As others have argued that over forty per cent of slave deaths can be attributed to gastrointestinal diseases – contemporaneously often commonly lumped together as "flux" – cleaning and providing uncontaminated food can be seen to have been a major part of the success of a voyage from a merchant's point of view.[24] This is true even if the absolute causes of such diseases and the preventative measures against them were unknown at the time. Thus such chores were not just random necessities, but an essential part of the job of the seaman as seen from the point of view of their employer, the merchant. If job descriptions had existed for seafarers in the eighteenth century these duties would have featured prominently. In the bigger picture, however,

[23] Robin Haines and Ralph Shlomowitz, "Explaining the Mortality Decline in the Eighteenth-Century British Slave Trade" *Economic History Review* (2000) 262–83, quote 275.

[24] See Richard H. Steckel and Richard A. Jensen "New Evidence on the Causes of Slave and Crew Mortality in the Atlantic Slave Trade" *Journal of Economic History* 46 (March 1986) 57–77.

keeping the slaves in the appalling conditions that required these tasks was part of their attempted subjection into slavery.

It is patent that not many sailors, who were renowned as hard men, nurtured sympathy towards those they perceived to be the cause of these hated chores. Two sailors from the ship *Africa* reported that "an elderly [slave] woman" who was suffering from dysentery had done "some dirt upon deck" for which she was whipped until "her back was as raw as beef steak". She "in her own Language begged Pardon" and then tried to throw herself overboard to escape the whipping but a member of the crew jumped after her and took her back on deck to whip her some more. She was then thrown back overboard.[25] Cleaning out the faeces from the women's and men's rooms, a job which was unpleasant at the best of times, cannot be imagined when a cargo of say, three hundred or more slaves crammed in a dark, airless room was suffering from dysentery – a common occurrence on slave ships. One seaman claimed that he had only made one voyage in the slave trade "because I could not bear with the nasty filthiness".[26]

Of course the misery for those who lived in this mess incomparably exceeded that of those who just had to clean it, but it is not hard to imagine too that sailors, men who at the best of times exhibited little in the way of tenderness, often lost their tempers when faced with the non-stop task of clearing up the excrement of those they considered to be their cargo. Surgeon Ecroyde Claxton recounted that sailors "inhumanely beat" the captive Africans "either with their hands or a cat [-o'-nine-tails]" when forced to clean up their mess.[27] In fact the work did pass from utterly unpleasant to thoroughly dangerous given that hygiene was minimal and that most of the major gastrointestinal killers are passed fecal-orally. Cruelty not sympathy abounded. A slave ship's ghastly hold was not a suitable environment for human beings, much less was it conducive to humanity.

Some of the seamen's work was clearly intended to depersonalize the captives, to ritually dishonour them. One entry in the *Mary*'s journal reads "Men Emp[loye]d tending Slaves, Shaving and triming them etc etc, also making mats and Sundry Necessaries."[28] A sailor recorded how he had been involved as "the heads of all slaves, without distinction of age or

[25] HCA 1/23.
[26] ZHC 1/87 121.
[27] ZHC 1/87 34.
[28] Donnan, *Documents* III 360–78.

sex, were shaved and they were then scrubbed with sand while standing in the water".[29] Another seaman noted, "began yesterday to shave them all and this morning finished".[30] The log of the *Sandown* states that on Thursday, 10 April 1794 the men were "Employ'd cleaning ship shaving slaves & filling up salt water".[31] A similar task was the removal of any clothing the Africans might be wearing when they first embarked on the ship.[32] Slave ship captains often claimed these things were done solely for health reasons, but Job Ben Solomon was closer to the truth when he remembered the shaving of his hair and beard, prior to his embarkation on a slave ship, as "the highest Indignity".[33] Carrying out these tasks, a seaman's identification with his own occupational group increased, and his pride in a tar's clothing and hairstyle became the symbols not only of his work and his skills, but also of his free status in the Atlantic world. In executing the removal of a captive's identity – central to the loss of his or her personal honour – seamen began more than ever to value the characteristics considered unique to maritime workers.

Similarly, sailors' body markings, tattoos, which represented a pride in their job and their ties to home, came to have added significance. They were in stark contrast to the African captives' branding marks which signified their bodily ownership by another, and their imposed removal from the tribes whose markings they might also bear. A sailor's tattoos were proudly worn "vocational badges" often showing ships, mermaids or anchors. Moreover, while a slave's markings represented his forced alienation from his previous existence, a sailor's tattoos often declared his love for a woman back home, his country or his god.[34] A seaman's tattoos indicated that he sold his labour on the open market; a slave's branding marks showed that his or her whole being was to be sold in the same way. It is probably not co-incidental that Kru seamen from Sierra Leone used tattooing as a means of displaying to all that they were free workers and not enslaved cargo.[35]

[29] Richard Drake, "Revelations of a Slave Smuggler: Being the Autobiography of Capt. Richard Drake, an African Trader for Fifty Years – from 1807 to 1857" George F. Dow, *Slave Ships and Slaving* (Westport, CT: Negro Universities Press, 1927) 206.

[30] Quoted in Earle, *Sailors* 78.

[31] National Maritime Museum Log/M/21.

[32] ZHC 1/82 220.

[33] Donnan, *Documents* I 21.

[34] Simon P. Newman, "Reading the Bodies of Early American Seafarers" *William and Mary Quarterly* 55 (1998) 59–82; Ira Dye, "The Tattoos of Early American Seafarers, 1796–1818" *American Philosophical Society Proceedings* 133 (1989) 520–54.

[35] Diane Frost, "Migration and Work: The Making of West African Kru Sailors" unpublished paper presented to the Southern Labor Studies Conference, Miami, April 2002;

Just as branding and shaving had a theoretical cause in addition to the more obvious economic one, so barbarity was not an unfortunate consequence of the slave trade but rather one of its founding principles. Violent subjugation was central to the process of commoditizing human beings. Putting a whip in a sailor's hands was the regular method of processing the debasement of African captives. One required part of their daily duty, for example, was to flog the slaves until they danced. Captives were forced to do this, at least in fine weather, ostensibly because the physical and mental health benefits of jumping up and down were considered to be great. Seamen themselves often danced on board ship as entertainment, but captives were made to do so against their will and often while shackled. Numerous sailors would later recall this part of their work when the slave trade was investigated by parliament. John Ashley Hall of the *Neptune* of London admitted that the slaves were forced to "dance" by using the cat-o'-nine-tails. Hall though was perceptive and honest enough to mention that "what I have heard called dancing" could more aptly be described as "being made after each meal to jump up and down upon the beat of a drum". It was not, he added, "to music of their own".[36]

Such practice was common throughout the eighteenth century. Slaver surgeon Alexander Falconbridge recalled that slaves who refused to "dance" were flogged, and that when the drums wore out they improvised with the buckets their food had been served in.[37] On 7 July 1756 the captain of the slaver *Venus* bought a "Negro Drum for slaves" as a tool of this peculiar form of torture.[38] Clement Noble stated that the slaves were made to dance "as best they can in irons, hands and legs tied together."[39] Ecroyde Claxton of the *Garland* in 1788 reported that the African captives were "compelled to dance by the cat" even when they had "the flux, scurvy, and such edematous swellings in their legs as made it painful to them to move at all".[40] The dual needs of keeping men and women captives alive, and of breaking their spirit meant that sailors were required to work as jailers or guards, and to subjugate through the

see also Diane Frost, *Work and Community among West African Migrant Workers since the Nineteenth Century* (Liverpool: Liverpool University Press, 1999).

[36] ZHC 1/85 519.
[37] Falconbridge, *Account* 23.
[38] New York Historical Society, Slavery Collection Box 2, Folder 14: Papers of Samuel and William Vernon, Trade Book of the Snow *Venus* 1756–7.
[39] ZHC 1/84 119.
[40] Anon., *An Extract of the Evidence delivered before a Select Committee of the House of Commons in the years 1790–1791* (Edinburgh, 1791) 39.

use of the same instruments of punishment that were frequently used on themselves.

For similar reasons, and with similar results, sailors also flogged the captives until they sang. What the Africans sang, though, could not be controlled by any means, and were more "melancholy lamentations of their exile" than the upbeat morale boosting tunes for which their captors hoped.[41] Few captives, noted a man who was a passenger on a slave ship, would sing or dance without at least the threat of a whipping, and even then some "were content to have the *cat* smartly applied across their shoulders several times, before they would so much belie their feelings as to make merry, when their heart was sad".[42] Surgeon Claxton, when asked whether the slaves on his ship ever "amused" themselves by singing, answered:

I believe they very seldom amuse themselves by it – they were ordered to sing by the captain, but they were songs of sad lamentations. The words of the songs used by them were Madda! Madda! Yiera! Bemini! Bemini! Madda! Aufera! that is to say, they were all sick, and by and by they should be no more; they also sung songs expressive of their fears of being beat, of their want of victuals... and of never returning to their own country.[43]

Seamen saw that the exceptional singing and dancing performances they had sometimes witnessed in Africa had been reduced to a parody of painful shuffling and moaning. Rather than feeling compassion for those under their control, this sordid diminution sometimes induced derision among seamen. The 1790 poem "The Sorrow of Yomba", penned by an unknown slave reads:

> At the savage Captain's beck,
> Now like brutes they make us prance:
> Smack the Cat about the Deck,
> And in scorn they bid us dance.[44]

The last sentence is especially revealing. Scorn, disdain and mockery marked the sailors' attitude towards captive Africans at such times. The proud men and women for whom singing and dancing had central cultural

---

[41] Falconbridge, *Account* 23.
[42] Rev. John Riland, *Memoirs of a West India Planter* (London: Hamilton, Adams and Co., 1827) 52.
[43] ZHC 1/87 36.
[44] Rare Book Collection, Cornell University, Ithaca, NY; quoted in Geneviève Fabre, "The Slave Ship Dance" Maria Diedrich, Henry Louis Gates Jr. and Carl Pedersen *Black Imagination and the Middle Passage* (New York: Oxford University Press, 1999) 37.

roles infused with meaning had been reduced to jumping up and down laden with ironware in answer to the whip. Themselves largely at the mercy of the ship's officers, sailors saw that they had physical power over the African captives.

The savage inhumanity that was sanctioned in sailors' work did not end with this travesty of singing and dancing. They also had to prevent the captives from committing suicide, and could do so by virtually any means. Such work illustrated another peculiarity of slave trading to sailors, because no other kind of "goods" listed on the bill of lading ever resisted in the innumerable and diverse complex and clever ways that human cargo did. No other attempted self-destruction because they "prefer[ed] death to slavery".[45] On the other side of this divide, seamen had their own incentive for preventing suicide, for, as mentioned in Chapter 1, if a captive managed to jump overboard, the sailors who should have been on watch duty could be charged the computed cost.

Those Africans who lost the will to live and stopped eating – which could have been because the food was often strange to them and anyway barely edible, or because of depression, seasickness or shock – were simply forced to eat. Often captains and their crews believed that the slaves were deliberately starving themselves as a means of escape, and had very little sympathy indeed for their predicament.[46] Sailor John Radcliffe later recalled how on the *Moth* food was pushed down a slave's neck with the handle of the cat-o'-nine-tails. "She was an elderly woman", he remembered of the victim.[47]

This was no ad hoc occurrence: the trade in slaves had adopted its own assortment of tools with which to subjugate. Captive Africans who refused to eat would be flogged until they did, or sometimes the *speculum oris* was used on them. This was an implement of torture, initially invented as a remedy for lockjaw or tetanus, which was readily available in shops in Liverpool and London at the height of the trade.[48] Isaac Wilson, who

[45] Olaudah Equiano, *The Interesting Narrative of Olaudah Equiano or Gustavus Vassa, the African* (Norwich: Printed for, and sold by, the Author, 1794); reprinted in Henry Louis Gates Jr. and William L. Andrews (eds.) *Pioneers of the Black Atlantic: Five Slave Narratives from the Age of Enlightenment, 1772–1815* (Washington, D.C.: Civitas, 1998) 221.

[46] William D. Piersen, "White Cannibals, Black Martyrs: Fear, Depression and Religious Faith as Causes of Suicide Among New Slaves" *Journal of Negro History* 62 (April 1977) 147–59. In contrast to the crew of the boat, the surgeon sometimes did express dismay at the treatment of slaves in forcing them to eat in this way.

[47] HCA 1/23 f.52.

[48] W.N. Boog Watson, "The Guinea Trade and some of its Surgeons" *Journal of the Royal College of Surgeons of Edinburgh* 14 (1969) 203–14.

sailed on slave ships during the 1780s related that he had once tried to force a young male slave to eat firstly with "mild means" then by whipping him, then with the *speculum oris*, and finally with a bolus knife, but to no avail. Wilson stated that he had often to whip them to get them to eat, yet "in the very act of chastisement they looked up to him with a smile, and in their own language have said, 'presently we shall be no more'".[49] Unfortunately, for each captive who resisted in such a manner, there was a seaman willing to stretch the margins of his inhumanity ever more.

Even the normal boundary of halting torture prior to a victim's death was not insuperable, as sometimes murder was part of a sailor's work. There is little doubt that many of the captives must have thought themselves in hell, for the trade led to some simply horrendous inversions of reasoning, and no less often to the abandonment of human compassion. In the same wooden craft where men and women were cast to their deaths so that merchants could claim on their insurance policies, others were forced to eat so as not to deny the opportunity for sale. Attempted suicides were dragged back on board and murdered for trying to cheat the merchant of his profit, as in the twisted logic of the officers and crew this was their prerogative alone. Sometimes a slave was killed as an example to the others not to rebel or disobey, or sometimes one of the crew's acts of torture simply went too far and a captive died.

At other times a captain coldly decided that it would be more profitable for the slaves to be dead than alive. The result of this peculiar mixture of an ancient labour form with modern economics, seamen were sometimes employed in the task of throwing slave men, women and children to their deaths for financial reasons. The rationale was simple: insured as merchandise at such institutions as Lloyd's of London, slave losses by drowning would be paid for by the insurers, but those lost aboard ship to sickness and disease were not covered. Naturally, the ones who did the work of throwing the men and women overboard were the seamen whose paid employ such reprehensible action encompassed, and whose own billet was not insured, being of a far more easily replaceable nature. It represented the ultimate in the reduction of human to commodity in the modern world, and illustrated to all the crass sacrifice of Africans to Western riches.

By far the most well-known case of live slaves being thrown overboard was that of one hundred and thirty-two slaves alleged to have been drowned from the *Zong* in 1781. Originally Dutch owned, an unknown

---

[49] Anon, *Extract of the Evidence* 45.

Bristol slave ship took it as a prize and then sold it on to the owners of another slaver, the *William,* while they were all still at the African coast. The *William*'s surgeon, Luke Collingwood, was made the captain of the *Zong,* taking possession of not only the vessel but also the two hundred and forty slaves that were already aboard, plus sufficient trading goods to purchase many more. Finally, the ownership resolved and the trading done, the vessel departed on 6 September 1781 with a total of four hundred and fifty-nine people aboard. One of these was named Stubbs, who would later play a major part in testifying to the horrifying events. Stubbs claimed that he had been "bred to the Sea" but after a long career as a sailor he had been appointed to the government of Anomabu where he lived until taking his passage to Jamaica in the *Zong.*[50]

Stubbs did not know what a controversial voyage he had chosen to ship out on. A severely inexperienced captain, ill for most of the voyage, Collingwood almost certainly had limited navigational skills. Predictably, the journey would end in disaster. After ten weeks and three days they reached Tobago but, as Stubbs would later testify, they did not anchor because they heard a rumour that the French had recently taken the island from the British. Choosing instead to head for Jamaica, they mistook that island for Hispaniola, and sailed past. By now acutely short of potable water, deaths started to wrack the ship: it would later be stated that sixty-six slaves and seven crewmembers had already been lost, and many of the remainder were sick.[51]

Such events were hardly rare on slave ships, but Collingwood's solution would become infamous. Gathering together the ship's officers, he proposed that they throw the sick slaves overboard. Although Chief Mate James Kelsal apparently at first objected to the plan, at length they all submitted to the captain's suggestion and began to separate the sick from the healthy. On the first day of the massacre fifty-four live slaves were thrown overboard; the following day another forty-two followed them. On the final day of the atrocity thirty-six more men and women slaves were cast overboard to their death. Legend has it that one man survived by clinging to a rope when thrown into the sea, climbing back aboard, and then disguising himself back among the remainder of the "cargo".[52]

---

[50] National Maritime Museum, File 19, *Zong* Records; Prince Hoare, *Memoirs of Granville Sharp* (London: Henry Colburn and Co., 1820) 236–247 and appendix VIII; Robert Wisebord, "The Case of the Slave-Ship *Zong,* 1783" *History Today* (1969) 561–7.

[51] Ibid.

[52] Ibid.

The jettisoning of goods, or murder? How did seamen see these events? Notably, while the former tar, Stubbs, did not take part in the murders he seemed unabashed about admitting that he had "amused himself with seeing them out of the Cabin Windows plunging into the Sea". It is also pertinent that one commentator on the *Zong* case has written that when James Kelsal was questioned at the trial he displayed an "almost Eichmann like" detachment from the crime, stating that "he thought such orders enough warrant for doing anything, without considering whether it was criminal or not". Clearly even the chief mate, never mind the common seaman, considered that the orders of the captain should be followed no matter what. Indeed they had good reason to believe this, for disobedience to the captain constituted mutinous behaviour, for which the Admiralty court could try them. Defying the captain was indisputably an offence. Throwing the sickly slaves of the *Zong* overboard, on the contrary, was an act of such legal ambiguity that the civil courts were unable to come to a firm conclusion about it.[53] The laws of their nation unwilling to condemn their crime, whatever the economic claims of the underwriters and merchants, the seamen had acted within the boundaries their job mandated. There is of course irony in this, for these were men who so often disobeyed the captain's orders, whatever the consequences. Among reasons to rebel, saving the lives of slaves obviously did not rank highly.[54]

Further incertitude in the seamen's reaction to such events is evident in other accounts of similar murders. One passenger on a slave ship claimed to have heard "a sullen debate among the crew" about who would do the unpleasant job of throwing sickly slaves overboard after the ship ran short of water. Although some of the crew seemed reluctant to commit this act of murder, most of the comments seem to have related to the imputed nastiness of the task – to the men being "squeamish" – rather than to any moral outrage.[55] In a comparable case on the *Polly* of Rhode Island, the crew agreed with the captain, James DeWolf, that a slave woman with smallpox should be jettisoned so that the disease would not spread among the "Crew and Cargo". Only those among the crew who had previously had smallpox were enlisted to assist in this activity, but all were adamant that they were behind the captain's decision. Two crewmembers, Isaac Shortman and Henry Claning, later testified at St. Eustatius that "so far from having been accompanied by malice or wantonness or want of due

---

[53] Ibid.
[54] Ibid.
[55] Riland, *Memoirs* 63–5.

consideration, the Captain and whole Crew were equally affected by the circumstance".[56] Not enough to make any attempt to save the woman's life evidently.

Mostly seamen appear to have cared less about what heinous acts they were ordered to perform than that they would not end up in court. Perhaps their own legendary unlawfulness led them to fear even appearing as witnesses. In a case where a slave was allegedly murdered by a captain, for example – an incident that came to trial through the dedicated opposition to the trade of William Wilberforce – the third mate of the vessel would later state that the slave's death "was not a matter of Conversation". The dead girl had been suffering from gonorrhoea when she had been taken aboard the *Recovery*, and had some problem or deformity in her legs which meant that she walked poorly. Fearing that this would lead to her attracting a bad price in the West Indies, Captain John Kimber apparently ordered her to be tied up and her legs stretched straight by the seamen.

Later Stephen Devereux, a man who had already been discharged from the slave ship *Wasp* for mutiny, declared that out of fear nobody mentioned the incident when the ship was at Grenada, or in fact immediately after it returned to England. Yet "every seaman must have heard of it", he declared, and in fact he had "heard it spoken of on board". A drawing of this incident published contemporaneously indeed shows two seamen discussing the whipping as it occurred, saying that Kimber should have raped the woman rather than killed her. Their feelings are ambiguous even in this interpretation, however, as one sailor says to his mate, "I'm almost sick of this black business". In reality, only when abolitionist support was evident did anybody make a complaint about this incident. Sailors evidently preferred to keep quiet and do their job. They had good reason: the two men who testified against Captain Kimber were, after his acquittal, imprisoned so that Kimber could prosecute them for perjuring him.[57]

The reality was that many a slave trade sailor too was ultimately thrown overboard to a burial in "Davy Jones's Locker". Kimber was certainly known to treat his men harshly, as even the abolitionists at Sierra Leone, known far more for their hatred of slave trading than their

[56] Jay Coughtry (ed.) *Papers of the American Slave Trade* (Bethesda, MD: University Publications of America, 1996) A/2/l9/468–9.

[57] HCA 1/61 ff.166–172; Marcus Wood, *Blind Memory: Visual Representations of Slavery in England and America, 1780–1865* (New York: Routledge, 2000) 160–1.

support of seamen, witnessed. Some years after the court case when Kimber returned to the African coast, one man remarked that "he had never seen in any such savage ferocity so marked in Kimber[']s conduct toward his men on the most trivial occasions".[58] As seamen's labour became a commodity to be calculated by merchants along with all others, seamen found that if they were no longer required as workers they too could be cast aside, if generally in a less murderous way than slaves. So for men with as little authority as the average tar employed on a slave ship, the act of manhandling Africans overboard to their death was conclusive proof that commoditization had to be resisted at every opportunity, because its ultimate horror was that human life came second to profits. Freedom came to have real significance to these men in life and death terms rather than some notional theory, and hardly surprisingly, freedom, materially better living conditions, and the absence of corporal punishment became closely linked.

The fact that violence was central to the trade, as it was to all systems of slavery, was apparent in the crew's very make-up. More than any other individual task, aside from those associated with sailing the ship, slaver seamen were hired to guard against rebellion when captives tried to cast off their slave status and reclaim their ties of belonging. The need for security against such revolts was why slave ships recruited numbers of sailors far outweighing the needs of the ship, commonly carrying up to fifty per cent more crewmembers than a non-slaver of the same size. David Richardson has calculated that the additional wage cost involved in hiring extra men to defend against slave revolt accounted for eighteen per cent of the total costs of the middle passage.[59] This was another pivotal part of a slave trade sailor's role, a planned for contingency rather than an incidental occurrence.

Sailors had to be competent to man the armaments that all slaving vessels carried against slave insurrection. A central part of the instructions issued to a captain from a ship-owner usually focused on prevention against rebellion. Liverpool merchant Robert Bostock warned Captain Stephen Bowers of the *Kite* "to be continually watchful... to guard against an insurrection".[60] Captain Samuel Rhodes was counselled to "have a needful guard over your Slaves, and not put too much

[58] Macaulay, "Journal", file 18, 2 December–3 February 1797.

[59] David Richardson, "Shipboard Revolts, African Authority, and the Atlantic Slave Trade" *William and Mary Quarterly* 58:1 (2001) 69–92.

[60] Liverpool RO 387 MD 54: Letter Book of Robert Bostock.

Confidence in the Women nor Children lest they happen to be Instrumental to your being surprised which may be fatall".[61] Merchant David Tuohy warned the officers of the *Ranger* in 1767 to have "white people under arms" guarding over the male slaves to not give them any opportunity to "rise on the crew".[62] Leading merchants Thomas Leyland and James Penny instructed Captain Charles Wilson of the *Madam Pookata* in 1783 to be "uniformly watchful to guard against Insurrections, as they always proceed from Neglect, and will inevitably ruin the Voyage".[63] Such warnings would have been especially important to merchants because underwriters would not always insure against the loss of slaves as the result of rebellion.[64]

Consequently ship-owners equipped ships with vast amounts of goods designed to control their human cargo. When it left Liverpool in 1784 the *Comte du Nord* had "110 leg irons, 110 pairs of handcuffs" plus iron "collars, chains etc".[65] Other contemporary records list ships having blunderbusses and cannon ready to train on the captives when they were in their quarters on the ship.[66] When slaves were on deck either being fed or washed these precautions increased, so that "four or more [sentinels] were placed, with loaded blunderbusses in their hands, on top of the barricade, above the heads of the slaves: and two cannons, loaded with small shot, were pointed towards the main-deck through holes cut in the barricade to receive them".[67] One historian has written that slave ships had "all the characteristics of a floating Alcatraz".[68] Slave trade sailors were guards as well as seamen, prison warders as much as mariners.

This indeed was another of the reasons why sailors hated the "Guinea voyage" above all other deep-sea trades. Thomas Clarkson estimated during the final years of British trading that between approximately one fifth

---

[61] Quoted in Lorenzo J. Greene, "Mutiny on the Slave Ships" *Phylon* 5 (1944) 354–64.

[62] Liverpool RO 380 TUO 4/2: Papers of the Ranger 1767.

[63] Sydney Jones Library, Liverpool University Library, MS.10.47: Records of the *Madam Pookata* 1783.

[64] See for example C107/13: Papers of James Rogers, insurance on the *Fly* 9 October 1788, "The insurers free from any Loss or damage that may happen from the Insurrection of the Negroes." On the other hand the *Lumbey* in 1792–3 was apparently insured to the value of £1,200 for the ship and £1,800 for the slaves, and included "a clause in the Policy, stating, if there was a loss of slaves by insurrection exceeding 5 per cent. that loss was to be covered by the policy." *The Star* [London], 4 April 1796.

[65] Liverpool RO 387 MD 62/1.

[66] Falconbridge, *Account* 6.

[67] Riland, *Memoirs* 54.

[68] Okon E. Uya, "Slave Revolts in the Middle Passage: a Neglected Theme" *Calabar Historical Journal* (1976) 65–88, quote 66.

and one quarter of all slave trade seamen would die during the course of a voyage.[69] This is roughly backed up by modern estimates.[70] Naturally the majority of this huge mortality toll can be attributed to the dangers of the sea, the harshness of their treatment, and especially their lack of resistance towards diseases that are endemic on the West African coast. Yet a considerable proportion more were killed in slave revolts. The *Marlborough* of Bristol was "cut off by the Negroes" sometime after leaving Bonny and all the sailors except two were killed. Aboard the *King David* in 1750 the captives rebelled as it neared the Caribbean, "and killed the captain and all the crew, except four sailors" who managed to sail the ship to Guadeloupe.[71] The *William* from Massachusetts lost all but three members of the crew in a slave revolt. When the Rhode Island ship of Captain Bear had a rebellion all the crew was killed except the two mates who escaped by jumping overboard.[72]

These are just some random examples of sailor mortality from the estimated ten per cent of ships that suffered slave revolts.[73] African captives resisted their enslavement from the moment of capture, revolted against their sale to white traders, and attempted at all times to regain their liberty and return home. A crucial part of a mariner's job was to endeavour to ensure that they were unsuccessful. Upon the Atlantic Ocean a vast, prolonged, and desperately fought battle intermittently surfaced as the captive Africans tried to overcome their reduction to chattel. The men in the front line against this battle, the waged servants of the same economic reductionism, were mariners.

What is more, they fought this battle savagely, often going beyond the merchants' dictates. Fear of slave revolts imbued the whole slave trade with a sense of dread, feeding the brutality that anyway pervaded the trade to an almost unbelievable level. Slaves were harshly treated not just because they had rebelled, but because sailors feared that they would. The crew of the Rhode Island ship the *Rising Sun*, for example, on their guard because they had heard of two other American ships having slave

---

[69] Thomas Clarkson, *Grievances of our Mercantile Seamen: A National and Crying Evil* (Ipswich, 1845) 4.

[70] Behrendt, in "Crew Mortality" estimates a rate of 17.8% died on Liverpool ships between 1780–1807, but this does not include the 254 ships that failed to return at all, 54.

[71] Joseph E. Inikori, "Measuring the Unmeasured Hazards of the Atlantic Slave Trade: Documents Relating to the British Trade" *Revue Français D'Histoire D'Outre-Mer* 83 (September 1996) 53–92

[72] Greene, "Mutiny" 349–51.

[73] Richardson, "Shipboard Revolts".

insurrections while they had been on the African coast, severely whipped two slaves they feared were plotting to poison their rice.[74] On board the slave ship *Nancy* as the trade entered its final year of legality, one sailor is reported to have "fired the Pistol... imagining that the Slaves were about to rise" while he was on watch on deck at night. "The next Morning one of the Male Slaves was taken from below dead, and thrown overboard, who had been shot by the Pistol which had been fired off." The following night, again fearing that the slaves were just about to revolt, the same man apparently "stabbed another of the Slaves".[75]

In a separate incident, when a slave ship struck some shoals off Morant Keys, Jamaica, the crew abandoned it leaving the captive Africans shackled aboard. "When morning came, it was discovered, that the Negroes had got out of their irons, and were busy making rafts upon which they placed the women and children, whilst the men, and others capable of swimming, attended upon the rafts." Fearing that they might rebel seamen shot all but thirty-three or thirty-four as they approached the shore.[76]

The cruelty with which slave revolts were crushed by mariners also went beyond the mere quelling of rebellion, and was symptomatic of the fact that sailors regularly took the violence demanded by their employment and turned it into more personal sadism. Severe floggings were routine in cases of rebellion, and other more creative, harsher punishments were also commonly seen. On one slave voyage captained by John Atkins, a slave called Tomba was whipped as punishment for insurrection, while the female slave who had provided him with tools for his revolt was "hoisted up by the Thumbs, whipp'd, and slashed... with Knives, before the other slaves till she died".[77] Henry Ellison, who worked in the slave trade from 1758 to 1770, reported that he had seen a slave burned alive for rebelling.[78]

An unnamed seaman gave the following account of a slave revolt aboard his ship, the *Nassau*, and the way in which it was suppressed. The captives having revolted one day while they were being fed, they chased the majority of the crew up the rigging. However, the storyteller, the captain and another sick seamen were all down below, and "each took a loaded piece and fired at the slaves as often as we could, by which means many lay dead about the companion [deck], so that those fettered with

[74] Coughtry, *Papers* A/2/28/170–8.
[75] Donnan, *Documents* III 400–1.
[76] ZHC 1/87 258: Evidence of Hercules Ross.
[77] Donnan, *Documents* II 266.
[78] Anon, *Extract of the Evidence* 48.

them could not get away, of course they also, attempting to get down, soon shared the same fate". After most of the Africans had retreated back below decks to escape the firing, the doctor was ordered to search out the wounded, who, as they would not fetch a good price at market, were made to jump overboard. The supposed ringleader was "secured alone with irons on his feet and hands, his feet thus seized to the ring bolt on deck, and the burton tackle from the mainstay hook'd to the bolt of his manacles, and with that purchase so stretched or distended in a perpendicular posture, as nearly to dislocate every joint in his body; in this inhuman manner he was exposed naked to all the crew, and each at liberty to scourge him as he pleased". Even the seaman involved was prepared to attribute these actions to "a disposition stain'd with blood, and a spirit blackened by revenge".[79]

The point is not that such events occurred on every slave ship, for clearly these cases were uncommon enough to make it into letters home, newspapers or even the courts. But the trade did inculcate cruelty by its nature, and in so doing created a setting in which such events would occur all too frequently. The subjugation of man and woman to slave entailed a certain amount of physical suppression, but the ships that operated the transatlantic slaving route created a form of inhuman oppression in which evil could thrive. As John Newton put it, "the real or supposed necessity of treating the Negroes with rigour gradually brings a numbness upon the heart, and renders most of those who are engaged in [the slave trade] too indifferent to the sufferings of their fellow creatures."[80]

In so doing, seamen's actions to some extent ran counter to the economic motivations of the slaving merchant, as in their suppression of revolts or punishment of rebelliousness, numbers of captives were frequently killed and wounded over and above what was required to quell the insurrection. One hundred and ten captives died on a Rhode Island ship during a revolt and eighty were "forced overboard" during a rebellion on the *Sally*. Aboard the *Blakeney* after a rebellion the doctor was said to be occupied taking "out the Balls from the Slaves".[81] A Bristol slave captain ordered injured slaves overboard after a rebellion fearing that they would "have sold for little or nothing".[82] This rational can be explained by another case, when slave importer Munro MacFarlane wrote

---

[79] *Pennsylvania Gazette* 21 May 1788.

[80] ZHC 1/184 140.

[81] *Pennsylvania Gazette* 28 May 1794, possibly the *Ascuncion*, Eltis *CD-ROM*, 36570; HCA 15/55.

[82] Thomas Clarkson to Comte de Mirabeau, 9 September 1789, Thomas Clarkson Papers, Huntington Library.

to ship-owner James Rogers about the cargo on board his ship *Mermaid*. "A good many of the Slaves lost their lives [in the revolt], & many of those who lived to be brought to Market had wounds in this bodies which gave an unfavourable impression" he stated, justifying Rogers' poor return.[83] Each scar, every wound, represented lost revenue to the merchant and with every slave killed in quelling a revolt, their profit margins shrank.

A similar contradiction appeared in the treatment of slave women, for sailors hardly needed the authorization of their employment to mistreat their female captives. It was partly because of their captors' overtly masculine character that slave women simply had different experiences of the transatlantic crossing than their male equivalents. Demarked by their gender from the start, they were commonly left unshackled because they were considered good-natured or docile, and because it left them more at the mercy of the crew. Many of their experiences were wholly female. They conceived children, had miscarriages, gave birth, and had their children taken from them. The rhythms of life continued aboard a slave ship, set surreally against the looming spectre of death. Let the distress and sorrow of many be represented by the known few. On the *Liberty* a woman died in childbirth, and the child surviving its mother was fed on flour and died two days later.[84] A woman aboard the *Hudibras* had "an abortion" after being severely beaten.[85] Another lost her nine-month-old child, who was flogged and burned to death, and then she herself was beaten when she refused to throw the body overboard.[86] On the *Neptune* the boatswain requested permission to throw a six week old baby overboard because its crying disturbed him.[87] The suffering was endless.[88]

---

[83] C 107/6.

[84] House of Lords, Papers 1979; Riland, *Memoirs* 52.

[85] William Butterworth, *Three Years Adventures of a Minor in England, Africa, the West Indies, South-Carolina, and Georgia* (Leeds: Edward Baines, 1822) 83.

[86] ZHC 1/84 122–3: Evidence of Isaac Parker.

[87] ZHC 1/85 558: Evidence of John Ashley Hall.

[88] Catherine Clinton, *The Plantation Mistress* (New York: Pantheon, 1982) 201. Nell Irvin Painter's exploration of 'Soul Murder' is useful in understanding that whatever the men involved in the trade considered about the inevitability of such things, they also played an enormous role in the suffering of slave women. Painter lists a range of psychological effects that abused women today are known to suffer, including revictimization, depression, feelings of isolation, poor self-esteem, and self-contempt, and poignantly notes that "it is doubtful that slaves possessed an immunity that victims lack today." Nell Irvin Painter, "Soul Murder and Slavery: Towards a Fully Loaded Cost Accounting" Linda K. Kerber, Alice Kessler-Harris and Kathryn Kish Sklar (eds.) *U.S. History as Women's History: New Feminist Essays* (Chapel Hill: University of North Carolina Press, 1995) 138; also Deborah Gray White, "Revisiting Ar'n't I a Woman?" *Ar'n't I a Woman?* (New York: W.W. Norton, 1999) 1–13.

The sexual exploitation of woman slaves subtly differed, in theory if not in nature, from the many other forms of abuse inflicted on the captive Africans transported across the Atlantic because it could in no way be said to have constituted part of the job for which seamen had been hired. It contributed towards the women's degradation – certainly a central aspect of slavery – but did so outside the prevailing necessity of providing untarnished commodities for market. The sexual abuse of women on slave ships was more a demanded perquisite of the job of seafaring than a depredation impelled by the fiscal drive of a merchant in his counting house.

The slave trade institutionalized violence, but this abased attitude towards women was part of all seafaring culture. It did not need the violence of the middle passage to legitimize it. Seaborne society – black and white, ruler and ruled – was devastatingly masculine in character.[89] That the debasement of captive women on slave ships cannot be separated from their African origin is self-evident of course – their racial designation accounted for their presence. What is equally clear, though, is that the sons of Neptune had a reputation for treating women of all races and ethnicities cavalierly, and that such treatment was acceptable,

---

Many fewer women than men were transported as slaves to the Americas, chiefly, it would seem, because they were more in demand as domestic slaves within Africa, and therefore were sold to transatlantic captains in smaller numbers than men. This factor varied along the coast and over time, however. In the 1790s the Bight of Biafra supplied a high percentage of women to English slave ships. Herbert S. Klein, "African Women in the Atlantic Slave Trade" Claire C. Robertson and Martin A. Klein (eds.) *Women and Slavery in Africa* (Madison: University of Wisconsin Press, 1983) 29–38.

[89] It is an interesting comment on the gender stratification of the era that when two hundred and thirty-seven British and Irish women convicts were shipped to Australia in 1789, the *Times* of London announced that each sailor of the ship on which they were to travel was "allowed to select a mate" from among them to be his sexual partner for the duration of the voyage. In anticipation of the outcome, the government sent out sixty sets of baby clothes with the ship. Siân Rees, *The Floating Brothel* 103; *Times* 4 August 1789.

The reactions to the few women who dressed as men and went to sea aboard slaving vessels are also pertinent. When Hugh Crow discovered that one of his seamen was really a woman named Jane Roberts, he declared her to be "a very beautiful young woman ... landed with all possible gentleness." Although he was amazed that before her discovery she had drunk alcohol, chewed tobacco and sung songs with the other sailors, he did not censure her behaviour. Hugh Crow, *Memoirs of the late Captain Hugh Crow, of Liverpool; comprising a narrative of his life, together with descriptive sketches of the western coast of Africa; particularly of Bonny* (London: Frank Cass, 1970) 60. The same cannot be said, however, of Captain Potter of the *Neptune*, who, upon finding a woman amongst his crew declared her to be "a scandal to her sex ... and a wretch of the most abandoned morals." *Williamson's Liverpool Advertiser and Marine Intelligencer* 20 January 1769.

even regularized, in maritime culture. Certain deference might be distantly offered to the captain's wife and daughters, but common to eighteenth-century shore-based society, even this was not founded in any notion of equality.[90]

As the evidence of sailors on shore in Africa also suggests, the exploitation of women was simply the norm. When coupled with the denigration that black skin came to be associated with in the Atlantic setting, it was clearly considered even less deplorable to violate African women than others. They were doubly damned, being both female and dark skinned. Or perhaps they were thrice damned, for those who had undergone female genital mutilation before their sale doubtless suffered immense physical pain if brutally forced to submit to sex, quite apart from the mental torment. That seamen were frequently infected with venereal diseases that could cause infertility in women just adds to the cataclysm that befell female captives.

It is notable that among men who have left their accounts of the slave trade, even those who were among the most humane, unified by their having completely opposed the trade after their preliminary involvement, reveal appalling ambiguity in the treatment of women. Alexander Falconbridge claimed that "common sailors" were only "allowed to have intercourse with such of the black women whose consent they can procure" while "the officers were permitted to indulge their passions among them at pleasure". They were "sometimes guilty of such brutal excesses, as disgrace human nature", he added.[91] Pious John Newton, thought odd by his fellow mariners for his sensibilities and fastidiousness, and who spent his time writing ardent letters back to his future wife Mary, wrote in his diary, "William Cooney seduced a woman slave down into the room and lay with her brutelike in view of the whole quarter deck". He continued, "if anything happens to the woman I shall impute it to him, for she was big with child. Her number is 83."[92] Thus was the horror of a viciously raped pregnant woman reduced to the potential economic loss of a nameless number.

Well within the captain's omnipresent power was the ability to sexually exploit the women he had purchased as his cargo. The captain of the *Ruby*

[90] Suzanne J. Stark, *Female Tars: Women Aboard Ship in the Age of Sail* (Annapolis, MD: Naval Institute Press, 1996).

[91] Falconbridge, *Account* 24.

[92] John Newton, *The Journal of a Slave Trader 1750–1754*. Bernard Martin and Mark Spurrell (eds.) (London, 1962) 75; for an insightful discussion of this particular journal entry from Newton, see Wood, *Slavery, Empathy and Pornography* 58–60.

apparently made a "general practice" of calling all newly purchased slave women to his cabin to sexually assault them. One young slave girl was chosen to stay in his cabin with him, but later he "whipped her so severely with the cat, and beat her so unmercifully with his fists, that she threw herself against the pumps". She died three days later, at which time, "she had then been living with him as his mistress for five or six months".[93] On the *Scipio* Captain Roach apparently "purchased a black girl for his own use".[94] Captain Evans of the *Hudibras* had two "favourites" among the women slaves, one of whom he named Sarah.[95] Ottobah Cugoano wrote that a revolt on his ship was betrayed "by one of our own countrywomen, who slept with some of the head men of the ship" "It was common", he remembered, "for the dirty filthy sailors to take the African women and lie upon their bodies".[96]

Other fragments of historical record survive. The chief of the mutineers on the *Polly*, for example, "asked the Captain's Girl for the Key of the Chest & Cask & took some Liquor out". He used the alcohol to make the men swear allegiance to him.[97] On the infamous ship the *Brookes* one night in the 1780s "a woman who lived in the cabin" supplied the male slaves with a knife so they could cut themselves out of irons.[98] Embedded in the last two cases is evidence that women slaves were sometimes able to use exploitation to their own advantage.

Common seamen did not of course wield the captain's range of authority aboard. If Falconbridge's comment above is considered to have any truth, then their sexual exploitation of the women was restricted, if for financial rather than humanitarian reasons. As John Newton's diary entry infers, seamen were apparently not supposed to have sexual relations with the slave women not out of any concern for their well-being but because it could detrimentally affect the price they would fetch at market. This, however, runs contrary to most of the evidence of the reality rather than the theory. That the sailors would consider the women to be sexually

[93] BT 6/11; Dow, *Slave Ships and Slaving* 174.
[94] Silas Told, *The Life of Mr. Silas Told* (London, 1796) 20–1.
[95] Butterworth, *Three Years Adventures* 80.
[96] Ottobah Cugoano., "Thoughts and Sentiments on the Evil and Wicked Traffic of the Human Species, Humbly Submitted to the Inhabitants of Great Britain" Henry Louis Gates Jr. and William L. Andrews (eds.) *Pioneers of the Black Atlantic: Five Slave Narratives from the Enlightenment, 1772–1815* (Washington D.C.: Civitas, 1998) 94.
[97] HCA 1/58 ff. 107–8.
[98] ZHC 1/84 86.

available was considered inevitable – a sop involving no financial outlay to keep these infamously rebellious men placid. Divisions of class
origin separated the captain and his officers from his men, but in this they
appear to have been united: slave women were "fair game". Whether
free black sailors had more scruples than their white counterparts is
unknown.[99]

When seamen were prevented from reaching the slave women by the
barricades designed to prevent rebellion they simply broke them down.
On board the ship *Mary* in 1796 it was noted that "This morning found
our women Slave Appartments had been attempted to have been opened
by some of the Ships crew, the locks being Spoild or sunderd."[100] They
did not all use such brute force though; some had more gentle means
of persuasion. When the *Antelope*'s crew mutinied, for example, among
their crimes was tearing up some of the Indian cloth in the cargo and
distributing it "among the Woman Slaves on board the said Ship".[101]
Access to slave women may even have presented a reason to try and
ascend the power structure of the ship, by legal means or otherwise. When
John Wynne "turned Pyrate" and took command of the *Polly* he mim-
icked the actions of a captain in ways other than dressing in his clothes,
for by the time he went ashore at Prampram to try to trade, he took
with him "his Girl."[102] Mixed in with this degradation were fragments
of the same kind of lurid appreciation for black women that they had
displayed on the African coast: on the *Recovery* the crew named one girl
"Venus".[103]

The complexities of such interaction, however, are illustrated by the
fact that it was not only for sexual purposes that seamen sought individual
relationships with female slaves. On occasion sailors also called upon the
surmised gentleness and empathy of the women slaves. In times of sickness
particularly, seamen sought tender nursing from the women. Young sailor
William Butterworth was sent to the female slaves when he was sick, and
likewise the chief mate of the *Ruby* "became sick and went to the steerage,

---

[99] Jeffrey Bolster argues that "sexual prowess played no small part in black sailors' identity
formation." "An Inner Diaspora: Black Sailors Making Selves" in Ronald Hoffman and
Fredrika J. Teute (eds.) *Through a Glass Darkly: Reflections on Early Identity in Early
America* (Chapel Hill: University of Chapel Hill Press, 1997) 432.

[100] Donnan, *Documents* III 374.

[101] HCA 1/58.

[102] HCA 1/58 f.109–110.

[103] HCA 1/61.

among the women, for shelter".[104] Slaves were also used to ease the men's workload. All seamen were expected to be able to make and mend their own clothes while at sea, opposing the usual on-shore designation of needlework as women's labour. At least two men who had worked on slaving vessels testified to the Houses of Parliament that slaves had sewn clothing for them.[105] Ali Eisami, who was sold to a slaving vessel after the British and Americans had legally abolished the trade, confirmed this. He later remembered "one of the white men ... liked me, and would give me his shirts to mend, and then gave me food, he being a benefactor".[106] In a similar way female slaves were sometimes used in the preparation and serving of food.

The general picture regarding a seaman's views of, and actions towards, those he was paid to transport to the Americas is therefore complex and enigmatic. In the overall scheme directed by merchants in London, Liverpool, Bristol and Rhode Island, slave trade seamen were employed not just to ensure that the ship sailed successfully across the seas, but also as central participants in the creation of slavery. Their non-seafaring tasks were laden with this reality. Removing the captives' clothing, shaving their heads, and shackling them were rituals through which the outward display of their identity and personality was stripped away in preparation for the transformation to slave. When they were whipped into dancing or singing, forced to eat or beaten for rebelling, the seamen who performed this work had authority over those whose personal power and honour was to be replaced by the state of slavery.

Also inherent to many of sailors' tasks was the truth that violent subjugation was central to the process of commodifying human beings. This was true of other forms of enforced bondage too, but in its transatlantic variant it coupled particularly uneasily with the pent up frustrations of those hired to oversee this transformation. Slave trade seamen were anyway accustomed to outright force in their working lives. The cat-o'-nine-tails was a perpetual presence aboard ship, governing their behaviour as much as the wages they would receive. Many slave ships went out equipped with a Letter of Marque that entitled them to capture enemy ships as prizes during war, which normally meant a deadly battle.

---

[104] Butterworth, *Three Years Adventures* 90; Dow, *Slave Ships and Slaving* 175.
[105] ZHC 1/85 45: Evidence of James Fraser; ZHC 1/85 582: Evidence of Alexander Falconbridge.
[106] H.F.C. Smith, D.M. Last and Gambo Gubio, "Ali Eisami Gazirmabe of Bornu" Curtin (ed.) *Africa Remembered* 199–216, quote 213.

Impressment into the Royal Navy, known as "uncle" to the men, was an omnipresent threat, and one which meant that they had to be ready to fight for their country.[107] Tellingly, those who sought to defend the trade before the British Parliament in the late eighteenth-century argued that it was necessary because it was "a nursery for seamen" for the Navy.[108] In other words – although clearly this is not what was meant – not only did it teach men the business of working a ship, it also brutalized them to prepare them for combat. Maritime society was harsh, and the men often ready to resort to physical violence. Within the demands of the slave trade was the opportunity to inflict pain on others, and to root their own lack of freedom in their allotted superiority over those even lowlier, or, to put it another way, for the flogged to flog. It was an opportunity many took.

Although the slave trade institutionalized violence, it should be explicitly stated that despite the setting the actors remain culpable. We may ask how men tolerated such levels of depravity towards their fellow humans, and the answer to such a question may reveal something fearful in the human psyche, but nothing can excuse the individual acts that comprised the whole. Brutality and cruelty pervaded seamen's lives anyway – these were men who were swift to fight – and as in so many other cases and settings those who are cruelly treated became actively cruel. Economic expediency and the resort to abject cruelty found common cause somewhere in a Guinea seaman's paid employ.

Yet the involvement of sailors in the "production" of slaves for sale at market, or, to put it another way, in the commoditization of human beings, caused them to value intensely their own notional freedom. It equated, what is more, to a feeling that their own brutal treatment at the hands of captains and mates was intolerable not only in itself, but because it symbolized slavery. Likewise, their poor conditions were hated because they represented a lack of the fruits of liberty. It is hardly surprising that sailors were at the forefront of battles for freedom around the Atlantic in the era when slave trading reached its peak, for they had seen up close

---

[107] Samuel Robinson, *A Sailor Boy's Experience Aboard a Slave Ship* (Wigtown: G.C. Book Publishers, 1996) 97.

[108] For example, ZHC 1/85 410: Evidence of Marriott Arbuthnot. Two other maritime industries, whaling and the Newfoundland fishery, were also given this epithet, Jerry Bannister, *The Rule of the Admirals: Law, Custom and Naval Government in Newfoundland, 1699–1832* (Toronto: University of Toronto Press, 2003). I am grateful to a reviewer for this reference.

what this asset, or rather the lack of it, represented in real terms. As Edmund S. Morgan argues in a different setting, men "may have had a special appreciation of...freedom...because they saw every day what life without it could be like".[109]

[109] *American Slavery, American Freedom: The Ordeal of Colonial Virginia* (New York: W.W. Norton and Co., 1975) 376.

6

Lives for Sale

Of this mixture [gunpowder, lemon-juice, and palm oil] the unresisting captive received a coating, which by the hand of another sailor, was rubbed into the skin, and then polished with a "danby-brush," until the sable epidermis glistened like a newly-blacked boot.——Page 28.

FIGURE 7. Sailors polishing slaves' skin prior to sale. Original in Mayne Reid, *The Maroon, or, Planter Life in Jamaica* (New York, 1864). Reprinted by permission of New York Public Library.

When Olaudah Equiano wrote his account of the middle passage – information he possibly gleaned from his parents – he wrote that when they first sighted Barbados the sailors "gave a great shout, and made many signs of joy".[1] They had doubtless been eagerly awaiting the first indications of landfall for some time, all eyes staring excitedly to the horizon, impatient to spy the land that would bring the end of the danger-ridden middle passage. The ship's officers shared this anxious expectation of land. After he had been sailing westward for around five weeks, Captain John Newton noted in his diary every day that he was avidly looking out for flying fish and Sargasso as signs that land was near. Newton, like all others sailing before the 1760s, could calculate only inaccurately his longitudinal position and, in desperate anticipation, wrote that he "began to think long for the land" when it did not appear on the horizon at the moment he had predicted.[2] Similar sentiments were shared by the slave ship surgeon who had written upon leaving Africa that he wished "never to think of these dread voyages more", and now noted the "joyful sight of the Long wish'd for Land" as he glimpsed New York in the distance.[3]

Common seamen had many reasons to be high-spirited as they approached the Americas, and not only because the treacherous voyage from Africa was almost completed. Contained in the whoops of glee was not just celebration of having survived slave revolt, disease and

---

[1] Olaudah Equiano, "The Interesting Narrative of Olaudah Equiano, or Gustavus Vassa, The African, Written by Himself" Henry Louis Gates, Jr. and William L. Andrews (eds.) *Pioneers of the Black Atlantic: Five Slave Narratives from the Enlightenment, 1772–1815* (Washington D.C.: Counterpoint, 1998) 221. Recently Equiano's story has been challenged by Vincent Carretta, who argues that Equiano was probably born in South Carolina and claimed an African birth to give his *Interesting Narrative* authority. As he doubtless drew on accounts he had heard of the middle passage from his parents or other slaves in America, his account still provides much useful information relative to the experience of being carried from Africa to the New World. Carretta, "Olaudah Equinao or Gustavus Vassa? New Light on an Eighteenth-Century Question of Identity" *Slavery and Abolition* 20:3 (1999) 96–105; Caretta, "Naval Records and Eighteenth Century black biography: with particular reference to the case of Olaudah Equiano (Gustavus Vassa)" *Journal for Maritime Research* (November 2003); Catherine Obianju Achonolu, "The home of Olaudah Equiano – a Linguistic and Anthropological Search" *Journal of Commonwealth Literature* 22 (1987) 5–16; S.E. Ogude, "No Roots Here: On the Igbo Roots of Olaudah Equiano" *Review of English and Literary Studies* 5 (1989) 1–16.

[2] John Newton, *The Journal of a Slave Trader, 1750–1754* Bernard Martin and Mark Spurrell (eds.) (London: The Epworth Press, 1962) 57.

[3] Darold D. Wax, "A Philadelphia Surgeon on a Slaving Voyage to Africa 1749–1751" *Pennsylvania Magazine of History and Biography* 92 (1968) 492.

shipwreck, but also the sailors' delight at the imminent arrival of their "liberty". Soon they would be paid part of the wages owed to them, and would be free to spend this money on drink, food, prostitutes and general rabble-rousing. They eagerly anticipated these times. During the transatlantic passage, while the captives had fretted below decks as to their fate, sailors had dreamt of the license and licentiousness of the Americas as a way of enduring their own privations.[4] As they carried out the hated tasks of slave commoditization, thoughts of their own liberty sustained them.

The spatial and situational separation invoked in these actions was not, however, consistent with the ongoing reality. By the late eighteenth century, the islands where most British slave ships disgorged their human cargo were places where dockside communities of free blacks, runaway slaves, soldiers who had deserted, seamen, small-time merchants and dealers, and any number of other transient characters lived side by side, ready to welcome the latest influx of rowdy tars with money to spend.[5] And the wild dealings of this world had a dark underside. The willingness of sailors to interact with black men and women in the Caribbean was not just a part of their wider cosmopolitan egalitarianism, but often also a matter of necessity. Capitalist enterprise demanded an unassailable division between slave and free – and certainly there was a profound difference in these two states – but at the point at which sailors' work to commoditize Africans was deemed to be completed, their own service to the trade was found to be rather in excess. Many a sailor found that after the slaves had been sold his contribution to the trade, his labour, was no longer needed. In the slave societies of the American continent Africans were reduced to commodities, but at the same time seamen faced the harsh reality of the commoditization of their own labour.

Of course the seamen's position overall was far superior to the slaves they had transported aboard their ships. The desperation of slave men to escape to sea and work as sailors is more than ample evidence of that. A seaman benefited from infinitely more opportunities and advantages than a slave. Nonetheless, sailors were often in desperate situations if abandoned in the Caribbean, and in their time of need patronized slave markets and African health care workers, as well as living among the

---

4 Samuel Robinson, *A Sailor Boy's Experience Aboard a Slave Ship* (Wigtown: G.C. Book Publishers, 1996) 60.
5 Between 1776 and 1800 43.3% of the total slaves disembarking from British slave ships did so in Jamaica. The next largest group arrived in Grenada, at which 9.95 of the total number transported on British ships arrived. Eltis, *CD-ROM.*

dockside community of countless runaway, manumitted and hired out bondsmen and women. Freedom hinged on the possession of white skin in the Atlantic plantation societies, but as seamen were increasingly finding in their homelands too, it also depended upon the possession of material wealth. This was something of which the average tar had very little. In fighting for freedom and justice, moreover, seamen sometimes found common cause with slaves, allying their campaign with those they had originally been paid to subjugate.

If any single event symbolized chattel slavery it was not the long days toiling in the fields with no pay, nor even the scores of a whip upon a slave's flesh, but the act of selling men, women and children as if they were simply merchandise. Selling slaves cut to the very heart of slavery as an institution, for it illustrated their dual economic role as both capital investment and worker, and in reducing slaves to their value in these terms it took no account of them as people with personalities, families, religious beliefs and cultures. In many ways sale marked the nadir of the slave experience, so that when the institution of slavery had developed a whole ideology of justifying rhetoric in the antebellum American South the paternalism of the slaveowners allowed no place for slave sale, even though it remained quintessentially important to their economy and society.[6] The buying and selling of the slaves that arrived on British and American slave ships at the end of the eighteenth century made no pretence towards paternalistic notions, but instead in the impenitent manner of Caribbean slavery rested purely on economic reckoning. It was the ultimate estrangement for which the actions of the middle passage had aimed to prepare them.

As the islands that would be the scene of the Africans' eternal exile hove into view, final attempts were therefore made to prime them for market. This did not, predictably, mean that any effort was made to reconcile them mentally to their fate, much less to try and ameliorate their suffering. Rather, these last minute preparations revolved around ensuring the best possible price for them. More food was commonly given to slaves at this time, and as much water as could be spared. Some captains handed out rum, sugar and tobacco.[7] While the captain and the surgeon advised, seamen primped and polished their goods so that they would fetch a good

---

[6] Walter Johnson, *Soul by Soul: Life Inside the Antebellum Slave Market* (Cambridge: Harvard University Press, 1999) 19–44.

[7] Silas Told, *The Life of Mr. Silas Told, Written by Himself* (London: G. Whitfield, 1796) 19.

return for the investors. One observer, upon going aboard a Liverpool slave ship that had arrived in Barbados noted "her cargo had been made up, for market, by having their skins dressed over three or four times with a compound of gun-powder, lime-juice, and oil". This was done not only to make them look "sleek and fine", but also to cover up their scars from "cra-cra" [yaws].[8]

Such tactics were not rare. Slaves were prepared for sale just as a market trader might shine apples. When the two hundred and fifty surviving slaves of the *Hudibras* arrived in Grenada in February 1787, not only were they washed and rubbed with palm oil to make their skin gleam, the seamen were also engaged in outright trickery. As the cabin boy put it, "Those whom age or grief had rendered grey were selected, when, with a well-primed blacking brush, the silvery hairs were made to assume a jetty hue."[9] Others were employed in similar acts of deception, such as closely shaving and buffing the faces of the men to make them appear younger than they really were.[10] One Liverpool captain boasted of having cheated planters over the sale of his "refuse slaves" who were suffering from dysentery by ordering the men to "stop the anus of each of them with oakum". This deception was discovered soon after their sale, "the excruciating pain which the prevention of a discharge of such an acrimonious nature occasioned, not being borne by the poor wretches, the temporary obstruction was removed".[11]

Slaves who died during this period had to be disposed of as quickly and inconspicuously as possible, so that their death would not frighten off possible purchasers fearing that disease would wrack their newly purchased possessions. Two young boys aboard one ship were put to work "under very arbitrary authority; and the quickest and simplest plan" was the one they favoured to do this work. Their scheme was to "fasten a rope round the body, lower the body into the water, fasten the rope around the stern of the boat, tow it ashore and bury it in the sand". They justified this by the "disgusting" nature of touching a "naked mass" that had died from smallpox, and "the state of the subject to be disposed of".[12]

[8] Pinckard, *Notes* I 238.
[9] William Butterworth, *Three Years Adventures of a Minor in England, Africa, the West Indies, South-Carolina, and Georgia* (Leeds: Edward Baines, 1822)132–3; Eltis, *CD-ROM*, 81890.
[10] ZHC 1/87 95.
[11] Alexander Falconbridge, *An Account of the Slave Trade on the Coast of Africa* (London: James Phillips, 1788) 35–6.
[12] Robinson, *Sailor Boy* 102–3.

Some tasks were more innocuous. When he was Fourth Mate of the *Spy*, William Richardson was sent onshore with a hundred of the healthiest male slaves "to give them an airing, but more with the intent of letting the planters see what fine slaves we had". The slaves were so pleased to be free of their confinement that they "jumped with wild enthusiasm and pleasure into a pond so that they could wash".[13] Other seamen were involved in scrubbing down the ship, which was especially important if slaves were to be sold directly from the deck rather than being taken on land for viewing.

These final acts of commoditization not only embraced the hopes and desires of merchants waiting anxiously for news of their investments, they also manifested a fundamental part of eighteenth century Atlantic slavery. Planters distanced themselves from the ugly, disreputable process of enslavement by considering the men, women and children they purchased in the American slave markets as previously commoditized. In the rhetoric of the plantation economy, Africans were already separated from their humanity by the time they stood on the auction block. This was essential in the late eighteenth century markets not only because, as commodities, slaves' bodies incorporated the fetishist desires of planters and also because capitalism "recognizes no extra-economic differences among human beings". Thus when sailors were involved in the final acts of Atlantic commoditization, they were enacting part of the process which not only turned human being into commodity, but which rendered him or her less than human.[14] It was a final act of shaping Africans into the particular kind of victims that were devoured by transatlantic capitalism and modern, racial slavery.

There was much about the arrival of ships at the slave markets, accompanied as this time was by the final acts of slave commoditization, that revealed the ultimate difference in the condition of captive slave and "galley slave", whatever the seaman's skin colour. In the slave markets of the Americas could be found an ultimate, irreparable nay-say to the seamen's comparison of their own situation to slavery. The markets embodied the culminating crescendo of racism that the slave trade's injustices endowed. No matter how much seamen may have suffered aboard ship,

---

[13] William Richardson, *A Mariner of England: An Account of the Career of William Richardson from Cabin Boy in the Merchant Service to Warrant Officer in the Royal Navy, 1780–1817* Colonel Spencer Childers (ed.) (London: John Murray, 1908) 64–5.

[14] Ellen Meiksins Wood, "Capitalism and Human Emancipation" *New Left Review* 167 (1988) 1–21; Robin Blackburn, *The Making of New World Slavery: From the Baroque to the Modern, 1492–1800* (London: Verso, 1997) 16.

and more importantly how much they perceived they had suffered in comparison to the captives, the overwhelming majority of sailors would not be sold at market. Instead, when planters and merchants arrived to survey the newly disembarked chattels, sailors were on the side of free men, a final part of their current employment often being the guarding of slaves for inspection by prospective purchasers.

The divergence between slave and sailor upon reaching the Americas is evidenced by the terminology: one was sold into eternal chattel slavery, while the other regained his liberty. In contrast to the sailors who cheered with joy upon reaching Barbados, Olaudah Equiano wrote that the captives were "all put under the deck again, [so] there was much dread and trembling among us, and nothing but bitter cries to be heard all night from these apprehensions".[15] They were right to feel such foreboding. Indeed, their suffering was not over when they were finally able to leave behind the disease-infested stinking slave rooms and escape the endless pitching and rolling of the ship, but rather entering a whole new phase. If the middle passage had been captivity, the time after sale was unqualified, backbreaking, murderous, demeaning slavery. Put another way, if the transatlantic crossing had been "purgatory" for them, the islands they were about to be delivered to were the scenes of sheer "hell".[16]

For sailors, by contrast, arrival often proved well worth the wait, at least initially. Samuel Robinson wrote that for him and his crewmates this time "was a turn of fortune we durst hardly dream of". Robinson was rhapsodic about the fresh food available when his ship reached Carlisle Bay, Barbados, writing that "no language ... can at all describe the luxury of the feast, no one can *feel* it till he has been for many weeks under a vertical sun fed on salt junk and mouldy biscuits, and stinking blue water to drink" [emphasis in original]. "To have fresh meat, with an unlimited supply of sweet wholesome water", he recalled, was all he could have wished for.[17]

Such benefits, however, often proved ephemeral. There was often not much to envy in many seamen's circumstances after they arrived in the Caribbean. This is not to compare the sufferings of slaves with those of sailors – certainly a dubious venture if viewed with retrospection – but to

[15] Equiano, *Interesting Narrative* 222.
[16] This phraseology was used by Father Laurent de Lucques, who travelled on a Portuguese slave ship and wrote, "I don't know if we should characterize that ship as hell or purgatory." He decided on the latter, as "Hell, apparently, would begin for the slaves after the ship reached Brazil." Robert Harms, *The Diligent: A Voyage Through the Worlds of the Slave Trade* (New York: Basic Books, 2002) 314.
[17] Robinson, *Sailor Boy* 96.

place in context the different kind of scourges inflicted on the two groups by this particular branch of Atlantic commerce. Slaves were required to be less than human commodities, who could be "pent up together like so many sheep in a fold" at market, where they would be "obliged to go through every sort of motion" by the prospective purchasers "to try their flesh and soundness".[18] Sailors, by contrast, were neither considered to be bodily commodities, nor less than human. What the slave trade did do to seamen, however, was to wilfully display in its fiscal rationale that their labour was purely a commodity. After the middle passage, their toil no longer required, seamen were "turned adrift to get, steal or starve" after the slaves had disembarked.[19]

Thus the tragedy for those who had been sold as slaves was that they were now an investment, an economic reckoning. The tragedy for seamen was that they, or rather their labour, no longer were part of this calculus. Some of the men who had been employed to commoditize captive Africans found that the commoditization of their own labour, which they fought so boldly against, literally left them marooned once the job of shipping slaves to the Americas was completed. Sailors had been fighting against this all around the Atlantic rim since at least the early eighteen hundreds, but by the last decades of the century the battle was practically lost, and many of the negative consequences of this caught up with men who were abandoned from slave ships after the middle passage.[20] Scores of seamen had outlived their usefulness to their employers, and could be hastily discarded. Unlike under pre-capitalist working relationships, in late eighteenth century long distance trade a person was only useful because of the labour he provided, the employer acknowledging no greater responsibility to the actual person performing the toil.

There were a number of reasons for captains to divest the ship of some of its crew in the Caribbean. Just as in Africa, some ships were wrecked, damaged or condemned as unseaworthy upon arrival in the Americas.

---

[18] Equiano, *Interesting Narrative* 222; Richard Drake, "Revelations of a Slave Smuggler: Being the Autobiography of Capt. Richard Drake, an African Trader for Fifty Years – from 1807 to 1857" George F. Dow(ed.) *Slave Ships and Slaving* (Westport, CT: Negro Universities Press, 1927) 208.

[19] Thomas Clarkson, *Grievances of our Mercantile Seamen: A National and Crying Evil* (Ipswich, 1845) 5; see also Daniel P. Mannix and Malcolm Cowley, *Black Cargoes: A History of the Atlantic Slave Trade 1518–1865* (New York: Penguin, 1962) 131–52; John Laney, "The Other Victims of the Slave Trade: English Seamen in the Eighteenth Century" unpublished MA Thesis, University College London (1992).

[20] Marcus Rediker, *Between the Devil and the Deep Blue Sea* (London: Cambridge University Press, 1987) 75.

Other vessels were sold purely because they had succeeded in making the voyage the merchants had desired, and with the slaves sold they preferred to convert the ship into ready cash. At other times the ship let the seamen go because it would be so long before it was ready to sail homeward. The captain of the *Florida*, for example, "discharg'd most of his hands" after arriving in St. Johns, Antigua, "because he could not get his Cargo of Sugar aboard till the ensuing Crop".[21] Letting one crew go and hiring a new, smaller one when the ship was ready to sail again meant that only a skeleton force had to be paid while the ship was docked, when few hands were needed. In addition ships that had been taken by an enemy privateer sometimes took their captive seamen to the nearest Caribbean isle. For all these reasons, seamen often found themselves in the West Indies without an organized passage home, and often with little means of support.

On many other occasions, however, seamen were discharged from their ships quite simply because far fewer crewmembers were needed for the journey back across the Atlantic than for the middle passage. With a cargo of slaves safely delivered to the Americas, it no longer mattered to the merchants in their offices in Liverpool or Rhode Island whether some of those they had shipped as crew lived or died. The work they had been employed to do had been concluded. Just as Liverpool merchant Thomas Leyland was pleased that his ship the *Enterprize* was wrecked at Annatto Bay, Jamaica after arriving with its human cargo, once the middle passage was over seamen too had accomplished what they were required to do. Merchants like Leyland spared no thought for their future.[22]

Logically the economic principles of the trade suggested that the men no longer needed were simply paid off so that they could look for a new employer aboard another ship. But in the disreputable, squalid world of slave trading, the end of a seaman's economic usefulness often took on an altogether darker hue. There was considerable incentive not to pay seamen off in the recognized manner, but to abandon as many excess men as possible after the slaves had been sold. This is reinforced by evidence that some *officers* were abandoned against their will in the West Indies, so firmly challenging the image of seamen who had been legitimately paid off, and were forced into destitution after squandering their wages.

Officers who were abandoned in this manner wrote to their employing merchant to protest at having been forsaken, and if this was their fate it

---

[21] British Library Add Mss 39946.
[22] Liverpool RO 387 MD 59.

was surely one far more commonly suffered by Jack Tar. William Linley, the surgeon of the *Fame* wrote a letter to merchant James Rogers protesting that he had been left on shore in Kingston, and pleading that he did not know the reason. "I am certain I did more than my Duty as surgeon on board", he plaintively beseeched. He was not without resources however, for he succeeded in getting the chief mate of his ship to witness before an attorney that he had been cast aside with no support.[23] It would seem that the merchant's influence could often be brought to bear in cases where officers had been abandoned. In 1731, slave merchant Humphrey Morice wrote to Captain Keate, chastising him that his "Conduct in turning yr Chief Mate ashore in an Island beyond the Seas, is obvious & notorious to the whole world, & cannot be justified".[24]

For common seamen clearly there was no chance of winning the merchant's sympathy if they were ejected from the ship in the West Indies. On the contrary, this was an accepted, even demanded, part of a slaving voyage. Liverpool slave merchant David Tuohy specifically told Captain Alexander Speers to get rid of any men that he found unacceptable, but not until after the slaves had been sold.[25] In 1761 the investors in the voyage of the *Tyrrell* told Captain William Hindle, "By the time you get to the West Indies you'll know who and which of your men are worth keeping, and who are not".[26] The implication, of course, was that they were not expecting all of the men who left with the ship to return with it, quite apart from the high mortality that normally ensued among seamen on board slave ships. William Richardson's description of events after his ship arrived in Jamaica is telling. "Having got clear of the slaves", he wrote, "our captain now began to get clear of those of the ship's company that he did not like."[27]

This fiscal dividend consequently intersected with other facets of a sailor's woes – his maltreatment aboard ship, and particularly the poor health many seamen were in by the time they reached the slave disembarkation ports. Those who were sick might be retained aboard at the African coast because they were still needed for the westward journey across the Atlantic, but ruthless captains saw little reason to keep them when that voyage was completed. Seamen often were put off the ship not so much for their own recovery, but simply to dispatch them from the

---

[23] C107/5.
[24] Bank of England: Humprey Morice Papers, VIII, letter dated 26 July 1731.
[25] Liverpool RO 380 TUO 4/6: Papers of David Tuohy.
[26] Liverpool University Library: David Davenport Papers, MIC 392.
[27] Richardson, *Mariner of England* 65.

muster roll. Men being abandoned from slave ships became the rule. It "was not uncommon for the masters of Guinea ships, a few hours previous to their sailing, to send on shore their lame, ulcerated, and sick seamen, and leave them behind, where they must have perished but for the humanity of the community of Kingston", remembered one observer. It was, in fact, such a common practice that it became "a very great nuisance to the community at Kingston", to the extent that a law was passed stopping captains from doing this, or making them liable for the costs of keeping their seamen so left behind.[28]

Many of those who travelled to the Caribbean islands during the late eighteenth and early nineteenth centuries related that seamen congregated around the docks in an appalling state of health, often having previously been employed on slaving vessels. Commonly called "wharfingers" or "scowbankers", these men were a visible section of Caribbean society. They loitered around the waterfront in all the major disembarkation points, "sick on the harbors with legs swelled" as one observer recalled.[29] Another man told of seeing such men at Roseau, Dominica and again while his own vessel was in careenage at Grenada. At the latter, he stated, "there were seven men from on board a Guineaman that was lying there, they were exceedingly emaciated and full of sores".[30] A man named Thomas Clappeson claimed before the parliamentary committee investigating the slave trade that he had been a wharfinger in Jamaica for many years stretching between the 1760s and 1780s, earning a sporadic income by working as a pilot for arriving ships.[31]

Certainly many slave trade sailors were suffering awfully by the time they arrived in the islands. John Ashley Hall, who worked as a mate on the *Neptune*, described the seamen disembarking from slave ships after their transatlantic voyages as "the most miserable objects I have ever met with in any country in my life". He recalled that he had "frequently seen them with their toes rotted off, their legs swelled to the size of their thighs, and an ulcerated state all over".[32] It was the same story for those who arrived on the American mainland. George Baillie, a merchant and planter in South Carolina and Georgia reported that seamen arriving on slave ships had often "received great injury in their health; as might be seen

---

[28] ZHC 1/87 259.
[29] ZHC 1/84 134–5.
[30] ZHC 1/87 134.
[31] ZHC 1/87 207.
[32] ZHC 1/85 521.

from their squalid countenances, and ulcerated limbs".[33] Even the Royal Navy, notorious for being extremely avaricious in its endless demand for workers, sometimes refused to take men arriving on slave ships. One naval captain stated that often they were simply unemployable, and described them by saying, "besides their cadaverous looks, they were the most filthy vagabonds I ever saw".[34]

Such sentiments are backed up by statistics from West Indian hospitals. In Kingston, Jamaica, where 60.1 per cent of British slave ships delivered their captives in 1790, sailors constituted 84 per cent of hospital in-patients the following year.[35] In 1792, partly as a rejoinder to Thomas Clarkson's arguments that the slave trade was so fatal to seamen, the Assembly of Grenada voted to extend the services of the county hospital to sailors arriving from Africa. Two years later Montego Bay, Jamaica decided to build a special hospital purely for seamen on the site of the former Fort Frederick.[36] There was clearly a huge need for medical treatment among the seamen arriving on slave ships.

The treatment in such hospitals was rather rudimentary, and lives were lost there as often as saved. Those suffering from malaria and yellow fever found that little could be done for them, and indeed these two diseases were not distinguished as separate conditions in this time period. Chinoma bark, from which quinine is derived, was known to be a relatively effective treatment for malaria but when it was mistakenly used to treat a yellow fever outbreak in Grenada in the 1790s with obvious failure, opposition to its use grew. Doctors fell back on the old practice of bleeding, which was actually extremely harmful as malaria causes anaemia.[37] The treatment for those suffering from dysentery was also woefully inadequate. Many who had hoped for freely flowing alcohol and female company instead endured fevers and bloodletting.

Countless other seamen arrived with the lacerations from their gashes and abrasions needing urgent care. A sailor on one American slaver

---

[33] ZHC 1/84 182.

[34] ZHC 1/84 12.

[35] Eltis, *CD-ROM*; Julius S. Scott III, "The Common Wind: Currents of Afro-American Communication in the era of the Haitian Revolution" unpublished PhD Dissertation, Duke University (1986) 61. There was a total of 301 seamen in the hospital in that year, the next highest proportions being 21 people who worked on plantations, 8 merchants, 7 shopkeepers and 5 blacksmiths. They shared the wards with 1 tavern keeper, 1 sail maker, 3 hairdressers, 1 rat killer, 1 "bird-teacher" and 2 tailors. *Royal Gazette* 19–26 January 1793.

[36] *Cornwall Chronicle* [Jamaica] 30 June 1792; 7 June 1794.

[37] Philip D. Curtin, "The White Man's Grave: Image and Reality, 1780–1850" *Journal of British Studies* 1 (1961) 94–110.

bound to Savannah, Georgia, showed George Pinckard "three desperate wounds" he had received during a slave revolt, inflicted by a rebel slave swinging an axe which previously had been used to decapitate the captain.[38] Presumably seaman Thomas Davis was in critical need of treatment after losing a leg in a shark attack while he was employed on the slaver *Nancy*, which arrived in Antigua in 1775.[39] In the same way, after a battle with another ship "in the latitude of Tobago" in December 1806, Captain Hugh Crow had his "wounded whites...carefully conveyed to the hospital" upon reaching Port Royal, Jamaica. Despite the care, some of them "prematurely paid the debt of nature", he wrote.[40] Those who had been wounded in shipboard accidents or slave revolt, injured during privateer or pirate attack, or bore the scars of maltreatment, could probably expect less harmful nursing than those afflicted with some unidentified tropical pyrexia, but nevertheless they could still suffer from the frightfully low hygiene standards in hospitals. Although of course it would be ridiculous to claim that only mariners were detrimentally affected by the era's health care inadequacies, slave trade sailors arriving in the Americas certainly justified the old adage that "Sea men are...to be numbered neither with the living nor the dead".[41]

Besides discharging crewmembers because of sickness, other underhand tactics were also used to reduce the wage burden of ships after the captives had been sold. Disenchanted sailor James Field Stanfield claimed that on a slave ship, both death and desertion among the crew were actively "encouraged".[42] If the former seems to be overstating the facts, it is clear that not all seamen, quite apart from Stansfield himself, perceived it to be so. An Italian sailor who became very sick after the British slave ship he had sailed on reached Demerara clearly thought he was going to be drowned. Two thirds of the crew were already dead from an unidentified plague which given the descriptions of men covered with mosquito stings was probably malaria or yellow fever. When "all those who could get away from the doomed ship had fled for their lives," the captain ordered two healthy sailors to take the Italian man "to the wharf, where the hospital officials would take care of him". The sick man

---

[38] Pinkard, *Notes* I 236.

[39] BT 98/35 197.

[40] Hugh Crow, *Memoirs of the late Captain Hugh Crow, of Liverpool; comprising a narrative of his life, together with descriptive sketches of the western coast of Africa; particularly of Bonny* (London: Frank Cass, 1970) 105, 118, 128.

[41] Rediker, *Between the Devil* 3.

[42] James Field Stanfield, *Observations on a Guinea Voyage: A Series of Letters Addressed to the Rev. Thomas Clarkson* (London: James Phillips, 1788) 3.

obviously feared a far worse fate, however, for when they tried to put him in the boat he imagined that they had been ordered to drown him. "Never shall I forget the imploring looks of those large black eyes, and the distracting cry for mercy of the poor fellow", remembered one who lived to tell the tale. So great was the fear in this situation that the educated Samuel Robinson was reminded of Shakespeare's poignant description of life as "a tale, Told by an idiot, full of sound and fury, Signifying nothing".[43]

Most seamen realized that their fate was unlikely to be a watery death once the slaves had been sold, but it is clear that many were "encouraged" to abscond. In fact some captains speciously claimed that men had run away when in fact they had just departed temporarily. Many capricious sailors simply ambled around the harbours of the New World surveying their opportunities, looking for other possible ships to sign upon, and enjoying all the things they had been deprived of aboard. If they dallied for too long, however, they could soon be judged to have deserted from their vessel. Some captains took advantage of a sailor's desires to enjoy life ashore, with one man claiming that captains often deemed that any man who was away on land for more than forty eight hours had deserted, and would not be let back on board.[44]

Many seamen undoubtedly did run for positive reasons when their ships reached the West Indies. Because they commonly had been paid part of the wages due to them at that point, this was a popular time for seamen to abscond. Additionally, compared to the west coast of Africa, the islands were appealing and agreeable to the average tar, and many felt that his life would be improved by staying. Given the humble background most came from in their homelands, here was a chance for a different life. Some sailors desired to stay but found themselves without the means to do so, like the unnamed sailor who spent three months on Antigua after his slaving voyage ended, and wished to settle, but was forced by his "indifferent circumstances" to sign on another ship.[45] Some had more personal reasons to stay – John Shutter, boatswain's mate on the *Daniel and Henry*, married after the ship reached Jamaica.[46]

---

[43] Robinson, *Sailor Boy* 60–2.

[44] Jonathan Press, *The Merchant Seamen of Bristol, 1747–1789* (Bristol: Bristol Branch of the Historical Society, 1975 and 1995) 9.

[45] British Library Add Mss 39946.

[46] Nigel Tattersfield, *The Forgotten Trade: Comprising the Log of the Daniel and Henry of 1700 and Accounts of the Slave Trade From Minor Ports of England, 1698–1725* (London: Pimlico, 1991) 57.

Many more, however, as in Africa, ran to escape ill-treatment, to avoid being pressed into naval service, or because they feared that disease or slave revolt would afflict them aboard their vessels. Many were desperate enough to run with nothing, despite having "upwards of thirty pounds due" and having to leave everything, including their hammocks, on board.[47] Whatever the reasons that caused seamen to desert – and positive and negative reasons were not necessarily exclusive to one another – it is clear that they were vastly less likely to be sought out and returned to their ship if they deserted after the slaves had been sold than if they fled prior to the middle passage. Although catchers sometimes tracked seamen in a similar way to which slaves were hunted down – in Virginia for example, captains offered a premium for seamen deserters – men from slave ships were unlikely to be tracked in this way.[48] Captains were unlikely to lament the loss of men they no longer needed for the voyage back home, but rather welcomed their desertion.

Because they wished to reduce crew numbers after the middle passage was completed, a ship's officers, and the captain particularly, had little reason to curb their harsh behaviour towards seamen as they approached the West Indies. On the contrary, they had cause to encourage a terrible level of misery and despair among the hired hands. The excesses of the middle passage grew largely from the necessity of keeping men, women and children enslaved and from breaking their spirit, but if a side-effect was that seamen were encouraged to run, minus their owed wages, when the ship reached the Caribbean, then evidently that was no negative thing in the eyes of the captain. Seamen, it was reported at St. Vincent, were "frequently so ill treated during the latter Part of their Voyage, that they are induced to run away from their ships".[49] Captains could abuse with impunity, knowing that seamen were unlikely to find an island, or mainland, magistrate willing to listen to their complaints. Many, such as the man who, upon arrival in the West Indies, "carried his shirt, stained with blood which had flowed from his wounds, to one of the magistrates on the island" often found little sympathy among the Caribbean's judiciary.[50]

Sometimes in fact a captain would use the islands' magistrates to take yet more sailors off his hands by having them imprisoned for trifling

[47] ZHC 1/82 120; ZHC 1/82 85; Robinson, *Sailor Boy* 62, 97.

[48] Peter Earle, *Sailors: English Merchant Seamen 1650–1775* (London: Methuen, 1998) 72.

[49] Extract of a Letter from Mr. Chief Justice Ottley to Sir William Young, dated August 6, 1788, *Privy Council Report* (1789) pt. III (St. Vincent); quoted in Scott, "Common Wind" 141.

[50] Falconbridge, *Account* 43.

offences, which might have been otherwise overlooked had they not needed to reduce crew numbers. Robert Barker was imprisoned in jail at Antigua after the first mate, who allegedly had taken a violent dislike to him during the passage, claimed that he "had been in the rebellion in the North of England". The jailer tried to get Barker's wages from the ship to pay for his keep, but was told that they had already been forfeited because he was guilty of mutiny.[51] In 1786 three seamen were imprisoned in St. Vincent for refusing to obey the captain's orders until they had received "some Refreshment" after completing the long voyage from Africa. This captain not only got rid of part of his crew in jail – others were so disgusted at the inequity of this, they deserted without either their wages or their sea chests.[52] Some crewmen from the *Recovery* were sent to jail in Grenada in 1791 and then appeared before the local magistrate.[53]

Those who sat in judgement over alleged criminals in the plantation colonies were often themselves planters and slaveowners, or their close associates from the cream of white island society. Like judges in Britain they were predisposed to favour the captain over the common tar. Some men did succeed in having their captain "put into the Admiralty" for "some treatment that appeared to us a little too rough." Captain Godfrey of the Rhode Island ship *Hare*, for example, was incarcerated in this way during the 1750s.[54]

The odds were generally stacked against them however. Those seeking justice for themselves or for their crewmates who they believed had died from mistreatment generally found little backing. Some of the men of the *Lilly* of Liverpool protested the death of one of their colleagues at the captain's hands when the ship reached Charleston, South Carolina, but the accused was acquitted for lack of evidence.[55] When the men of a Liverpool ship also named *Hare* tried to protest the alleged murder of the carpenter, carpenter's mate, cook and another seaman when they arrived in Virginia in 1761, their complaint was not even heard. They were "immediately ordered" back aboard, "or else to the whipping

---

[51] Robert Barker, *The Unfortunate Shipwright, or Cruel Captain. Being a faithful narrative of the unparallel'd sufferings of Robert Barker, late carpenter on board the Thetis Snow, of Bristol, in a voyage to the coast of Guinea and Antigua* (London: Printed for, and sold by the Sufferer, 1760) 27–9.

[52] Scott, "Common Wind" 140.

[53] HCA 1/61 f.166.

[54] Elizabeth Donnan (ed.) *Documents Illustrative of the Slave Trade to America* (Washington D.C.: Carnegie Institute, 1931) III 172.

[55] ZHC 1/87 29–30.

post". "It is almost impossible for Guinea seamen to gain redress in those ports, to which the slaves are consigned for sale", lamented one of the sailors.[56]

The truth for many white sailors was that although in some senses their skin colour gave them stature in the Caribbean – most importantly it protected them from enslavement and announced to all the free status of the owner – divisions of class also cut an extremely brutal swath through white society in plantation colonies. The impression fostered by the white minority flexing its (metaphorical and real) whip over the bent backs of enslaved African sugar workers rather concealed the fact that in Caribbean plantation society class cleaved almost as sure a division as race. Planters saw little commonality with poor white sailors – until the time of slave rebellion at least – and held them in contempt. Planters were, or more commonly aspired to be, part of the English gentry and regarded with acute disapproval these men who so obviously did not live up to the definition of "gentlemen".

This scorn and disapproval cut both ways. For seamen too there was little identification with the *grand blanc* way of life. In fact, in the very act of enjoying their "liberty" or suffering their abandonment, sailors displayed an alternative moral and ethical code to that of powerful slaveowners, who aspired to be English gentlemen. Seamen were a large and visible part of the "masterless" class of men who roamed the Caribbean islands living their lives in opposition to the ruling class's ethics. Despite having participated in plantation society through their employment transforming Africans into slaves, soon after arrival sailors quickly reverted to their true maverick, dissident lifestyle, and certainly did not fit quietly into the social structure that planters sought to impose. Sailors did not dwell on vast plantations with servants and riches, but were much more commonly found lying in the dives and dens around the harbour. Jamaican newspapers reported with disgust the "riotous and disorderly" conduct of sailors in the island's ports, who displayed their anti-authoritarianism in the Caribbean just as they did in North America and Europe.[57]

In seeking to restrict the excesses of the seamen, slaveowners instituted laws that reveal all too clearly the way in which the ties of class cut across those of race. As Julius S. Scott phrases it, "in every island colony, town guards, workhouses and other instruments of social control designated primarily to regulate the enslaved majority were used to keep sailors in

---

[56] ZHC 1/87 29; Clarkson, *Substance of the Evidence* 59.
[57] *Royal Gazette* 7 July 1792; quoted in Scott, "Common Winds" 62.

check."[58] In Grenada, for example, the 1789 Police Act aimed to control the entertainment of male slaves, free blacks and sailors, who, if "found in gaming houses could be imprisoned for two to fifteen days, and such individuals who were found on the streets between 9:00 P.M. and 4:00 A.M. without a lighted lantern risked being taken to the guardhouse until the following morning".[59]

Legislators in Jamaica also attempted to severely limit seamen's access to alcohol in the 1790s, believing that it "was the source of seducing seamen from their duty" and the cause of many of their fights. "An order was made also, directing the constables to apprehend any sailor, who shall be found in a grog shop, and carry him away to the workhouse", which was also where runaway slaves were kept until their masters collected them. The captains of ships were required to ring their ship bells at six o'clock to enable the magistrates to enforce a law passed over a century before "for inflicting a penalty of forty shillings for every seaman found in grog shops after ringing of the bell."[60] The militia in Kingston, whose main purpose was slave control, frequently had to be used to restrain rowdy sailors in the town.[61]

Planters' difficulty with seamen was not just that, in their view, they disgraced the image of white men, but more importantly that they interacted with slaves and free blacks in ways that they considered to be far too free. Although his comments were made with no sense of censure, the words of small time Irish merchant James Kelly are instructive. He wrote "Sailors and Negroes are ever on the most amicable terms", enjoying "mutual confidence and familiarity". They had, he said, a "feeling of independence in their intercourse", leading him to the oft-quoted declaration, "in the presence of the sailor, the Negro feels as a man".[62] This was clearly anathema to the plantation aristocracy, who lived by a set

---

[58] Julius S. Scott, "Crisscrossing Empires: Ships, Sailors and Resistance in the Less Antilles in the Eighteenth Century" Robert L. Paquette and Stanley L. Engerman (eds.) *The Lesser Antilles in the Age of European Expansion* (Gainsville: University of Florida Press, 1996) 130–1.

[59] Edward L. Cox, *Free Coloreds in the Slave Societies of St. Kitts and Grenada, 1763–1833* (Knoxville: University of Tennessee Press, 1984) 94–5.

[60] *Cornwall Chronicle* [Jamaica] 7 July 1794.

[61] Scott, "The Common Wind" 62.

[62] James Kelly, *Voyage to Jamaica* (Belfast, 1838) 29–30; quoted in Philip D. Morgan, "Encounters between British and 'Indigenous' Peoples c. 1500–1800" Martin Daunton and Rick Halpern (eds.) *Empire and Others: British Encounters with Indigenous Peoples, 1600–1850* (Philadelphia: University of Pennsylvania Press, 1999)195, and Marcus Rediker, "Common Seamen and the Histories of Capitalism and the Working Class" *International Journal of Maritime History* 1 (1989) 355.

of values based directly on notions of racial supremacy. As Kelly's words reveal, this was simply not replicated among the poorer, itinerant population in the urban areas around the ports. The near-absolute division of black as slave and white as free, rendered by the slave markets, was part of the fiction of the planters' delusive worldview, just like the conception of slave as uncomplicated commodity. The reality was that all around the harbours of the West Indies runaway slaves, free blacks, sailors, soldiers and a host of other indigents of indeterminate legal freedom lived side by side with a degree of equality that dismayed slaveowners.

It is hardly surprising that the sailors from slave ships, despite having taken part in the process of enslavement through their employment, would joyfully embrace this subversive culture. Most would have recognized its code of beliefs and the make-up of its population as a variant of that in Britain's port cities. Furthermore, far from living lives separate from Africans other than as coerced sexual partners and domestic servants, as planters did, sailors in the slave trade worked alongside men (and sometimes women) with black skin at every stage of their journey. Just as in Africa and less frequently during the middle passage, the circumstances that prevailed when slave ships docked in their New World disembarkation ports brooked no absolute divide between black and white. Personal acquaintance between European slaver seamen and black maritime workers continued in the West Indian ports of call just as it had in Africa. Soon after arrival in the Americas, additional workers were hired from the dockside community to assist with the work on board slaving vessels.

Men were needed in exactly the same roles as free Africans had been hired before the ship crossed the ocean. When the *Lady Nelson* arrived at Jamaica in 1803 it hired a pilot to see them through the "sandbanks [that] lie along the coast" and guide them safely into Port Royal. Samuel Robinson later wrote of this man that he "could not help taking stock of the face of the black beauty...his nose as flat as a pancake...high cheek bones and a long chin; ears like saucers, but with lovely eyes and teeth". Later the ship also engaged two black men who looked after the sick slaves, and buried the dead. At least six further men were also hired to do general ship duty.[63]

Likewise the Liverpool slaver *Fortune* which arrived in New Providence, Bahamas in 1805 with a cargo of 343 slaves, hired a number of local men to supplement the already huge number of seamen aboard. The man named "Doctor O Rourke" who was paid "for his attendance on

---

[63] Robinson, *Sailor Boy* 100, 104, 114–15.

Slaves from 28 April to 31 July and taking care of Slave Yard and Slaves from 31 Mar to 20 May 50 days" was almost certainly European or of European descent, but those paid to do more menial and less prestigious work were listed in the account book simply under the heading "Negro hire" or "Negroes on shore".[64]

The slaver *Sally*, under the command of Captain John Mortimer, was forced to hire additional carpenters in the Caribbean to make the ship seaworthy for the journey home. It proved rather a wasted effort as a Spanish privateer captured it before reaching Liverpool.[65] Another ship of the same name that had sailed from the same port a year earlier recorded "Two Negroes employed scraping" on 14 November, and then "Got 6 Negroes to work on board" on the 24th of that month.[66] Although all these examples come from the final five years of legal trading, the hiring of black men in the West Indies to assist the crewmembers was not a new practice. The *Anne*, which arrived in 1725 hired a carpenter for eight and a half days because their own was too sick to work, then hired a canoe and some black men for two days, plus another four Afro-Caribbean men for six and a half days to help with unloading and reloading the ship. They were all paid standard wage rates.[67]

Evidence as to how European seamen directly interacted with such latterly hired men is scanty, not least because after departing from their ships, seamen left, temporarily at least, the larger capitalist world and so tend to also leave the historical record. We can surmise that Afro-Caribbean maritime workers were treated with the same kind of rough and ready, caustic egalitarianism with which humble seagoing men generally dealt with their black fellow travellers. Many of the notions that had led seamen to conceive their African co-workers as rather outlandish people were tempered by the fact that most Caribbean blacks knew at least a smattering of English. As in Britain, witnesses noted the multiracial disposition of the seafaring community. One European observer in the West Indies noted that the good relations between sailors and slaves "were proverbial".[68]

[64] Liverpool RO 387 MD 44: Accounts of the *Lottery*; Eltis, *CD-ROM*, 81497.

[65] Merseyside Maritime Museum, DX 1150.

[66] C108/214: Papers of John Leigh.

[67] Bank of England: Humphrey Morice Papers, 7/11.

[68] Philip D. Morgan, "British Encounters with Africans and African-Americans circa 1600–1780" Bernard Bailyn and Philip D. Morgan (eds.) *Strangers within the Realm: Cultural Margins of the First British Empire* (Williamsburg: Institute of Early American History and Culture, 1991) 157–219.

There was certainly much interaction between sailors and slaves, both those who were directly involved with arriving crews and those who were not. One seaman, when employed on a merchant vessel named *Cotton Planter* (not a slave ship) took beef and ships' biscuits to slaves on plantations while the vessel was in harbour at Grenada. In return they invited him and some of his fellow tars to join in their entertainments. "I never in my life was happier", wrote the seaman, "I esteemed them in my heart."[69] On the other hand, sailors seeking extra food provided an important market for the produce that slaves cultivated on their own private provision grounds. They were happy to attend slave markets and barter for these foodstuffs in a way that rich white planters would certainly not have condescended to do. Every culinary exchange between sailor and slave was part of a much bigger saga in which, as a direct result of the trade in slaves, crops, fruits, vegetables and knowledge of cultivation were transferred and popularized around the Atlantic rim.[70]

Besides conveying foodstuffs, seamen also tested traditional medicine in their various ports of call, and occasionally even sought respite and nursing among the female slaves during the middle passage. In keeping with the belief that black women would show them care and tenderness, some sailors who arrived sick on slave ships entrusted themselves to local health care. Samuel Robinson, who had injured his ankle during his voyage, was put "under the care of an old lady, in a street called Rum Lane". This woman worked as a kind of makeshift doctor who also had an income from her daughter, "a very pretty, handsome young woman" who lived as a "temporary wife" to visiting planters, naval men and soldiers.[71] Another man who had injured his leg during the passage across the Atlantic first of all arranged care with "a black woman, who ranked as a doctress" before cajoling his captain to arrange for hospital treatment for him, where he was kept company by twelve

[69] John Nicol, *The Life and Adventures of John Nicol, Mariner* Tim Flannery (ed.) (Edinburgh: Cannongate Books, 2000) 65–70.

[70] Richard B. Sheridan, "Captain Bligh, the Breadfruit, and the Botanic Gardens of Jamaica" *Journal of Caribbean History* 23:1 (1989) 28–50. Robert C.-H. Shell paints a similar picture of Cape Town in the decades after 1770, when market gardens manned by African slaves provided produce for passing seamen. "While the male slaves around the port labored outside to produce and deliver vitamin C for the sick seafarers, the female slaves in the ubiquitous boarding houses ministered to the needs of the revitalized sailors and officers. Again, the result was to concentrate young slaves in and around the port." *Children of Bondage: A Social History of the Slave Society at the Cape of Good Hope, 1652–1838* (Hanover and London: Wesleyan University Press, 1994) 168.

[71] Robinson, *Sailor Boy* 110–13.

other sailors.[72] It is of course entirely possible that such women provided care equal to, or greater than, that of the island hospitals. Contemporary western medicine frequently may have proved inferior to traditional cures.

Those who did not survive the diseases they suffered also needed slaves to carry out their last needs. Several commentators claimed that when the destitute seamen known as "wharfingers" or "scowbankers" died, slaves took care of their final worldly affairs by carrying their bodies off for burial. Henry Ellison, who had worked aboard a slave ship, reported that he had seen dead seamen being carried away by blacks while in the West Indies, to be buried at a site he named only as "Spring Park".[73] Ninian Jeffreys, who had resided in Jamaica, also recounted that when wharfingers died they were carried away and buried by slave men. The slaves simply termed these sad, broken sailors "poor Buchra" men, he related, and he insisted that they performed the interments of their own accord, not at the biding of their masters. Many slave trade seamen were buried "in an adjoining spot" to blacks in the "negroe cemetery".[74] This is debatable and cannot be verified, but nonetheless it is probable that some men who had worked on slave ships as sailors, at the end of their lives, had words spoken over their graves that had their origins in the African continent.

Seamen's collective identity stereotypically involved looking for "women in every port", and along with alcohol and entertainment, they certainly sought female company among the Afro-Caribbean dockside communities around the West Indies. Sailors' demands created a fringe industry, as some slaveowners allowed or forced their female slaves, especially young, attractive, light-skinned ones, to work as prostitutes, and sometimes sent them out to ships to earn money in this way.[75] In Barbados several taverns run by free black women became famous among sailors. They provided alcohol and lodgings for common seamen, as well as being "houses of debauchery, a number of young women of colour being always procurable in them for the purposes of prostitution". Often these women were slaves of the tavern owner.[76] These female publicans, furthermore,

---

[72] Butterworth, *Three Years* 144–5, 148, 152, 157.
[73] ZHC 1/84 372.
[74] ZHC 1/84 244; Clarkson, *Substance of the Evidence* 92.
[75] Suzanne J. Stark *Female Tars: Women Aboard Ship in the Age of Sail* (London: Pimlico, 1988) 10.
[76] Jerome S. Handler, *The Unappropriated People: Freedmen in the Slave Society of Barbados* (Baltimore: Johns Hopkins University Press, 1974) 133–8.

were certainly not without power and authority, and it should not be assumed that the seamen were necessarily in the dominant societal role. Unquestionably this was one area in which seamen's ideas of leisure were not very different to that of the Caribbean's white slaveowners and merchants, the vast majority of whom were male. Planters too appropriated, with various degrees of coercion, the sexual favours of slave women. Yet even while sharing this same tendency, the gap between seamen and slaveowner was still apparent. Planters exercised a different level of public admittance and disparity of influence than the seamen did in their dalliances. The former tried to keep their sexual activities with black women somewhat covert, hidden at least from polite society. While the image of a Jack Tar who bellowed about his sexual conquests and bragged about his sexual prowess was part of the negative stereotypes about seamen, nonetheless there is evidence that seamen sought plenty of female company in the Caribbean. What is different in their attitudes to those of planters was that they did not hide their relationships with women of African origin.[77] Moreover, while sex was undoubtedly sometimes a commodity to sailors, black women themselves were not bodily commodities in the same way that they were to merchants and planters.[78] Egalitarianism towards females, and especially black females, is not part of this picture, but what is clear is that sailors' interaction with slave and free black women was of a different nature than planters' sexual encounters with such women. It probably included relatively settled relationships with women of colour. It is possible, for example, that John Shutter's Jamaican wife was of African descent.[79] Certainly on that island "coloured births were most common among slaves employed on wharves".[80]

So, mingling freely with blacks in taverns around the harbour, Jack enjoyed his liberty just as he did in all other ports of call. He procured the

[77] Valerie Burton, "The Myth of Bachelor Jack: Masculinity, Patriarchy and Seafaring Labor" *Jack Tar in History: Essays in the History of Maritime Life and Labor* Colin Howell and Richard Twomey (eds.) (New Brunswick: Acadiensis Press, 1991); David Cordingly, *Women Sailors and Sailors' Women: an Untold Maritime History* (New York: Random, 2001) 200–12; W. Jeffrey Bolster, "'Every Inch a Man': Gender in the Lives of African American Seamen, 1800–1860" *Iron Men, Wooden Women: Gender and Seafaring the Atlantic World, 1700–1920* Margaret S. Creighton and Lisa Norling (eds) (Baltimore: Johns Hopkins University Press, 1996).

[78] Edward E. Baptist, " 'Cuffy,' 'Fancy Maids,' and 'One-Eyed Men': Rape, Commodification, and the Domestic Slave Trade in the United States" *American Historical Review* 106:5 (December 2001) 1619–50.

[79] Tattersfield, *The Forgotten Trade* 57.

[80] Quoted in Rediker and Linebaugh, *Many-Headed Hydra* 321.

company of women, drank, and not infrequently got into alcohol-fuelled brawls. But while the average sailor did not modify his usual onshore behaviour while in the Caribbean, the implications of his actions cut deeper there than elsewhere because authorities in the Caribbean had graver reason to fear seamen's disobedient nature than most. Plantation society's rule was rather tenuous, and depended precariously on hard line definitions of racial superiority.[81] Numerically far weaker than those they ruled over, planters needed to believe that sailors would reinforce their rule in times of need, most significantly in the event of slave rebellion.

In fact sailors occupied an unpredictable role in eighteenth century Caribbean history for they vacillated between bolstering the minority white power on the islands and themselves being a feared force of subversion. They were, to use a suitable combat metaphor, rather loose cannons. In 1733 it was reported in the English news that rebel slaves had been "driven into the Mountains by a Body of Sailors sent after them". Forty slaves and eleven sailors were killed in the fight.[82] In all likelihood seamen often supported white control of slaves in many unrecorded, extemporized ways.

Yet they also sometimes showed ambivalence towards slave rebellion. Although the rumour that circulated during Tacky's Revolt in Jamaica in 1760 was that the captain of a slave ship had first spotted the symbol of insurrection – a "wooden sword adorned with parrot's feathers" which he surmised was "the signal of union [in] some part of Guinea" – common seamen were less diligent.[83] They were forced into the militia to put down the revolt, but, as a slave rebel declared, "As for the sailors, you see they do not oppose us, they care not who is in possession of the country, Black

[81]   Richard S. Dunn, *Sugar and Slaves: The Rise of the Planter Class in the British West Indies, 1624–1713* (Chapel Hill: University of North Carolina Press,1972); David Barry Gaspar, *Bondmen and Rebels: A Study of Master-Slave Relations in Antigua* (Baltimore: Johns Hopkins University Press, 1985); B.W. Higman, *Montpellier, Jamaica: A Plantation Community in Slavery and Freedom, 1739–1912* (Kingston: University of the West Indies Press, 1998); Michael Craton, *Searching for the Invisible Man: Slaves and Plantation Life in Jamaica* (Cambridge: Harvard University Press, 1978); William Dusinberre, *Them Dark Days: Slavery in the American Rice Swamps* (Oxford: Oxford University Press, 1996); Michael Mullin, *Africa in America: Slave Acculturation and Resistance in the American South and the British Caribbean, 1736–81* (Urbana: University of Illinois Press, 1992); Peter Kolchin, *American Slavery, 1619–1877* (London: Penguin, 1995).
[82]   *Gentleman's Magazine* November 1733.
[83]   Douglas Hall, *In Miserable Slavery: Thomas Thistlewood in Jamaica, 1750–86* (London: MacMillan Press, 1989) 104.

or White, it is the same to them".[84] Certainly Thomas Thistlewood's comments in his diary seem to suggest that most of the sailors who passed by his plantation as part of the militia were more interested in drinking and occasionally pillaging than in suppressing rebellion. On 26 May 1760, for example, Thistlewood recorded that while soldiers went after the rebel slaves, sailors stopped at his plantation to drink and "in the hurry" took a silver spoon.[85]

A similarly ambiguous picture emerges of seamen's part in the Haitian Revolution. The *Gentleman's Magazine* reported that "about fifty" British seamen had joined some Americans who had gone to try and subdue the rebellious slaves in St. Domingue.[86] Clearly some sailors were prepared to support the slaveowners. But this was a tiny percentage of all the seamen who potentially could have volunteered to go and fight the rebel slaves. Most chose to stay away. Julius S. Scott in fact claims that seamen working on board slave ships were sources of information for blacks about the spread of revolutionary thinking in France, and abolitionism in Britain. A Frenchman who had lived in St. Domingue stated that merchant seamen were "the agents of the negrophiles" in France and, in keeping with their English counterparts, were "always together" with the local slaves, making the harbour a "cauldron of insurrection."[87] Scott argues that some English seamen likely got caught up in this seditious exchange of information, especially as the French sailors, temporarily escaping the fighting across the sea, drank away their troubles in Jamaica's waterfront taverns.[88]

On a smaller scale too seamen showed ambivalent feelings towards individual slaves in the West Indies. Their relationship was one where they supported the weaker slave as the underdog, but also did not hesitate to brutally beat slaves if a fellow seaman, honour, or money was at stake. When a black sailor went on a bloody rampage in the late 1750s in St. Eustatius, he first stabbed a white man with whom he was working,

---

[84] Quoted in Peter Linebaugh and Marcus Rediker, *The Many-Headed Hydra: Sailors, Slaves, Commoners, and the Hidden History of the Revolutionary Atlantic* (London: Verso, 2000) 222.

[85] Ibid; 98; Douglas Hall, *In Miserable Slavery: Thomas Thistlewood in Jamaica 1750–86* (London: MacMillan Press, 1989) 98.

[86] 62 (1792) 270.

[87] [Félix Carteau], *Soirées Bermudiennes, ou entretiens sur les événements qui ont opéré la ruine de la partie Français de L'isle Saint Domingue* (Bordeaux, 1802) 75–8; quoted in Scott, "Common Wind" 170; Linebaugh also credits seamen with spreading anti-slavery ideas among slaves, *London Hanged* 136–8.

[88] Scott, "Common Wind" 182.

then killed an English sailor he met walking around the harbour, whom he "instantly cut across the belly, so that his bowels appeared". Following the stabbing of a man in a nearby draper's shop, he ran back out onto the street and wounded "one or two others". Clearly the man's murderous rage fully incorporated, and was even triggered by, white seamen. Likewise, when the governor offered a reward for anyone who would take the man alive or dead, it was an English sailor who undertook the challenge, doubtless interested both in avenging the death of two of his fellow tars, and in the reward that was offered. The black seaman was captured and hanged the next day "upon a gibbet, in irons, alive, where he continued in the greatest agonies, and shrieking in the most terrible manner, for near three days".[89]

Yet sailors could undoubtedly also react in hot-headed ways to protect those who were the "underdog", which could quite easily incorporate slaves and free blacks. These actions may or may not have been sustained by any larger ideological regard for those being protected, and were partially a sport, part of their collective impetuous, fiery identity, as much as any dedication to multiracialism. The sailors on *HMS Proteus*, for example, defended a sick female slave who had come aboard their vessel to sell fruit and was flogged by a slave driver arriving to collect her. A body of the men on the ship "knocked him overboard" and he "sunk like a stone", at which the sailors "gave a hurra!" reported the ship's cooper.[90] Later this sailor reported that one of his shipmates beat a slave driver who was thrashing a woman slave.[91]

On other occasions still, sailors and slaves fed off each other's rebelliousness to oppose the authorities. The approximately twenty-one thousand sailors who arrived in the Caribbean during the 1780s – of whom around sixty per cent arrived on slave ships – formed a large part of the "Caribbean underground".[92] Perhaps few went as far as the Liverpool seaman Robert "Runwell" Barrow who fifty years earlier had deserted from his slave ship in Antigua and gone to live among the maroons.[93] But it is overstating to suggest that his case was unique. Bryan Edwards wrote of sailors in Old Harbor, Jamaica, rescuing a runaway slave who

[89] *Gentleman's Magazine* February 1759.
[90] Nicol, *Life and Adventures* 37.
[91] Ibid 65–70.
[92] Scott, "Common Winds" 60, 135.
[93] Rediker, "Common Seamen" 355.

was being pursued.[94] American newspapers occasionally listed runaway slaves as having been assisted by sailors.[95] Clearly there were angles of both sailors' and slaves' protests against authority that could, and did, converge.

The line between the two groups was most blurred, however, when slaves ran away to sea to work as sailors. Ex-slave seamen bodily crossed the lines between sailor and slave. This was perhaps the ultimate aspect of the paradox by which interracial understanding was fostered by the slave trade on an individual level, while its overall result was one of grossly exaggerated racial disharmony. Jeffrey Bolster notes that all captive Africans who were transported across the Atlantic "came face to face" with seafaring skills.[96] Others, who were too old to be free to wander the deck and see "the use of the quadrant" did not witness the secrets of European seafaring but were cunning enough to learn the occasional word of a shanty, terminology or some seafaring colloquialism that would later allow them to talk their way into a shipboard position.[97] Some of the ships they joined, moreover, were slaving vessels. That they had been involved in the trade in Africans was something of a moot point by this time, for laden with rum and sugar, they were no more morally offensive to runaways than any other merchant vessel and provided an important escape route.

So those who had been transported across the sea as captives to be sold as commodities, and their descendents, sometimes escaped to sea by using the knowledge they had picked up during the hellish crossing, and employing ships that had been employed in the repugnant trade in African flesh as the craft of their freedom. The irony did not end there, however, as in these acts black men incorporated themselves into the relatively unified body of mariners, and so increased the egalitarian tolerance of Europe's tars through close contact. What is more, given white seamen's willingness to help those at the bottom of society, their disobedience of authority, and their rebellious tendencies, some of the slaves who escaped to sea on

---

[94] Bryan Edwards, British Library Add Mss 12413; quoted also in Morgan, "Encounters" 195.

[95] For example, *Maryland Gazette* 2 August 1762; quoted in Lathan A. Windley, *Runaway Slave Advertisements: A Documentary History from the 1730s to 1790* (Westport: Greenwood Press, 1983) volume 2, 46–7.

[96] W. Jeffrey Bolster, *Black Jacks: African American Seamen in the Age of Sail* (Cambridge: Harvard University Press, 1997) 57.

[97] Equiano, *Interesting Narrative* 221–4.

slave ships did so with the connivance of the crew. Many white crewmembers simply "turned a blind eye" to Africans stowing away, or agreed to support a runaway's claims to be a free man and an experienced sailor.[98] Slaves who had not encountered maritime skills while being transported as captives from Africa could nonetheless easily learn enough applicable words or phrases to pass as a seaman if aided in his subterfuge by a sailor. All around the harbours of the Caribbean where white sailors and blacks mingled freely, there were ample opportunities for men to build up the kind of affiliations through which such information could be shared. A European seaman's pride in his nautical skills, his anti-authoritarianism, and his multi-ethnic worldliness – along with some tongue-loosening alcohol to create some drunken boasting – could easily present slaves with the glimpse of an escape route.

Ironically, seamen also occasionally used slavery to escape their old bugbear, the naval press. A naval seaman sent out to press men in Kingston, Jamaica, in 1795 was told that many slave trade seamen "disguise themselves, sometimes as American women, at other times as tradesmen". This in fact was the least of their artifices. In one house he found a seaman disguised as a dying woman and while his crewmates pretended to be mourners around the deathbed. A sixteen year old sailor was even posing as a baby in a crib. Most pertinently of all, the press gang also found a mulatto seaman who they recognized as a deserter from *HMS Thorn*. Aptly, this man was posing as a slave to avoid recapture by the navy.[99] It is not hard to see how this particular man might have mixed together humour and desperation in deciding on this role. A free man trying to escape the Royal Navy, he tried to subvert the prevalent notions of inferiority his race conveyed to his own advantage. He evidently hoped that as a slave the press gang would ignore him, seeing him as beyond their reach because his labour power belonged to his master alone and could not be demanded by the navy.

One of the paradoxes of slave commoditization was that those who had been employed to enact the process – in this case, seamen – could not see all Africans unambiguously or solely as merchandise. In order to support the social order their economics demanded, planters needed to believe that

---

[98] Donnan, *Documents IV* 39.
[99] Captain Fredrick Hoffman, *A Sailor of King George: The Journals of Captain Frederick Hoffman, RN, 1793–1814* (Annapolis: Naval Institute Press, 1998) 45.

slaves arrived at the marketplace formed into ready-made commodities, but sailors were not fooled by this fiction. Nineteenth century legal arguments questioning whether a slave had a will of his or her own would have been thoroughly nonsensical to those whose employment hinged on the possibility of slave insurrection.[100] The notion that a slave would have no social capacity, but live solely through his or her owner was not appropriate in the hold of a slave ship, where there were no slave masters.[101] While planters had yet to address the fact that a slave was a person with an individual will, and who could use it to reject their status as a thing, seamen had dealt with this since African captives were first loaded onto their vessels. It was what they had been hired to prevent, for each slave insurrection was a manifestation of their rejection of the status of slave, and a refutation of their reduction to commodity.

Over and above not engaging with the idea of an African as a commodity, after their shipboard duties were completed, seamen lived alongside runaway slaves and free blacks throughout the American disembarkation points. Whilst it is certainly a mistake to see interracial contact as necessarily egalitarian – the sending out of female plantation slaves to ships for the sailors' sexual gratification was clearly neither of these things – nonetheless there was an element of equality to much sailor/slave interaction that both horrified and terrified the ruling planter classes. Like all people, seamen had shifting multi-faceted identities, and this meant that they regularly applauded the rebelliousness of slaves once they were no longer held accountable for any who escaped. Black seamen, as Bolster argues, were "racial go-betweens straddling black and white worlds", and white sailors too appear on occasion to have interacted with Africans with surprising parity.[102] Again the example of Olaudah Equiano is pertinent. He acknowledged that slaves who made the Atlantic crossing would have feared the sailors that worked the vessel carrying them into exile, but he was treated "very kindly" by other tars when he joined the crew of the *Industrious Bee* in Virginia. This experience he wrote was "quite contrary

[100] Eugene D. Genovese, *Roll, Jordan, Roll: The World the Slaves Made* (New York: Vintage, 1976) 28–30.
[101] Emma Christopher, "The Slave Trade and Social Death" unpublished MA Thesis, University College London (1995) 6; Orlando Patterson, *Slavery and Social Death: A Comparative Study* (Cambridge: Harvard University Press, 1982) 45–51.
[102] W. Jeffrey Bolster, "An Inner Diaspora: Black Sailors Making Selves" Ronald Hoffman, Mechal Sobel and Frederika J. Teute *Through a Glass Darkly: Reflections on Personal Identity in Early America* (Chapel Hill: University of North Carolina Press, 1997) 421.

to what I had seen of white people before; I therefore began to think that they were not all of the same disposition."[103]

The heady days of Caribbean piracy might have been long gone, but the spirit of rebellion that these men personified had certainly not been totally crushed. In fact many of the causes that sailors agitated for around the Atlantic littoral – better wages and working conditions, freedom and justice for labouring men – played out in extreme ways on the western edge of the ocean. Sailors fought in, and transmitted news about, the American Revolution, the French Revolution, the Haitian Revolution, slave revolts, sailor mutinies and innumerable smaller-scale strikes and disputes. They might also have passed on news about the progress of British abolitionism to West Indian slaves.[104] What is more, the conditions and consequences of the trade in slaves played a central part in shaping seamen's protests, and determined those that they took as allies in their fight. In some cases their rebellion found common ground with that of slaves, to the profound dread and revulsion of planters, merchants and all others whose livelihood depended upon the race-based slave system of modern times.

[103] Equiano, *Interesting Narrative* 225.
[104] Scott, "Common Wind" 170.

FIGURE 8. Slaves arriving in Suriname.
From John Gabriel Stedman, *Narrative of a Five Year's Expedition against the Revolted Negroes of Suriname* (London, 1796). Reprinted by permission of the New York Public Library.

Conclusion

Ned Ward, who liked to be known as a "Manly Plain-dealer", described seamen as "the chaff of the world, being tossed here and there by every blast that bloweth".[1] It is an apt metaphor. Sailors were indeed well travelled and international; they could hardly be otherwise, for these features were inherent to their labour. When the wind changed direction and blew the men and their vessels onwards in new directions, it took with it newly gathered men and women, while those who had previously been broadcast were deeply changed by their travels. The crews of sailing ships, to use Linebaugh and Rediker's phrase, were thoroughly "motley", in every sense of that term.[2] Seamen's origins might have been overwhelmingly humble, but their horizons were vast. Their culture, while distinctly plebeian, was garnered from a truly cosmopolitan range of sources. They embodied the multiethnic from their Tahitian tattoos to their African shanties, and in the diverse origins of the people that they incorporated into the seafaring brotherhood.

To sailors the Atlantic was "bond" rather than "barrier" with its three and a half thousand miles of deep blue sea being the scene of shared experiences, the source of common dangers and the setting of possible triumphs.[3] Seamen were the original global citizens. More than simply

---

[1] Ned Ward, *The Wooden World Dissected* (London, 1798) 5.

[2] Peter Linebaugh and Marcus Rediker, *The Many-Headed Hydra: Sailors, Slaves, Commoners, and the Hidden History of the Revolutionary Atlantic* (Boston: Beacon Press, 2000) 27–8. The authors suggest not only the "multicoloured" aspect of the term motley, but also point to "the subversion of power and the poverty of appearance" implicit in its meaning.

[3] Bernard Bailyn, "The Idea of Atlantic History" *Itinerario* 20:1 (1996) 19–43; see page 27.

"working men who got wet" they represented a vitally important means of contact in an era before mass immediate communication.[4] In the late eighteenth century this meant spreading reports of revolutions, the cause of anti-slavery and working-class agitation as well as information about other events. They also took part in many of those actions, therefore fighting for liberty while also being employed in the process of enslavement. As on the American mainland, those who were closest to slavery knew only too well what the absence of freedom meant, and valued all the more both the abstract ideal of liberty and its practical tenets: fair pay, reasonable working conditions and the absence of barbaric physical punishments. The sea routes across the Atlantic Ocean reveal where concepts of liberty spread as well as where non-free persons were forcibly transported. Seamen were closely engaged in both.

Sailors' pressing demands for better treatment eventuated from the fact that their working conditions were worst when African enslavement was closest. Slave ships had a tradition of being especially unpleasant places to work with their officers particularly likely to rule through violence and cruelty. The human costs of the slave trade were borne by those who made the Atlantic crossing in shackles and chains, but that suffering rebounded on those paid to guard them, and from thence back again, redoubled, onto the original victims. Sailors, therefore, generally hated work aboard slave ships, with its harsh rule, deadly disease environments, unpleasant tasks that were unrelated to maritime work and the omnipresent risk of slave revolt. Correspondingly, more had to be trepanned aboard ship to make up a crew, and equally they increasingly asserted their status as free men by absconding, demanding better treatment or rebelling. As the Liverpool sailors' strike showed, slaving merchants were generally loathed by those who were their lowliest employees.

What David Brion Davis calls "the great American paradox": "slavery and democracy marching ahead to the same beat" could, therefore, also be characterized as ships bobbing on the seas, moving forward by harnessing the same winds.[5] Slavery was not a "peculiar" institution in the United States – a flaw on the nation's otherwise impeccable freedom – rather

---

[4] Rosemary Ommer and Gerald Panting, (eds.) *Working men who got wet: Proceedings of the fourth Conference of the Atlantic Canada Shipping Project, July 24–July 26, 1980* (St. John's: Maritime History Group, Memorial University of Newfoundland, 1980).

[5] Davis, "Broader Perspectives" 459; Edmund S. Morgan made a similar argument in *American Slavery, American Freedom: The Ordeal of Colonial Virginia* (New York: W.W. Norton and Co., 1975).

freedom in this period was symbiotically dependent upon slavery.[6] Both advanced together with sails unfurled.

The racial perspective was also, in some ways, contradictory. Without doubt the slave trade was built on xenophobia and escalated it into an odious brand of racism which could enshrine people of African origin as property in the constitution of a nation founded on ideals of liberty and equality. Later it would develop a whole branch of science dedicated to trying to explain that alleged inferiority. On slave ships men of European origin could learn not only that a person's skin colour could be considered the only determinant of his or her race, but also that their white skin was not merely significant, it would be the core of their identity. Among the most oppressed men in England, subjugated by a class system that they would very rarely be able to climb, they found that their skin colour gave them status both aboard a slave ship and in the Americas when their human cargo was unloaded. Whiteness came to have significance because it was what saved seamen, however badly they themselves were treated, from the slave markets and auction blocks of the Caribbean and mainland plantation societies.

Unlike most poor white men for whom whiteness came to be a defining factor in North America, however, sailors on slave ships also had inconsistent influences on their ability to conceive race in such clear terms. Having had men, and sometimes women, with darker skin as their crewmates and having spent months anchored off the African coast, they knew Africans not just as degraded members of the vessel's freight, but as sovereign human beings. They were people to whom they had turned in times of distress, had nursed them while they were sick and had disciplined them while they were insubordinate to their captain. Those who joined the ship and made the crossing as crewmembers may have helped fight a slave revolt, joined in some petty trickery to supplement the men's food or even been welcomed by Neptune and initiated into the seafaring fraternity. In the Caribbean too they worked alongside black workers as their colleagues and workmates to a degree few other white men of the era did.

Ira Berlin's award-winning book *Many Thousands Gone: The First Two Centuries of Slavery in America* shows how slavery demanded the creation and constant recreation of ideas about race and racial superiority.[7] This recreation was going on in miniature aboard the

[6] Kenneth M. Stampp, *The Peculiar Institution: Slavery in the Ante-Bellum South* (New York: Knopf, 1956).
[7] (Cambridge: Harvard University Press, 1998).

microcosmic society of a slave ship as it circulated the ocean. A man's skin colour held different significance as he made landfall at various ports around the Atlantic, but he took with him ideologies from other regions. Engaged in the trade which fed the plantation booms, used human beings as saleable commodities and ensured that African men in the Americas were identified as inferior, "black" chattels, a seaman nonetheless also knew that men of African origin could be very faithful brother tars.

The history of the men who worked on British and American transatlantic slave ships is therefore one of paradox and contradiction. Just as the wind could quickly change direction and blow a ship off course, so the currents of the slave trade ran in inconsistent and conflicting directions. Slave ships introduced many sailors to the notion that their white skin was the root of their status while all the time making them among the most debased white men of the era. Regularly kidnapped aboard their vessel, ruled with the whip and shackles, and at constant risk of enslavement in North Africa, the men who made transatlantic slavery were themselves the white men closest to bondage. They responded by being one of the most anti-authoritarian, militant, unruly professional groups, and could and did, on occasion, extend their activism to spread news of slave revolts and abolitionism and help runaway slaves. While being engaged in a trade which created the racial, chattel slavery of the Americas, working on ships where their skin colour came to have predominant salience and status, they also became the occupation most known to be tolerant of black men as co-workers. Such was the paradox of Jack Tar, a man who stood over the captive Africans with a whip, while his shirt hid the scars from that same instrument which were welded into his own flesh. Primarily the abusers in the trade which has become seen as a crime against humanity, they were also constantly abused.

Appendix 1

Black Sailors on Liverpool Slave Ships, 1794–1805

Name	Occupation	Ship	Year	Abode	Joined ship	Description	Outcome	Source
Richard Harper		Bell	1794	Africa				BT 98/55
R Slater		Ann	1794	Isles de Los				BT 98/55
April Chenie		Ann	1794	Africa			Impressed	BT 98/55
Charles Williams		Hinde	1794	Africa	Liverpool			BT 98/55
Henry Douglas		Hinde	1794	Africa	Liverpool			BT 98/55
Peter Hewitt		Mary Ellen	1795	Africa				BT 98/56
Quadgeo		Mary	1795	Cape Coast	Cape Coast			BT 98/56
Peter Coast Guinea		Ann	1795					BT 98/56
Joseph Noble		Crescent	1795	Africa	Liverpool			BT 98/56
John Bendis	Cook	Mary	1797	Grenada				BT 98/58
John James	3/4 Seaman	Mary	1797	Africa				BT 98/58
Black Tom		Lightening	1797	Anabon	Anabon			BT 98/58
Bigg Tom		Lightening	1797	Anabon	Anabon			BT 98/58
John Kelly		Diana	1797	Africa				BT 98/58
George Williams		Fisher	1797	Liverpool	Liverpool	Black man		BT 98/58
Anthony Dixon		Hamilton	1797	St. Kitts	Liverpool			BT 98/58
Frank Mullin	Apprentice?	Kingsmill	1797	Africa				BT 98/59
Peter Annabona		Kingsmill	1797	Africa				BT 98/59
Tobias Brown		Infant Ann	1797	Africa	Liverpool			BT 98/59
Ben Johnson	Apprentice	Infant Ann	1797	Africa	Africa			BT 98/59
Peter Parker		Neptune	1797	Africa	Liverpool			BT 98/59

(continued)

231

Appendix 1 (continued)

Name	Occupation	Ship	Year	Abode	Joined ship	Description	Outcome	Source
John Liverpool		Goodrich	1799	Africa				BT 98/60
William Grey		Goodrich	1799	Africa				BT 98/60
John Sabally		Goodrich	1799	Africa				BT 98/60
Simon Gold		Henrietta	1799	Antigua	Antigua	Free black man		BT 98/60
John Cock	Chief mate	Rosalind	1799	West Indies				BT 98/60
(Name unknown)		Willy Tom Robin	1799	Gorée				BT 98/61
John Brown		Lord Nelson	1800	Africa				BT 98/61
Jem Anabona		Polly	1800	Annobon	Annobon			BT 98/61
Mat Anabona		Polly	1800	Annobon	Annobon			BT 98/61
Ambree		Two Sisters	1800	Annobon				BT 98/61
Baggy		Two Sisters	1800	Africa				BT 98/61
Bassanta		Two Sisters	1800	Africa				BT 98/61
John Dido		Mercury	1800	Africa	Liverpool		Died at Suriname	BT 98/61
Edward Caroll		Commerce	1801	Senegal				BT 98/62
George Anderson		Commerce	1801	Barbados				BT 98/62
John Johnson		Blanche	1801	Martinique				BT 98/62
Robert Slater		Elizabeth	1801	Africa				BT 98/62
Henry Sargeant		Elizabeth	1801	Jamaica			Deserted in Suriname	BT 98/62
Tusker Bridge		William	1801	Africa				BT 98/62
James Amacre		Amazon	1801	Africa	Liverpool			BT 98/62
Edward King		Earl of Liverpool	1801	Jamaica				BT 98/62
John Kelly		Earl of Liverpool	1801	Africa				BT 98/62
Mich Gray		John	1801	Gambia				BT 98/63
John Witby		Alexander	1801	Africa				BT 98/63
Joseph Samuel		Elizabeth	1802	Island Princes	Liverpool			BT 98/63
James Blue	Runaway slave	Blanche	1802	Barbados	Liverpool		Taken by owner	BT 98/63

Dick Sam		Eclipse	1803	Africa	West Indies			BT 98/64
Richard Haynes	Cook	Ann	1803	West Indies				BT 98/64
Jack Williams	Cook	Otter	1803				Sent ashore in Africa	BT 98/64
Cato Johnson	Cook	Hamilton	1803			A black		BT 98/64
Alfred	Seaman	Mars	1803		Liverpool			BT 98/64
Thomas Tittle	Seaman	Hibernia	1803			Black seaman		BT 98/64
Peter Tittle	Seaman	Hibernia	1803			Black seaman		BT 98/64
Anthony Cacandia	Seaman	Hibernia	1803			Black seaman		BT 98/64
Henry Caffir	Seaman	Hibernia	1803			Black seaman		BT 98/64
James Curtes	Seaman	Hibernia	1803			Black seaman		BT 98/64
John Banks	Seaman	Hibernia	1803			Black seaman		BT 98/64
Abraham Newland	Seaman	Hibernia	1803			Black seaman	Deserted in Africa	BT 98/64
John Thomas	Apprentice	Agnes	1803	Africa				BT 98/64
George Bonney	Cook	Governor Dowdswell	1803					BT 98/64
Law	Seaman	Minerva	1803	Africa	Africa			BT 98/64
Caulow	Seaman	Minera	1803	Africa	Africa			BT 98/64
Robin	1/2 Seaman	Minerva	1803	Africa	Africa			BT 98/64
Robert Slater	Cook	Princess Royal	1803	Africa				BT 98/64
William Mckneil	Apprentice	Roehampton	1804	Africa				BT 98/64
James Lowes	Apprentice	Frances	1804	Africa				BT 98/64
John Bailley	Cook	Ann	1804	Africa				BT 98/64
Peter Lewes	Cook	Egyptian	1804	Africa			Deserted	BT 98/65
Manuel		Woolton	1805	Annabon	Annabon	Black		BT 98/66
Anthony Lorentz	Cook	Princess Royal	1805	Sao Tome				BT 98/66
George Joseph	Cook	Diana John	1805	Africa				BT 98/66
John William	Cook	Retrieve	1805	Africa				BT 98/66
Peter Black	1/2 Seaman	Adventure	1805	Annabon	Liverpool			BT 98/66
John Irving		Frances	1805	Africa	Africa	Blackman		BT 98/66
Manuel Irving		Frances	1805	Africa	Africa	Blackman		BT 98/66

Appendix 2

Black Sailors on Bristol Slave Ships, 1748–1795

Name	Occupation	Ship	Year	Abode	Joined ship	Description	Outcome	Source
John Morris		Charming Betty	1748–9			Black man	Died at sea	MVA
John Goodboy		Peggy	1749–50	Guinea	Bristol	Black, 25 yrs old		MVA
Quacko		Indian Prince	1749–50	Bristol	Bristol	Negroe		MVA
Thomas Quacoe		Rainbow	1749–50	Gold Coast	Bristol			MVA
Thomas Jupiter		Black Prince x3	*	Africa	Bristol		Died at sea	MVA
Thomas Wesbury		Emporer	1751–2		Bristol	A black		MVA
William Brown		Indian Prince	1752–3		Bristol	Negro		MVA
William Watson		Indian Prince	1752–3		Bristol	Negro		MVA
Thomas Johnson		Williamsburg	1752–3		Bristol	A black		MVA
William Waters		Rainbow	1752–3		Bristol	A Bristol black		MVA
Bristol		Juba	1753–4		Bristol	A black		MVA
Henry Baker		Indian Prince	1753–4		Bristol	A black		MVA
George Lewes		Indian Queen	1754–5		Bristol	A Negroe		MVA
Jack Prince		Black Prince	1757–8	Africa	Bristol			MVA
Coffee	"Boy"	Jolly Batchelor	1757–8			Black, 20 yrs old		MVA
John Juqua	Cook	Jolly Batchelor	1757–8			Black, 45 yrs old		MVA
Nero		Tryal/Prince Tom	57–7 & 61–2					MVA

Name	Role	Ship	Years	Note	Origin	From	Remarks	
John Pompey		Amelia	1764–5		Africa	Bristol		MVA
George Black		Amelia	1764–5		Africa	Bristol		MVA
Chance		Polly	1772–3		Africa	Bristol	Disch. in Africa	MVA
Quafay		Hector	1776–7		Africa	Bristol		MVA
Same Joe		Brothers	1786–7		Africa	Africa		MVA
John Quacko		Sylvia/Jolly Batchelor		A free man				MVA
John Browne		Thomas	1785–6		Africa	Bristol		MVA
Samuel Yewman	Steward's mate	Pearl	1790–1		Bonny	Bristol	Died at sea	MVA
John Peters	Cook	Pearl	1790–1		Africa	Bristol	Left in Jamaica	MVA
John Robertson	Seaman	Flora	1792–3		Africa	Bristol		MVA
John Williams	Cook	Trelawny	1792–3		Africa	Bristol		MVA
Antonio	Seaman	Thomas	1793–4		Africa	Bristol		MVA
Thomas Jones		Nassau	1793–4		Africa	Bristol		MVA
Will Cary	Cook	Brothers	1794–5		Africa	Bristol	Left in Jamaica	MVA
John Davis	"Boy"	Thomas	1794–5	A black	Africa	Bristol	Disch. in Africa	MVA
James Jones		Thomas	1794–5	Black	Africa	Bristol		MVA
John Baptist		Thomas	1794–5	Black	Annobon	Bristol		MVA

* Thomas Jupiter sailed on the *Black Prince* three times, in 1751–2, 1752–3 and 1757–8.

Appendix 3

Black Sailors on Rhode Island Slave Ships, 1803–1807

Name	Occupation	Ship	Year	Age	Residence	Birth place	Description	Outcome	Source
Quash Briggs	Cook	Polly	1803	16	Newport	Africa	Black		NARA 36.3.1
Thomas Price	Seamen	Eagle	1804	18	Newport	Newport	Brown		NARA 36.3.1
Peter Louis	Cook	Eagle	1804	28	Newport	Africa	Black		NARA 36.3.1
Warren Gardnes	Seaman	Semiramis	1804	21	Newport	Massachusetts	Black		NARA 36.3.1
George Rogers	Cook	Semiramis	1804	25	Newport	Connecticut	Yellow	DROWNED	NARA 36.3.1
Prince Center	Steward	Semiramis	1804	35	Newport	Newport	Black	DROWNED	NARA 36.3.1
John Miti	Seaman*	Semiramis	1804		Newport				NARA 36.3.1
Henry Spencer	Seaman	Rising Sun	1804	19	Kingston	Rhode Island	Brown		NARA 36.3.1
Peter Lewis	Cook	Rising Sun	1804	24	Newport	Guadeloupe	Black		NARA 36.3.1
Stephen Gardner	Seaman	Rising Sun	1804	19	Kingston	Rhode Island	Black		NARA 36.3.1
John Clarke	Cook	Brayard	1804	23	Providence	Rhode Island	Black		NARA 36.3.1
James Cain	Seaman	Oneida	1804		Newport	Rhode Island	Black		NARA 36.3.1
William Wright	Cook	Bayard	1805	43	Newport	New York	Black		NARA 36.3.1
Peter Lewis	Cook	Eagle	1805	30	Newport	Africa	Black		NARA 36.3.1
Hercules Hunder	Seaman	John	1805	23	Rhode Island	Rhode Island	Yellow		NARA 36.3.1

236

Name	Occupation	Vessel	Year	Age	Port	Origin	Color	Source
James Thompson	Cook	John	1805	25	Newport	St. Croix	Black	NARA 36.3.1
Jeremiah Crawford	Cook	Marian	1805	22	Newport	New Jersey	Yellow	NARA 36.3.1
Titus Sheffield	Seaman*	Hope	1805	21	Newport	Rhode Island	Black	NARA 36.3.1
Stephen Gardner	Seaman*	Hope	1805	22	Kingston	Rhode Island	Black	NARA 36.3.1
John Oxford	Seaman	Hope	1805	33	Boston	Massachusetts	Black	NARA 36.3.1
Ebenezer Underwood	Cook*	Hope	1805	20	Newport	Massachusetts	Black	NARA 36.3.1
John Wright	Cook*	Marian	1806	27	Newport	Virginia	Yellow	NARA 36.3.1
Daniel Minss	Seaman	John	1807	33	Boston	Pennsylvania	Mulatto	NARA 36.3.1
Samuel Hazard	Seaman	John	1807	26	Newport	Rhode Island	Yellow	NARA 36.3.1
Peter Jackson	Cook	John	1807	24	Newport	Rhode Island	Black	NARA 36.3.1
James Watson	Cook	Polly			Kingston		Black	RIHS
Noah Howland		Nancy	1804	37			Black	RIHS
(Name unknown)		Mary	1804			Africa	Black	RIHS
Samuel Lippitt		Charlotte	1804	19	Providence		Black	RIHS
James Taylor		Charlotte	1804	21	Providence		Very black	RIHS
Charles Harrison		Charlotte	1804	19	Tiverton		Black	RIHS
Robin Carr		Charlotte	1804	29	Bristol		Black	RIHS
Abraham Rinewall		Charlotte	1804	32			Brown	RIHS

(continued)

237

Appendix 3 (continued)

Name	Occupation	Ship	Year	Age	Residence	Birth place	Description	Outcome	Source
Edward Jones		Lark	1804	24	Bristol	Pennsylvania	Brown		RIHS
John Pitt		Lark	1804	22		Pennsylvania	Brown		RIHS
Thomas Munro	*	Lavinia	1806		Bristol	Africa	Black		RIHS
Song Haskell		Hiram	1806	37	Bristol	Rhode Island	Black		RIHS
Samuel Cummings		Agent	1806	25			Black		RIHS
Caesar Freeman		Agent	1806	21			Black		RIHS
Nassar Ballard		Agent	1806		Africa	Africa	African boy		RIHS
Robert Howland		Concord	1806	16		Jamestown	Black		RIHS
Pero Morse		Concord	1806	37	Newport		Yellow		RIHS
Francisco Gomez		Vulture	1806	20		Cape Verde	Black		RIHS
Henry Staple		Heroine	1806		Providence	Africa	Black		RIHS
Caesar Ebow		Little Watt	1806	42	Newport				RIHS
Coggeshall Chase		Friendship	1806	19			Brown		RIHS
Caesar Miller		Lark	1806	25	Bristol		Black		RIHS
James Young		Newry	1806	25		New York	Brown		RIHS
James Taylor		Newry	1806	30		New York	Brown		RIHS
Alexander Northrup		Newry	1806	18	Providence		Black		RIHS

* Men who were also apprentices.

Index